Reviews of Artificial

"*Artificial Intelligence Engines will introduce you to the rapidly growing field of deep learning networks: how to build them, how to use them; and how to think about them. James Stone will guide you from the basics to the outer reaches of a technology that is changing the world.*"

Professor Terrence Sejnowski, Director of the Computational Neurobiology Laboratory, the Salk Institute, USA. Author of *The Deep Learning Revolution*, MIT Press, 2018.

"*This book manages the impossible: it is a fun read, intuitive and engaging, lighthearted and delightful, and cuts right through the hype and turgid terminology. Unlike many texts, this is not a shallow cookbook for some particular deep learning program-du-jure. Instead, it crisply and painlessly imparts the principles, intuitions and background needed to understand existing machine-learning systems, learn new tools, and invent novel architectures, with ease.*"

Professor Barak Pearlmutter, Brain and Computation Laboratory, National University of Ireland Maynooth, Ireland.

"*This text provides an engaging introduction to the mathematics underlying neural networks. It is meant to be read from start to finish, as it carefully builds up, chapter by chapter, the essentials of neural network theory. After first describing classic linear networks and nonlinear multilayer perceptrons, Stone gradually introduces a comprehensive range of cutting edge technologies in use today. Written in an accessible and insightful manner, this book is a pleasure to read, and I will certainly be recommending it to my students.*"

Dr Stephen Eglen, Cambridge Computational Biology Institute, Cambridge University, UK.

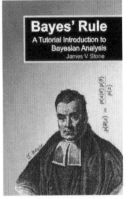

James V Stone is an Honorary Associate Professor at the University of Sheffield, UK.

Artificial Intelligence Engines

A Tutorial Introduction to the

Mathematics of Deep Learning

James V Stone

Title: Artificial Intelligence Engines
Author: James V Stone

©2019 Sebtel Press

First Edition, 2019.
Typeset in LaTeX $\partial 2_\varepsilon$.
Second printing.

ISBN 9780956372819

Cover background by Okan Caliskan, reproduced with permission.

For Teleri, my bright star

Contents

List of Pseudocode Examples   i

Online Code Examples   ii

Preface   iii

1   **Artificial Neural Networks**   1

   1.1   Introduction 1
   1.2   What is an Artificial Neural Network? 2
   1.3   The Origins of Neural Networks 5
   1.4   From Backprop to Deep Learning 8
   1.5   An Overview of Chapters 9

2   **Linear Associative Networks**   11

   2.1   Introduction 11
   2.2   Setting One Connection Weight 12
   2.3   Learning One Association 14
   2.4   Gradient Descent 16
   2.5   Learning Two Associations 18
   2.6   Learning Many Associations 23
   2.7   Learning Photographs 25
   2.8   Summary 26

3   **Perceptrons**   27

   3.1   Introduction 27
   3.2   The Perceptron Learning Algorithm 28
   3.3   The Exclusive OR Problem 32
   3.4   Why Exclusive OR Matters 34
   3.5   Summary 36

4   **The Backpropagation Algorithm**   37

   4.1   Introduction 37
   4.2   The Backpropagation Algorithm 39
   4.3   Why Use Sigmoidal Hidden Units? 48
   4.4   Generalisation and Over-fitting 49
   4.5   Vanishing Gradients 52
   4.6   Speeding Up Backprop 55
   4.7   Local and Global Mimima 57
   4.8   Temporal Backprop 59
   4.9   Early Backprop Achievements 62
   4.10   Summary 62

5 Hopfield Nets   **63**

5.1   Introduction 63
5.2   The Hopfield Net 64
5.3   Learning One Network State 65
5.4   Content Addressable Memory 66
5.5   Tolerance to Damage 68
5.6   The Energy Function 68
5.7   Summary 70

6 Boltzmann Machines   **71**

6.1   Introduction 71
6.2   Learning in Generative Models 72
6.3   The Boltzmann Machine Energy Function 74
6.4   Simulated Annealing 76
6.5   Learning by Sculpting Distributions 77
6.6   Learning in Boltzmann Machines 78
6.7   Learning by Maximising Likelihood 80
6.8   Autoencoder Networks 84
6.9   Summary 84

7 Deep RBMs   **85**

7.1   Introduction 85
7.2   Restricted Boltzmann Machines 87
7.3   Training Restricted Boltzmann Machines 87
7.4   Deep Autoencoder Networks 93
7.5   Summary 96

8 Variational Autoencoders   **97**

8.1   Introduction 97
8.2   Why Favour Independent Features? 98
8.3   Overview of Variational Autoencoders 100
8.4   Latent Variables and Manifolds 103
8.5   Key Quantities 104
8.6   How Variational Autoencoders Work 106
8.7   The Evidence Lower Bound 110
8.8   An Alternative Derivation 115
8.9   Maximising the Lower Bound 115
8.10 Conditional Variational Autoencoders 119
8.11 Applications 119
8.12 Summary 120

9 Deep Backprop Networks   **121**

    9.1   Introduction 121
    9.2   Convolutional Neural Networks 122
    9.3   LeNet1 125
    9.4   LeNet5 127
    9.5   AlexNet 129
    9.6   GoogLeNet 130
    9.7   ResNet 130
    9.8   Ladder Autoencoder Networks 132
    9.9   Denoising Autoencoders 135
    9.10 Fooling Neural Networks 136
    9.11 Generative Adversarial Networks 137
    9.12 Temporal Deep Neural Networks 140
    9.13 Capsule Networks 141
    9.14 Summary 142

10 Reinforcement Learning   **143**

    10.1 Introduction 143
    10.2 What's the Problem? 146
    10.3 Key Quantities 147
    10.4 Markov Decision Processes 148
    10.5 Formalising the Problem 149
    10.6 The Bellman Equation 150
    10.7 Learning State-Value Functions 152
    10.8 Eligibility Traces 155
    10.9 Learning Action-Value Functions 157
    10.10 Balancing a Pole 164
    10.11 Applications 166
    10.12 Summary 168

11 The Emperor's New AI?   **169**

    11.1 Artificial Intelligence 169
    11.2 Yet Another Revolution? 170

Further Reading   **173**

Appendices
A Glossary   **175**
B Mathematical Symbols   **181**
C A Vector and Matrix Tutorial   **183**
D Maximum Likelihood Estimation   **187**
E Bayes' Theorem   **189**
References   **191**
Index   **199**

List of Pseudocode Examples

Each example below refers to a text box that summarises a particular method or neural network.

Linear associative network gradient descent: One weight page 16.

Linear associative network gradient descent: Two weights page 22.

Perceptron classification page 35.

Backprop: Short version page 43.

Backprop: Long version page 47.

Hopfield net: Learning page 66.

Hopfield net: Recall page 67.

Boltzmann machine: Simulated annealing page 77.

Boltzmann machine learning algorithm page 82.

Restricted Boltzmann machine learning algorithm page 93.

Variational autoencoder learning algorithm page 118.

SARSA: On-policy learning of action-value functions page 160.

Q-Learning: Off-policy learning of action-value functions page 161.

Learning to balance a pole page 165.

Online Code Examples

The Python and MatLab code examples below can be obtained from the online GitHub repository at
`https://github.com/jgvfwstone/ArtificialIntelligenceEngines`
Please see the file README.txt in that repository.

The computer code has been collated from various sources (with permission). It is intended to provide small scale transparent examples, rather than an exercise in how to program artificial neural networks. The examples below are written in Python.

Linear network

Perceptron

Backprop network

Hopfield net

Restricted Boltzmann machine

Variational autoencoder

Convolutional neural network

Reinforcement learning

Preface

This book is intended to provide an account of deep neural networks that is both informal and rigorous. Each neural network learning algorithm is introduced informally with diagrams, before a mathematical account is provided. In order to cement the reader's understanding, each algorithm is accompanied by a step-by-step summary written in pseudocode. Thus, each algorithm is approached from several convergent directions, which should ensure that the diligent reader gains a thorough understanding of the inner workings of deep learning artificial neural networks. Additionally, technical terms are described in a comprehensive glossary, and (for the complete novice) a tutorial appendix on vectors and matrices is provided.

Unlike most books on deep learning, this is not a 'user manual' for any particular software package. Such books often place high demands on the novice, who has to learn the conceptual infrastructure of neural network algorithms, whilst simultaneously learning the minutiae of how to operate an unfamiliar software package. Instead, this book concentrates on key concepts and algorithms.

Having said that, readers familiar with programming can benefit from running working examples of neural networks, which are available at the website associated with this book. Simple examples were written by the author, and these are intended to be easy to understand rather than efficient to run. More complex examples have been borrowed (with permission) from around the internet, but mainly from the PyTorch repository. A list of the online code examples that accompany this book is given opposite.

Who Should Read This Book? The material in this book should be accessible to anyone with an understanding of basic calculus. The tutorial style adopted ensures that any reader prepared to put in the effort will be amply rewarded with a solid grasp of the fundamentals of deep learning networks.

The Author. My education in artificial neural networks began with a lecture by Geoff Hinton on Boltzmann machines in 1984 at Sussex University, where I was studying for an MSc in Knowledge Based Systems. I was so inspired by this lecture that I implemented Hinton and Sejnowski's Boltzmann machine for my MSc project. Later, I enjoyed extended visits to Hinton's laboratory in Toronto and to Sejnowski's laboratory in San Diego, funded by a Wellcome Trust Mathematical Biology Fellowship. I have published research papers on human memory[30;125], temporal backprop[116], backprop[71], evolution[120], optimisation[115;117], independent component analysis[119], and using neural networks to test principles of brain function[118;124].

Acknowledgements. Thanks to Steve Snow for discussions on variational autoencoders and the physics of Boltzmann machines. For debates about neural networks over many years, I am indebted to my friend Raymond Lister. For helping with Python frameworks, thanks to Royston Sellman. For reading one or more chapters, I am very grateful to Olivier Codol, Peter Dunne, Lancelot Da Costa, Stephen Eglen, George Farmer, Charles Fox, Nikki Hunkin, Raymond Lister, Gonzalo de Polavieja, and Paul Warren. Special thanks to Eleni Vasilaki and Luca Manneschi for providing guidance on reinforcement learning. For allowing me to use their computer code, I'd like to thank Jose Antonio Martin H (reinforcement learning) and Peter Dunne (for his version of Hinton's RBM code). Finally, thanks to Alice Yew for meticulous copy-editing and proofreading.

Corrections. Please email corrections to j.v.stone@sheffield.ac.uk. A list of corrections can be found at:
https://jim-stone.staff.shef.ac.uk/AIEngines

Once the machine thinking method has started, it would not take long to outstrip our feeble powers.
A Turing, 1951.

Chapter 1

Artificial Neural Networks

If you want to understand a really complicated device, like a brain, you should build one.
G Hinton, 2018.

1.1. Introduction

Deep neural networks are the computational engines that power modern artificial intelligence. Behind every headline regarding the latest achievements of artificial intelligence lies a deep neural network, whether this involves diagnosing cancer, recognising objects (Figure 1.1), learning to ride a bicycle[90], or learning to fly[28;93] (Figure 1.2). In essence, deep neural networks rely on a sophisticated form of pattern recognition, but the secret of their success is that they are capable of *learning*.

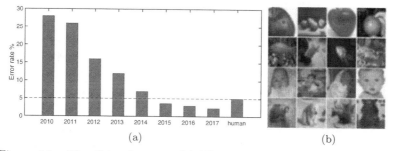

(a)   (b)

Figure 1.1. Classifying images. (a) The percentage error on the annual ILSVRC image classification competition has fallen dramatically since 2010. (b) Example images. The latest competition involves classifying about 1.5 million images into 1,000 object classes. Reproduced with permission from Wu and Gu (2015).

A striking indication of the dramatic progress made over recent years can be seen in Figure 1.1, which shows performance on an image classification task. Note that the performance of deep neural networks surpassed human performance in 2015.

1.2. What is an Artificial Neural Network?

An artificial neural network is a set of interconnected model neurons or *units*, as shown in Figure 1.3. For brevity, we will use the term *neural network* to refer to artificial neural networks. By analogy to the brain, the most common forms of neural networks receive inputs via an array of sensory units. With repeated presentations, a neural network

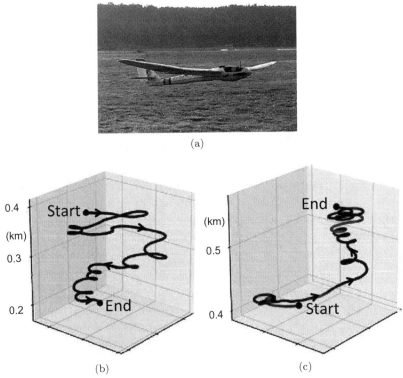

(a)

(b)   (c)

Figure 1.2. Learning to soar using reinforcement learning. (a) Glider used for learning. (b) Before learning, flight is disorganised, and glider descends. (c) After learning, glider ascends to 0.6 km. Note the different scales on the vertical axes in (b) and (c). Reproduced with permission: (a) from Guilliard et al. (2018); (b,c) from Reddy et al. (2016).

can learn to recognise those inputs so as to classify them or to perform some action. For example, if the input to a neural network is an image of a teapot then the output should indicate that the image contains a teapot. However, this simple description hides the many complexities that make object recognition extraordinarily difficult. Indeed, the fact that we humans are so good at object recognition makes it hard to appreciate just how difficult it is for a neural network to recognise objects. A teapot can vary in colour and shape, and it can appear at many different orientations and sizes, as in Figure 1.4. These variations do not usually fool humans, but they can cause major problems for neural networks.

Let's assume that we have wired up a neural network so that its input is an image, and that we want its output to indicate which object is in the image. Specifically, we wire up the network so that each pixel in the image acts as input to one *input unit*, and we connect all of these input units to a single *output unit*. The output or *state* of the output unit is determined by the image through the strengths or *weights* of the connections from the different input units to the output unit. In essence, the bigger the weight, the more a given input unit affects the state of the output unit. To make things really simple, we assume that the object is either a teapot or a cup, and that the state of the output unit should be 1 when the image contains a teapot and 0 when it contains a cup.

In order to get a feel for the magnitude of the problem confronting a neural network, consider a square (black and white) image that is $1,000 \times 1,000$ pixels. If each pixel can adopt 256 grey-levels then the

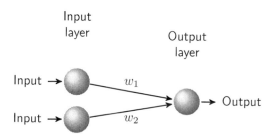

Figure 1.3. A neural network with two input units and one output unit. The connections from the input units to the output unit have weights w_1 and w_2.

3

number of possible images is $256^{1,000,000}$, which is much more than the number of atoms in the universe (about 10^{87}). Of course, most of these images look like random noise, and only a tiny fraction depict anything approaching a natural scene — and only a fraction of those depict a teapot. The point is that if a network is to discriminate between teapots and non-teapots then it implicitly must learn to assign a probability to each of the $256^{1,000,000}$ possible images, which is the probability that each image contains a teapot.

The neural network has to learn to recognise objects in its input image by adjusting the connection weights between units (here, between input and output units). The process of adjusting weights is implemented by a learning *algorithm* (the word *algorithm* just means a definite sequence of logical steps that yields a specified outcome).

Now, suppose the input image contains a teapot but the output unit state is 0 (indicating that the image depicts a cup). This *classification error* occurs because one or more weights have the wrong values. However, it is far from obvious which weights are wrong and how they should be adjusted to correct the error. This general problem is called the *credit assignment problem*, but it should really be called the blame assignment problem, or even the whodunnit problem.

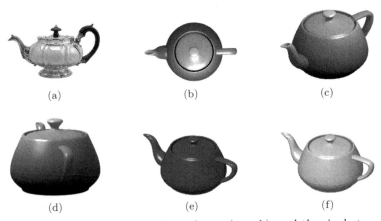

(a)   (b)   (c)

(d)   (e)   (f)

Figure 1.4. Teapots come in various shapes (a vs b), and the single teapot in (b)–(f) can appear with many different orientations, sizes, and colours (represented as shades of grey here).

In practice, knowing whodunnit, and what to do with whoever-did-do-it, represents the crux of the problem to be solved by neural network learning algorithms. In order to learn, artificial (and biological) neural networks must solve this credit/blame assignment problem.

Most solutions to this problem have their roots in an idea proposed by Donald Hebb[34] in 1949, which is known as *Hebb's postulate*:

> *When an axon of cell A is near enough to excite cell B and repeatedly or persistently takes part in firing it, some growth process or metabolic change takes place in one or both cells such that A's efficiency, as one of the cells firing B, is increased.*

1.3. The Origins of Neural Networks

The development of modern neural networks (see Figure 1.5) occurred in a series of step-wise dramatic improvements, interspersed with periods of stasis (often called *neural network winters*). As early as 1943, before commercial computers existed, McCulloch and Pitts[77] began to explore how small networks of artificial neurons could mimic brain-like processes. The cross-disciplinary nature of this early research is evident from the fact that McCulloch and Pitts also contributed to a classic paper on the neurophysiology of vision (What the frog's eye tells the frog's brain[68], 1959), which was published not in a biology journal, but in the *Proceedings of the Institute of Radio Engineers*.

In subsequent years, the increasing availability of computers allowed neural networks to be tested on simple pattern recognition tasks. But progress was slow, partly because most research funding was allocated to more conventional approaches that did not attempt to mimic the neural architecture of the brain, and partly because artificial neural network learning algorithms were limited.

A major landmark in the history of neural networks was Frank Rosenblatt's *perceptron* (1958), which was explicitly modelled on the neuronal structures in the brain. The *perceptron learning algorithm* allowed a perceptron to learn to associate inputs with outputs in a manner apparently similar to learning in humans. Specifically, the perceptron could learn an association between a simple input 'image' and a desired output, where this output indicated whether or not the object was present in the image.

Perceptrons, and neural networks in general, share three key properties with human memory. First, unlike conventional computer memory, neural network memory is *content addressable*, which means that recall is triggered by an image or a sound. In contrast, computer memory can be accessed only if the specific location (address) of the required information is known. Second, a common side-effect of content addressable memory is that, given a learned association between an input image and an output, recall can be triggered by an input image that is similar (but not identical) to the original input of a particular input/output association. This ability to *generalise* beyond learned associations is a critical human-like property of artificial neural networks. Third, if a single weight or unit is destroyed, this does not remove a particular learned association; instead, it degrades all associations to some extent. This *graceful degradation* is thought to resemble human memory.

Despite these human-like qualities, the perceptron was dealt a severe blow in 1969, when Minsky and Papert[79] famously proved that it could not learn associations unless they were of a particularly simple kind (i.e. *linearly separable*, as described in Chapter 2). This marked the beginning of the first neural network winter, during which neural network research was undertaken by only a handful of scientists.

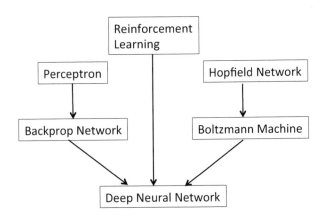

Figure 1.5. A simplified taxonomy of artificial neural networks.

The modern era of neural networks began in 1982 with the *Hopfield net*[47]. Although Hopfield nets are not practically very useful, Hopfield introduced a theoretical framework based on *statistical mechanics*, which laid the foundations for Ackley, Hinton, and Sejnowki's *Boltzmann machine*[1] in 1985. Unlike a Hopfield net, in which the *states* of all units are specified by the associations being learned, a Boltzmann machine has a reservoir of *hidden units*, which can be used to learn complex associations. The Boltzmann machine is important because it facilitated a conceptual shift away from the idea of a neural network as a passive associative machine towards the view of a neural network as a *generative model*. The only problem is that Boltzmann machines learn at a rate that is best described as glacial. But on a practical level, the Boltzmann machine demonstrated that neural networks could learn to solve complex toy (i.e. small-scale) problems, which suggested that they could learn to solve almost any problem (at least in principle, and at least eventually).

The impetus supplied by the Boltzmann machine gave rise to a more tractable method devised in 1986 by Rumelhart, Hinton, and Williams, the *backpropagation learning algorithm*[97]. A backpropagation network consists of three layers of units: an *input layer*, which is connected with connection weights to a hidden layer, which in turn is connected to an *output layer*, as shown in Figure 1.6. The backpropagation algorithm is important because it demonstrated the potential of neural networks to learn sophisticated tasks in a human-like manner. Crucially, for the first time, a backpropagation neural network called *NETtalk* learned to 'speak', inasmuch as it translated text to *phonemes* (the basic elements of speech), which a voice synthesizer then used to produce speech.

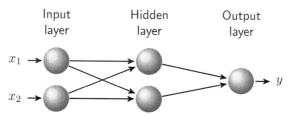

Figure 1.6. A neural network with two input units, two hidden units, and one output unit.

In parallel with the evolution of neural networks, *reinforcement learning* was developed throughout the 1980s and 1990s, principally by Sutton and Barto (2018). Reinforcement learning is an inspired fusion of game playing by computers, as developed by Shannon (1950) and Samuel (1959), optimal control theory, and stimulus–response experiments in psychology. Early results showed that hard, albeit small-scale, problems such as balancing a pole can be solved using feedback in the form of simple reward signals (Michie and Chambers, 1968; Barto, Sutton, and Anderson, 1983). More recently, reinforcement learning has been combined with deep learning to produce impressive skill acquisition, such as in the case of a glider that learns to gain height on thermals[28] (see Figure 1.2).

1.4. From Backprop to Deep Learning

In principle, a backprop network with just two hidden layers of units can associate pretty much any inputs with any outputs[12], which means that it should be able to perform most tasks. However, getting a backprop to *learn* the tasks that it should be able to perform in theory is problematic. A plausible solution is to add more units to each layer and more layers of hidden units, because this should improve learning (at least in theory). In practice, it was found that conventional backprop networks struggled to learn if they had deep learning architectures like that shown in Figure 1.7.

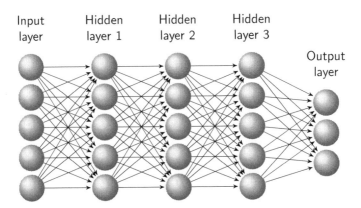

Figure 1.7. A deep network with three hidden layers.

With the benefit of hindsight, the field of artificial intelligence stems from the research originally done on Hopfield nets, Boltzmann machines, the backprop algorithm, and reinforcement learning. However, the evolution of backprop networks into deep learning networks had to wait for three related developments. To quote one of the inventors of backprop, the reason for the revolution in neural networks is because:

> *In simple terms, computers became millions of times faster, data sets got thousands of times bigger, and researchers discovered many technical refinements that made neural nets easier to train.*
> G Hinton, 2018.

1.5. An Overview of Chapters

In order to appreciate modern deep learning networks, some familiarity with their historical antecedents is required. Accordingly, Chapter 2 provides a tutorial on the simplest neural network, a *linear associative network*. This embodies many of the essential ingredients (e.g. *gradient descent*) necessary for understanding more sophisticated neural networks. In Chapter 3, the role of the *perceptron* in exposing the limitations of linear neural networks is described.

In Chapter 4, the *backpropagation* or *backprop* algorithm is introduced and demonstrated on the simplest nonlinear problem (i.e. the exclusive OR problem). The application of *recurrent backprop neural networks* to the problem of recognising sequences (e.g. speech) is also explored. The properties of backprop are examined in the context of the *cross-entropy error function* and in relation to problems of *overfitting, generalisation,* and *vanishing gradients*.

To understand the stochastic nature of deep learning neural networks, Chapter 5 examines *Hopfield nets*, which have their roots in statistical mechanics. In Chapter 6, the limitations of Hopfield nets are addressed in the form of *Boltzmann machines*, which represent the first *generative models*. The glacial learning rates of Boltzmann machines are overcome by *restricted Boltzmann machines* in Chapter 7. A recent innovation in the form of *variational autoencoders* promises a further step-change in generative models, as described in Chapter 8.

The use of convolution in backprop networks in the early 1990s foreshadowed the rise of *deep convolutional networks, ladder networks, denoising autoencoders, generative adversarial networks, temporal deep networks,* and *capsule networks,* which are described in Chapter 9.

In Chapter 10, the *reinforcement learning algorithm* is introduced and demonstrated on examples such as pole balancing. Ingenious variants of backprop were devised between 2000 and 2016, which, when combined with reinforcement learning, allowed deep networks to learn increasingly complex tasks. A particularly striking result of these developments was a deep network called AlphaGo[108], which learned to play the game of Go so well that it beat the world's best human players in 2016.

Finally, the prospect of an artificial intelligence revolution is discussed in Chapter 11, where we consider the two extremes of naive optimism and cynical pessimism that inevitably accompany any putative revolution.

Chapter 2

Linear Associative Networks

It is no good poking around in the brain without some idea of what one is looking for. That would be like trying to find a needle in a haystack without having any idea what needles look like. The theorist is the man who might reasonably be asked for his opinion about the appearance of needles.
HC Longuet-Higgins, 1969.

2.1. Introduction

In order to understand the deep learning networks considered in later chapters, we will sneak up on them slowly, so that what appears mysterious at a distance will seem obvious by the time it is viewed close up. Historically, the simplest form of artificial neural network consists of an array of input units that project to an array of output units. Usually, every input unit is connected to every output unit via a

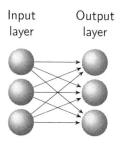

Figure 2.1. A neural network with three input units, which are connected to three output units via a matrix of nine connection weights.

matrix of connection weights, as shown in Figure 2.1. Depending on the network under consideration, the unit states can have either binary or real values. The capabilities of these networks were explored between the late 1950s and early 1970s as *perceptrons* by Rosenblatt (1958), *adalines* by Widrow and Hoff (1960), *holophones* by Longuet-Higgins (1968), *correlographs* by Longuet-Higgins, Willshaw, and Buneman (1970), and *correlation matrix memories* by Kohonen (1972).

2.2. Setting One Connection Weight

All of the networks mentioned above are variations on the theme of *linear associative networks*. A linear associative network can have many input and output units, which do not have thresholds, such that each output is a linear function of the input. To simplify matters, we dispense with all except one unit in the input layer and one unit in the output layer, as in Figure 2.2.

The state of the input unit is represented as x, and the state of the output unit is represented as y. Suppose we wish the network to learn a single association, such that when the input unit's state is set to $x = 0.8$, the output unit's state is $y = 0.2$. The desired *target value* of the output unit state is represented as ý, to differentiate it from the actual output unit state y.

The input and output units are connected by a single connection. Crucially, the strength, or weight, of this connection is the only thing that determines the output unit state for a given input unit state, because the output unit state is the input unit state multiplied by the value of the connection weight. More formally, if the input state is x and if the weight of the connection from the input unit to the output

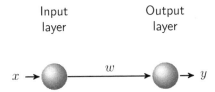

Figure 2.2. A neural network with two layers, each containing one artificial neuron or *unit*. The *state* x of the unit in the input layer affects the state y of the unit in the output layer via a connection weight w (Equation 2.1).

unit is w, then the total input u to the output unit is

$$u = w \times x. \tag{2.1}$$

We will omit the multiplication sign from now on, and write simply $u = wx$. In general, the state y of a unit is governed by an *activation function* (i.e. input/output function)

$$y = f(u). \tag{2.2}$$

However, in a linear associative network, the activation function of each unit is usually the identity function, which means that the state of the output unit is equal to its input, $y = u = wx$, as shown in Figure 2.3.

How should we adjust the weight w so that the input unit state $x = 0.8$ yields an output unit state $y = 0.2$? In this example, the optimal weight is

$$w^* = y/x = 0.25. \tag{2.3}$$

The optimal weight has an asterisk superscript, which is standard notation. We can check that this gives the desired output unit state: $y = w^* \times x = 0.25 \times 0.8 = 0.2$. If learning in a neural network is so easy, then what is all the fuss about? Well, we cheated in five ways:

1. we calculated the optimal weight value manually, rather than using a learning algorithm

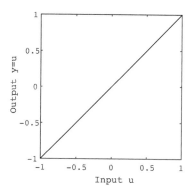

Figure 2.3. A linear activation function, $y = u$.

2. the network only 'learned' one association, rather than simultaneously learning many associations

3. the network had only one input unit, rather than the many units required to represent images at its input

4. the network used only two layers of units, rather than the many layers necessary for learning complex associations

5. because each unit has a linear activation function, the network provides a linear mapping between input and output layers.

The final point introduces the idea that the network, when considered as a whole, defines a function F that maps unit states in the input layer to unit states in the output layer. The nature of this function depends on the activation functions of the individual units and on the connection weights. Crucially, if the activation functions of the units are linear then the function F implemented by the network is also linear, no matter how many layers or how many units the network contains. In Chapter 3, we will see how the linearity of the network function F represents a fundamental limitation.

Next, we will incrementally remove each of the cheats listed above, so that by the time we get to Chapter 4 we will have a nonlinear three-layer neural network, which can learn many associations.

2.3. Learning One Association

We begin by describing an algorithm for learning a single association in the network shown in Figure 2.2. For simplicity, we refer to a network with one input unit and one output unit as a 1-1 network.

Suppose, as above, we wish the network to learn to associate an input value of $x = 0.8$ with a target state of y $= 0.2$. Usually, we have no idea of the correct value for the weight w, so we may as well begin by choosing its value at random. Suppose we choose a value $w = 0.4$, so the output state is $y = 0.4 \times 0.8 = 0.32$. The difference between the output y and the target value y is defined here as the *delta term*:

$$\delta \; = \; y - \text{y} \; = \; 0.32 - 0.2 \; = \; 0.12. \tag{2.4}$$

A standard measure of the error in y is half the squared difference:

$$E = \tfrac{1}{2}(wx - \mathsf{y})^2 \qquad (2.5)$$

$$= \tfrac{1}{2}(\mathsf{y} - \mathsf{y})^2 \qquad (2.6)$$

$$= \tfrac{1}{2}\delta^2. \qquad (2.7)$$

Below we will explore a method for adjusting the weight w automatically so that $\delta = 0$. However, in the simple case under consideration here, we can use Equation 2.5 to calculate the value of E for values of w between 0 and 0.5, and then plot a graph of E versus w, as in Figure 2.4. This defines a quadratic curve called the *error function*, which has its lowest point at $w^* = 0.25$, a point that corresponds to an error of $E = 0$. Because we can plot the entire error function, we can see that the solution lies at $w^* = 0.25$. This is not possible with more complex networks, because we cannot plot the entire error function. Nevertheless, we will continue to explore an automatic method for finding w^* using this simple network, which will hold good for cases where we cannot see the whole error function.

So if we cannot see the whole error function, how can we find the value of w that minimises E? The following trial-and-error method is not perfect, but it motivates the better methods described below. We begin by choosing the value of w at random, as in Figure 2.4 where we have chosen $w = 0.4$. How could we decide how to change w in order to reduce E? Well, even though we don't know which value of w minimises the value of E, there are only two possible ways to alter w: we can make it either bigger or smaller, which corresponds to the right and left directions in Figure 2.4. If we make w a little bigger then this increases E, so that is a bad idea. But if we make w a little smaller then this decreases E, so that is a good idea. And if we repeatedly make w smaller then E keeps on decreasing until $E = 0$.

This method works well if there is only one weight, because there are only two directions to choose from. But as the number of weights gets bigger, the number of possible combinations of directions grows exponentially, so this method becomes inefficient. Fortunately, there exists a more efficient method, called *gradient descent*.

2.4. Gradient Descent

Gradient descent is based on a simple *heuristic*: if you want to get to the bottom of a valley, you should take a step in a direction that takes you downhill, and then repeat this until there is no more downhill left.

To make this more like the gradient descent that occurs in neural networks, imagine you are standing in a dense fog on the error function at a point that corresponds to the randomly chosen value w_{rand}. The fog simulates any computer's view of the error function; the computer cannot see the whole function, but it can see a small region centred on a given value of w. For you, the fog means that you cannot see very far, but you can see a small region around yourself, so you can also see which direction points downhill. The obvious thing to do is to take a step in the *direction of steepest descent* (i.e. either left or right), and repeat this until the ground beneath your feet becomes horizontal, which means that you have reached the lowest point on the error function. But how does a computer know which direction is down?

Well, given the right tool, a computer can evaluate the slope or *gradient* at any given point on the error function. And the right tool is calculus, which can be used to find the gradient at any point w.

Gradient Descent for Figure 2.2:
Learning One Association
initialise network weight w to random value
set input unit states x to training vector x
set learning to true
while *learning* **do**
  get state of output unit $y = wx$
  get delta term $\delta = y - \mathsf{y}$
  get weight gradient for input vector $dE/dw = \delta x$
  get change in weight $\Delta w = -\epsilon\, dE/dw$
  update weight $w \leftarrow w + \Delta w$
  if *gradient $dE/dw \approx 0$* **then**
    | set learning to false
  end
end

Once the computer knows the gradient, it moves w a small step in the direction of steepest descent, re-evaluates the gradient, and moves w again. This is repeated until the gradient equals zero, at which point E is at a minimum value, and the weight has reached an optimal value $w = w^*$.

The gradient of the error function at a point w is approximated by $\Delta E / \Delta w$, as in Figure 2.4. An exact measure of the gradient is defined by the derivative of E (Equation 2.5) with respect to w:

$$\frac{dE}{dw} = (wx - y)\,x \tag{2.8}$$

$$\approx \frac{\Delta E}{\Delta w}. \tag{2.9}$$

It will prove useful to write Equation 2.8 in terms of the delta term:

$$\frac{dE}{dw} = \delta\, x. \tag{2.10}$$

The magnitude of the gradient indicates the steepness of the slope at w, and the sign of the gradient indicates the direction in which to move so as to increase E; a positive gradient (like that shown in Figure 2.4 at $w = 0.4$) means that increasing w increases E, so to decrease E we should decrease the value of w. It turns out that the direction of the gradient measured using calculus points uphill, and is called the

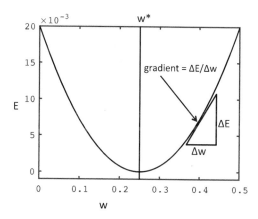

Figure 2.4. Gradient descent. The gradient at any point w is approximately $\Delta E / \Delta w$. The optimal weight is $w^* = 0.25$.

direction of steepest ascent. This means that in order to reduce E, we should change the value of w by a small amount Δw in the *direction of steepest descent*:

$$\Delta w = -\epsilon \frac{dE}{dw} \qquad (2.11)$$

$$= -\epsilon \, \delta \, x, \qquad (2.12)$$

where the size of the step is defined by a *learning rate parameter* ϵ. Equation 2.12 is known as the *delta rule*, the *Widrow–Hoff rule*, or the *least mean square* (LMS) rule. Thus, if the current value of the weight is w_{old}, then the new value should be set to

$$w_{\mathrm{new}} = w_{\mathrm{old}} + \Delta w. \qquad (2.13)$$

So far, gradient descent just seems like a very laborious method for solving a problem that could have been solved by dividing one number by another (as in Equation 2.3). But the true worth of gradient descent only becomes apparent when the problem cannot be solved so easily.

2.5. Learning Two Associations

To make things a bit more realistic, consider a neural network with two input units and one output unit, as shown in Figure 2.5. This network can learn up to two associations, as explained below. Each association consists of an input, which is a pair of values x_1 and x_2, and each corresponding output is a single value y. In this network, there are two connection weights w_1 and w_2.

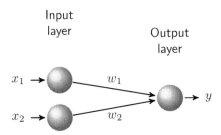

Figure 2.5. A neural network with two input units and one output unit.

Given one input (x_1, x_2), the output y is found by multiplying each input value by its corresponding weight and then summing the resultant products:

$$y = w_1 x_1 + w_2 x_2. \tag{2.14}$$

This can be written succinctly if we represent the weights as a vector, written in bold typeface:

$$\mathbf{w} = (w_1, w_2). \tag{2.15}$$

Similarly, each pair of input values can be represented as a vector, again in bold typeface:

$$\mathbf{x} = (x_1, x_2). \tag{2.16}$$

The state y for an input $\mathbf{x}$ is found from the *dot* or *inner* product,

$$y = \mathbf{w} \cdot \mathbf{x}, \tag{2.17}$$

which is defined by Equation 2.14 (see Appendix C). Notice that scalar variables are in italics, whereas vectors are in bold typeface.

As stated above, this network can learn two associations. Accordingly, we use subscripts to denote the association between an input vector $\mathbf{x}_1$ and the corresponding state y_1 of the output unit, and between an input vector $\mathbf{x}_2$ and the state y_2 of the output unit, such that

$$\begin{aligned} y_1 &= \mathbf{w} \cdot \mathbf{x}_1, \\ y_2 &= \mathbf{w} \cdot \mathbf{x}_2. \end{aligned} \tag{2.18}$$

The vector notation is succinct, but it can also hide the apparent complexity of the problem. So just this once, we will write the problem out in full. This requires using additional subscripts to represent each input vector, so that $\mathbf{x}_1 = (x_{11}, x_{21})$ and $\mathbf{x}_2 = (x_{12}, x_{22})$, and then the two Equations 2.18 become

$$y_1 = w_1 x_{11} + w_2 x_{21},$$
$$y_2 = w_1 x_{12} + w_2 x_{22}. \tag{2.19}$$

At this point, we can recognise the problem as two simultaneous equations with two unknowns (w_1 and w_2), so we know that a solution for w_1 and w_2 usually exists. We could find this solution manually, but because we know that the problems we encounter later will become unrealistic for manual methods, we will stick to using gradient descent.

To use gradient descent, we first need to write down an error function like Equation 2.5, but for two associations. The error function for the first association is

$$E_1 = \tfrac{1}{2} \left(\mathbf{w} \cdot \mathbf{x}_1 - \mathbf{y}_1 \right)^2, \tag{2.20}$$

and for the second association it is

$$E_2 = \tfrac{1}{2} \left(\mathbf{w} \cdot \mathbf{x}_2 - \mathbf{y}_2 \right)^2. \tag{2.21}$$

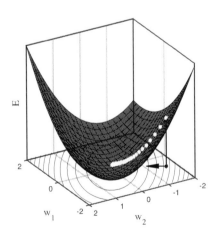

Figure 2.6. The error surface is obtained by evaluating Equation 2.24 over a range of values for w_1 and w_2. Given an initial weight vector $\mathbf{w} = (-0.8, -1.6)$, the direction of steepest descent is $-\nabla_{\mathbf{w}} E$ (shown by an arrow on the ground plane). The white dots depict the evolution of weights during learning using Equation 2.32.

The error function for the set of two associations is the sum

$$
\begin{aligned}
E & = E_1 + E_2 & (2.22) \\
& = \tfrac{1}{2}\left[(\mathbf{w} \cdot \mathbf{x}_1 - y_1)^2 + (\mathbf{w} \cdot \mathbf{x}_2 - y_2)^2\right], & (2.23)
\end{aligned}
$$

which can be written succinctly using the summation convention as

$$
E = \frac{1}{2}\sum_{t=1}^{2}(\mathbf{w} \cdot \mathbf{x}_t - y_t)^2. \tag{2.24}
$$

Gradient Descent For Two Weights. Just as we used gradient descent to find the optimal weight w^* in Equation 2.8, we can repeat this process to find the optimal pair of weights $\mathbf{w}^*$. This is achieved by finding the gradient of the error function with respect to each weight, and then combining these to obtain the direction of steepest descent.

Using the *chain rule*, the gradient of the error function with respect to w_1 for the tth association ($t = 1$ or 2) is

$$
\frac{\partial E_t}{\partial w_1} = \frac{\partial E_t}{\partial y_t}\frac{\partial y_t}{\partial w_1}, \tag{2.25}
$$

where $\partial E_t/\partial y_t = (\mathbf{w} \cdot \mathbf{x}_t - y_t)$, $y_t = \mathbf{w} \cdot \mathbf{x}_t$, and $\partial y_t/\partial w_1 = x_{1t}$, so

$$
\frac{\partial E_t}{\partial w_1} = (\mathbf{w} \cdot \mathbf{x}_t - y_t)\, x_{1t}. \tag{2.26}
$$

Given that the delta term for the tth association is

$$
\delta_t = (\mathbf{w} \cdot \mathbf{x}_t - y_t), \tag{2.27}
$$

we then have

$$
\frac{\partial E_t}{\partial w_1} = \delta_t\, x_{1t}. \tag{2.28}
$$

When considered over both associations, the gradient of the error function with respect to w_1 is

$$
\frac{\partial E}{\partial w_1} = \sum_{t=1}^{2}\delta_t\, x_{1t}. \tag{2.29}
$$

21

Similarly, the gradient with respect to w_2 is

$$\frac{\partial E}{\partial w_2} \quad = \quad \sum_{t=1}^{2} \delta_t \, x_{2t}. \qquad (2.30)$$

As was the case for a single weight, the gradients $\partial E/\partial w_1$ and $\partial E/\partial w_2$ point uphill. Therefore, the relative magnitudes of the two component gradients $\partial E/\partial w_1$ and $\partial E/\partial w_2$ determine the *direction of steepest ascent* with respect to the error function E. The direction of steepest ascent is a vector on the ground plane that points in the direction to go in order to increase the value of E as quickly as possible. This direction is represented by the *nabla* symbol (∇), which is a vector of scalar gradients:

$$\nabla_{\mathbf{w}} E \quad = \quad \left(\frac{\partial E}{\partial w_1}, \frac{\partial E}{\partial w_2} \right), \qquad (2.31)$$

where the subscript $\mathbf{w}$ indicates a derivative with respect to $\mathbf{w}$. As was the case for one weight, if the direction of steepest ascent is ∇E

Gradient Descent for a Network With Two Weights
initialise network weights $\mathbf{w}$ to random values
set learning to true
while *learning* **do**
    set recorder of weight change vectors $\Delta \mathbf{w}$ to zero
    foreach *association from $t = 1$ to 2* **do**
        set input unit states $\mathbf{x}$ to tth training vector $\mathbf{x}_t$
        get state of output unit $y_t = \mathbf{w} \cdot \mathbf{x}_t$
        get delta term $\delta_t = y_t - y_t$
        get weight gradient for tth input vector $\nabla E_t = \delta_t \mathbf{x}_t$
        get change in weights for tth input vector $\Delta \mathbf{w}_t = -\epsilon \nabla E_t$
        accumulate weight changes in $\Delta \mathbf{w} \leftarrow \Delta \mathbf{w} + \Delta \mathbf{w}_t$
    end
    update weights $\mathbf{w} \leftarrow \mathbf{w} + \Delta \mathbf{w}$
    if *gradient $|\nabla E| \approx 0$* **then**
        set learning to false
    end
end

then the direction of steepest descent is $-\nabla E$, as shown in Figure 2.6. Accordingly, if the current value of the weight vector is $\mathbf{w}_{\text{old}}$, then

$$\mathbf{w}_{\text{new}} \quad = \quad \mathbf{w}_{\text{old}} - \epsilon \nabla E. \tag{2.32}$$

Learning is achieved by repeated application of Equation 2.32, as depicted in Figure 2.6. Near the optimal weight vector $\mathbf{w}^*$, the magnitude of the gradient $|\nabla E| = ((\partial E/\partial w_1)^2 + (\partial E/\partial w_2)^2)^{1/2}$ is approximately zero (where $|\cdot|$ denotes vector length).

2.6. Learning Many Associations

It can be shown that a linear neural network with I input units and one output unit can learn up to I associations perfectly. However, visualising the error surface of such networks is difficult, if not impossible, for most mortals.

We can represent such a network as a number of distinct networks that all share the same input units, but where each network has its own output unit. This idea is shown in Figure 2.7a for a network with $I = 4$ input and $K = 4$ output units, which can be considered as four networks, each of which has (the same) four input units and a unique output unit (one such network is shown in Figure 2.7b).

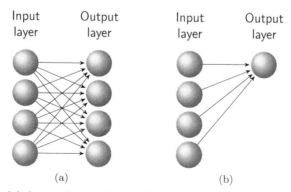

(a)   (b)

Figure 2.7. (a) A neural network with four input units and four output units (i.e. a 4-4 network) can be viewed as four neural networks like the one in (b), where each of the four neural networks has the same four input units but a different output unit (i.e. four 4-1 networks).

More generally, a network that has I input and K output units (i.e. an I-K network) can be represented as K distinct (I-1) networks, each of which has (the same) I input units and a unique output unit. Because the weights belonging to each output unit do not affect the state of any other output unit, each I-1 network can learn independently of the others. If we consider each output unit to be part of an I-1 network, then the collection of states of the output units is the network's response to an input vector $\mathbf{x}_t$. Specifically, the state of each output unit is given by an inner product, so the output states are

$$
\begin{aligned}
y_{1t} &= \mathbf{w}_1^\mathsf{T} \mathbf{x}_t, \\
&\vdots \qquad \vdots \\
y_{Kt} &= \mathbf{w}_K^\mathsf{T} \mathbf{x}_t,
\end{aligned}
\tag{2.33}
$$

where the *transpose operator* T is needed because we need to distinguish between row and column vectors (see Appendix C). Each column vector $\mathbf{w}_i$ represents the I weights connecting to one output unit:

$$
\mathbf{w}_i = (w_{i1}, \ldots, w_{iI})^\mathsf{T}.
\tag{2.34}
$$

If we represent the output states as a column vector

$$
\mathbf{y}_t = (y_{1t}, y_{2t}, \ldots, y_{Kt})^\mathsf{T},
\tag{2.35}
$$

then we can rewrite Equation 2.33 as

$$
\mathbf{y}_t = (\mathbf{w}_1^\mathsf{T}, \mathbf{w}_2^\mathsf{T}, \ldots, \mathbf{w}_K^\mathsf{T})^\mathsf{T} \mathbf{x}_t.
\tag{2.36}
$$

Combining the column vectors $\mathbf{w}_i$ defines the *weight matrix*

$$
W = (\mathbf{w}_1, \mathbf{w}_2, \ldots, \mathbf{w}_K)^\mathsf{T}.
\tag{2.37}
$$

We can now rewrite Equation 2.36 as

$$
\mathbf{y}_t = W \mathbf{x}_t,
\tag{2.38}
$$

which defines the output vector $\mathbf{y}_t$ in response to an input vector $\mathbf{x}_t$.

2.7. Learning Photographs

In order to demonstrate a linear neural network performing the task of learning photographs, we need a network in which each input unit represents the value of one image pixel. And, to show how a network can act as a content addressable memory, we can use a network with an output that is effectively an entire image, so there should be as many output units as there are image pixels. Thus, if an image $\mathbf{x}_t$ consists of $50 \times 50 = 2,500$ pixels, then the network must have $I = 2,500$ input units and $K = 2,500$ output units. Each input unit is connected to every output unit, so there are a total of $I \times K = 6,250,000$ weights. Despite these large numbers, this network has the same general architecture as in Figure 2.7a, but with 2,500 input and output

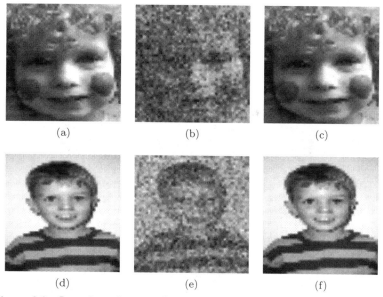

(a) (b) (c)

(d) (e) (f)

Figure 2.8. Learning photographs using a network with the same type of architecture as in Figure 2.7a. Each photograph $\mathbf{x}_t$ consists of 50×50 pixels. A linear network was used, with an array of $I = 50 \times 50$ input units and an array of $K = 50 \times 50$ output units. The network was trained to associate each of two training vectors (a and d) with itself, so that the input (a) yielded an output very similar to (a). Adding noise to (a) yielded (b), and when (b) was used as input to the network, the output was (c), showing that the network's memory is content addressable. Similarly, adding noise to (d) yielded (e), and when (e) was used as input to the network, the output was (f).

units rather than four. Given an input image $\mathbf{x}_t$, the output is obtained from Equation 2.38.

Such a linear network was trained on the two 50×50 images shown in Figure 2.8a and Figure 2.8d. Specifically, the network was trained to associate each image with itself, so if the input was the image $\mathbf{x}_t$ then the target vector at the output was $\mathbf{y}_t = \mathbf{x}_t$. Because this network was trained to associate its input with an output identical to the input, it is called an *autoassociative network*. After training, if the image in Figure 2.8a was used as input, then as expected this image is reproduced at the output; the same near-perfect performance was obtained for Figure 2.8d. This effectively demonstrates the ability of the network to recognise an image, or (more accurately) to discriminate between two images.

Next, instead of presenting the network with perfect input images, noise was added to the input images. The resultant noisy images are shown in Figures 2.8b and 2.8e. When Figure 2.8b was presented to the network, the output was Figure 2.8c. Similarly, when Figure 2.8e was presented to the network, the output was Figure 2.8f. Thus, by producing a denoised version of each input image, the network effectively recognised the underlying image.

Because each association is stored in all the weights, deleting some weights has no discernible effect on the results. Thus, even this simple neural network displays all three of the key characteristics of human memory described in Section 1.3.

2.8. Summary

Starting with the simplest possible neural network, consisting of one input unit and one output unit, we saw how a single association can be learned using gradient descent. We then applied this method to learn two associations in a neural network with two input units and one output unit. From this, it is a relatively trivial matter to extend gradient descent to any number of input and output units. This was demonstrated for two associations consisting of photographs, where it was shown that a neural network can reconstruct degraded images to their original forms.

Chapter 3

Perceptrons

By the study of systems such as the perceptron, it is hoped that those fundamental laws of organization which are common to all information handling systems, machines and men included, may eventually be understood.

F Rosenblatt, 1958.

3.1. Introduction

So far, we have used a neural network to learn associations between particular inputs and outputs. But we would like to be able to *classify* inputs that may be superficially different as belonging to the same class of objects. For example, given that there are many different possible images of a teapot (Figure 1.4), we would like a neural network to classify all of those images as belonging to the class called *teapots*. One of the first neural networks designed to learn this type of classification task was the *perceptron*. A crucial aspect of the perceptron was the way in which it appeared to mimic human memory:

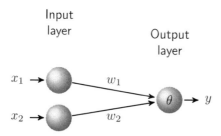

Figure 3.1. A perceptron with one output unit, which has a threshold θ.

The memory of the perceptron is distributed, in the sense that any association may make use of a large proportion of the cells in the system, and the removal of a portion of the association system would not have an appreciable effect on the performance of any one discrimination or association, but would begin to show up as a general deficit in all learned associations.
F Rosenblatt, 1958.

3.2. The Perceptron Learning Algorithm

A *perceptron* is essentially a linear associative network with many input units and one output unit, but with the addition of a threshold applied to the state of the output unit (Figure 3.1). If the total input u to the output unit exceeds this threshold then the output unit's state is $y = +1$; otherwise it is $y = -1$. To see how classification might be achieved, let's start with the simplest possible example: classifying input vectors into two possible classes.

For reasons that will become apparent, each input vector consists of just two elements, which can be interpreted as an image containing two pixels. However, images are rarely perfect, and they contain noise, which corrupts the original image. Consequently, we usually have a population of images, where each image contains a noisy version of the

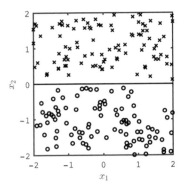

Figure 3.2. Defining two classes. Each data point $\mathbf{x} = (x_1, x_2)$ defines a location. All points on or below the line, defined by $x_2 \leq 0$, belong to class C_1, and all points above the line belong to class C_2.

original noiseless image. Our objective is to train a neural network to classify the entire population of images correctly.

If an image $\mathbf{x} = (x_1, x_2)$ belongs to the class C_1 then we would like the neural network output y to be the target value $\mathsf{y}_1 = -1$, and if $\mathbf{x}$ belongs to class C_2 then we would like the neural network output to be $\mathsf{y}_1 = +1$. For simplicity, we define all input vectors $\mathbf{x}$ in which $x_2 \leq 0$ as belonging to class C_1 (i.e. $\mathbf{x} \in C_1$) and all input vectors in which $x_2 > 0$ as belonging to class C_2 (i.e. $\mathbf{x} \in C_2$), as shown in Figure 3.2. This is written succinctly as

$$\mathbf{x} \in \begin{cases} C_1 & \text{if } x_2 \leq 0, \\ C_2 & \text{if } x_2 > 0. \end{cases} \tag{3.1}$$

Because each image consists of just two pixels with values x_1 and x_2, we can represent each input vector as a point in a two-dimensional graph of x_1 versus x_2. For each class, the population of images defines a cluster of points, as shown in Figure 3.2; in this case the points on or below the line belong to class C_1, and the points above the line belong to C_2.

For a perceptron with a weight vector $\mathbf{w}$ and an input vector $\mathbf{x}$, the total input u to the output unit is given by the inner product

$$u = \mathbf{w} \cdot \mathbf{x}. \tag{3.2}$$

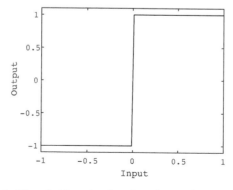

Figure 3.3. Threshold activation function with a threshold $\theta = 0$.

If this input exceeds the threshold θ then the output unit state is set to $y = +1$; otherwise it is set to $y = -1$, as shown in Figure 3.3. This arrangement is expressed succinctly as

$$
y \quad = \quad \begin{cases} -1 & \text{if } u \leq \theta, \\ +1 & \text{if } u > \theta. \end{cases} \tag{3.3}
$$

For simplicity, we assume $\theta = 0$ here.

The perceptron learning rule states that if an input vector is correctly classified then do nothing, but if it is misclassified then update the weights as follows: $\mathbf{w}_{\text{new}} \leftarrow \mathbf{w}_{\text{old}} + \Delta\mathbf{w}$, where

$$
\Delta\mathbf{w} \quad = \quad \begin{cases} -\epsilon\,\mathbf{x} & \text{if } \mathsf{y} < 0 \text{ and } y > 0, \\ +\epsilon\,\mathbf{x} & \text{if } \mathsf{y} > 0 \text{ and } y < 0. \end{cases} \tag{3.4}
$$

The perceptron learning algorithm is summarised on page 35 and (to modern eyes) would seem a complicated way to implement a form of gradient descent. If the classes are *linearly separable* (see below), then the *perceptron convergence theorem* guarantees that the optimal weights $\mathbf{w}^*$ are learned.

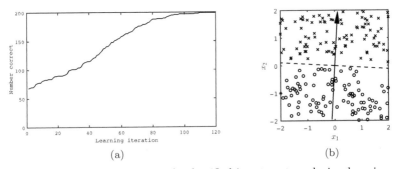

Figure 3.4. (a) Number of correctly classified input vectors during learning. (b) After training, the weight vector $\mathbf{w}$ (arrow) is nearly vertical, and the dashed decision boundary is perpendicular to the weight vector. If $|\mathbf{w}| = 1$ then the inner product $u_t = \mathbf{w} \cdot \mathbf{x}_t$ provides an orthogonal projection of each input $\mathbf{x}_t$ onto $\mathbf{w}$. All points above the decision boundary yield $u_t > 0$, whereas all points below the line yield $u_t < 0$, so all points are correctly classified.

As an example, a set of $N = 200$ input vectors to be classified consists of $N_1 = 100$ vectors belonging to C_1 and $N_2 = 100$ belonging to C_2. During training, the number of correctly classified input vectors increases, as shown in Figure 3.4a.

When the neural network has finished learning, the final weight vector can be drawn as a line in the input space (the arrow in Figure 3.4b), and a line perpendicular to this vector defines a *decision boundary*. In this example, the decision boundary is a line that is approximately horizontal, as shown by the dashed line in Figure 3.4b. The network classifies input vectors below the decision boundary as belonging to C_1 and inputs above the boundary as belonging to C_2.

The point is that any weight vector defines a decision boundary, and in the perceptron, this boundary is always a straight line. This matters because it means that any two classes which cannot be separated by a straight line cannot be classified by a perceptron. If two classes can be separated by a straight line then they are said to be linearly separable.

Now let's back up a little and work out why the decision boundary is perpendicular to the weight vector. To understand this, we need a geometric interpretation of the mapping from input to output. For an

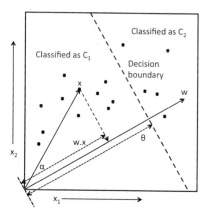

Figure 3.5. The decision boundary for the perceptron in Figure 3.1. The length of the orthogonal projection of a data point $\mathbf{x}$ onto a weight vector $\mathbf{w} = (0.89, 0.45)$ is given by the inner product $\mathbf{w} \cdot \mathbf{x} = |\mathbf{x}|\,|\mathbf{w}|\cos\alpha$, where α is the angle between $\mathbf{w}$ and $\mathbf{x}$, and $|\mathbf{w}| = 1$. If $\mathbf{w} \cdot \mathbf{x} \leq \theta$ then $\mathbf{x}$ is classified into class C_1, or else it is classified into C_2; the threshold θ corresponds to a length along $\mathbf{w}$.

31

input vector $\mathbf{x}$, the input u to the output unit is the inner product $u = \mathbf{w} \cdot \mathbf{x}$ (Equation 3.2). For convenience, we assume that the weight vector is maintained at unit length by setting $\mathbf{w} \leftarrow \mathbf{w}/|\mathbf{w}|$, where $|\mathbf{w}| = \sqrt{w_1^2 + w_2^2}$, so that $|\mathbf{w}| = 1$. Geometrically, if $|\mathbf{w}| = 1$ then the inner product is the length of the *orthogonal projection* of $\mathbf{x}$ onto $\mathbf{w}$, as shown in Figure 3.5, so the input u is simply a length measured along $\mathbf{w}$. If $u \leq \theta$ then $\mathbf{x}$ is classified as belonging to class C_1; otherwise it is classified as C_2. Just as u is a length measured along $\mathbf{w}$, so θ is also a length along $\mathbf{w}$. From Figure 3.5, any input vector $\mathbf{x}$ that projects to a point on $\mathbf{w}$ such that $u = \mathbf{w} \cdot \mathbf{x} > \theta$ gets classified as C_2. Geometrically, it can be seen that all such points lie to the right of the (dashed) line that is orthogonal to $\mathbf{w}$ and which intersects $\mathbf{w}$ at a distance θ from the origin, so this line is the decision boundary.

From Figure 3.4b, we can see that all points in class C_1 project to values u below $x_2 = 0$; similarly, all points in class C_2 project to values u above $x_2 = 0$. Once we have found the weight vector $\mathbf{w}$, the decision boundary is a line perpendicular to $\mathbf{w}$ that separates the two sets of projections onto $\mathbf{w}$.

3.3. The Exclusive OR Problem

The *exclusive OR problem* (XOR) was almost single-handedly responsible for what is now called the first *neural network winter*. An initial flurry of excitement over perceptrons rapidly faded after Minsky and Papert (1969) proved that perceptrons cannot solve this apparently simple problem.

The XOR problem can be summarised as four associations, where each association comprises an input vector $\mathbf{x}_t$ and a corresponding target value y_t:

$$\mathbf{x}_1 = (-1, -1) \rightarrow y_1 = -1, \quad \mathbf{x}_2 = (+1, +1) \rightarrow y_2 = -1, \quad (3.5)$$

$$\mathbf{x}_3 = (-1, +1) \rightarrow y_3 = +1, \quad \mathbf{x}_4 = (+1, -1) \rightarrow y_4 = +1. \quad (3.6)$$

This set of associations defines the *exclusive OR function*, depicted as four two-pixel images in Figure 3.6. It is called exclusive OR because the output unit has a state of $y = +1$ only if exactly one of the two input units has a state of +1; otherwise the output unit has a state of −1. More generally, this classification problem consists of classifying any input vectors within one pair of opposite quadrants as C_1, and input vectors within the other two quadrants as C_2, as shown in Figure 3.6.

However, whereas the classification examples in the previous section could be solved using a neural network with two input units and one output unit, this neural network cannot solve the XOR problem. The reason for this can be understood in terms of the decision boundaries possible with a perceptron.

We know that the only decision boundaries possible with a perceptron are straight lines. But the data points representing the class C_1 lie in two opposite quadrants of the input space defined by x_1 and x_2, as shown in Figure 3.6. Similarly, the data points representing the class C_2 lie in the other two opposite quadrants of the input space. This means that there is no straight line that can separate the data points in C_1 from those in C_2; and this means that it is impossible for a perceptron to classify these points correctly. Of course, we could try running a perceptron on these data, but the beauty of mathematical analysis is that it allows us to prove that there is no point in doing so.

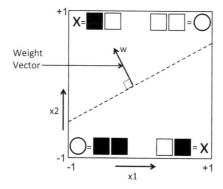

Figure 3.6. Geometric representation of the XOR problem, with each vector represented as a two-pixel image $\mathbf{x} = (x_1, x_2)$, where black $= -1$ and white $= +1$. A weight vector $\mathbf{w}$ defines a decision boundary (dashed) that splits the input space into two regions. If class C_1 contains two items (open circles) located at opposite corners $(-1, -1)$ and $(+1, +1)$, and C_2 has two items (crosses) at $(-1, +1)$ and $(+1, -1)$, then there is no straight-line decision boundary that can split the input space into C_1 and C_2. The weight vector shown defines a decision boundary that fails to separate the two classes.

3.4. Why Exclusive OR Matters

The fact that a perceptron cannot solve the XOR problem may seem trivial. Surely, the XOR problem is of purely academic interest? In abstract terms, the exclusive OR problem can be expressed as discriminating between two pairs of features: one pair includes X and not Y, whereas the other pair includes Y but not X. These features can be pixel values, as in the example above, or whole sets of connected pixels that define a visual feature. The point is that if two classes of objects are classified as different because one class has a feature X and not Y, and the other class has a feature Y and not X, then these classes represent an XOR problem.

For example, the letter H has a vertical bar on the right but no horizontal bar at the top, whereas F has a horizontal top bar but no vertical right bar, as shown in Figure 3.7. In contrast, the letter L has no top bar and no bar on the right, whereas an inverted L has both a top bar and a bar on the right. For brevity, we use L' to represent an inverted L. If we define a class $C_1 = (F, H)$ as containing F and H, and a class $C_2 = (L, L')$ as containing L and inverted L, then discriminating between these classes represents an XOR problem.

This classification task is not a fanciful vague analogy of the XOR problem, but an exact example of it. Consider two pixels located roughly at the arrow tips in Figure 3.7a. In an image of an L these two

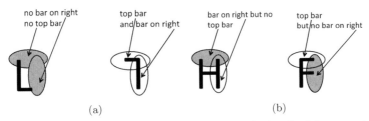

(a)   (b)

Figure 3.7. The exclusive OR (XOR) problem depicted with two sets of images. (a) The letters L and inverted L (represented as L') make up the class $C_1 = (L, L')$. (b) The letters F and H make up the class $C_2 = (F, H)$. Crucially, pixels at the arrow tips in (a) have values $(-1, -1)$ for L and $(+1, +1)$ for L', whereas the same pixels in (b) have values $(-1, +1)$ for H and $(+1, -1)$ for F; so these two pixels alone represent an XOR problem, which implies that C_1 and C_2 are not linearly separable.

pixels are both white, $(+1, +1)$, whereas in the image of an L' those same pixels are black, $(-1, -1)$. Similarly, these two pixels are white and black, $(+1, -1)$, in the image of an H, but they are black and white, $(-1, +1)$, in the image of an F, as shown in Figure 3.7b.

For the two-pixel image considered above, a linear network defines a line through the 2D input space. Similarly, if a letter resides in an image of, say, $8 \times 8 = 64$ pixels, this defines a 64-dimensional space, and each image is represented by a point in this space. Additionally, just as a line separates the space of two-pixel images into two regions, so a 63-dimensional plane separates images in the 64-dimensional space into two regions. We already know that if the image consisted only of the two pixels at the arrow tips in Figure 3.7a or Figure 3.7b, then a linear network could not divide the 2D space so that one region contains the

---

The Perceptron Learning Algorithm
if $\mathbf{x}$ belongs to class C_1 then target y $= -1$, else y $= +1$
initialise network weights $\mathbf{w} = (w_1, w_2)$ to random values
set learning rate $\epsilon = 0.01$
set learning $=$ true
while *learning* **do**
  set learning $=$ false
  foreach *association from* $t = 1$ *to* T **do**
    get tth training vector $\mathbf{x}_t = (x_1, x_2)$
    get input to output unit $u_t = \mathbf{w} \cdot \mathbf{x}_t$
    get state of output unit $y_t = \text{sign}(u_t)$
    (next: if any input is misclassified, set learning to true)
    if *($y_t < 0$ and $y_t > 0$)* **then**
      $\Delta \mathbf{w}_t = -\epsilon \mathbf{x}_t$
      set learning $=$ true
    end
    if *($y_t > 0$ and $y_t < 0$)* **then**
      $\Delta \mathbf{w}_t = +\epsilon \mathbf{x}_t$
      set learning $=$ true
    end
    update weights $\mathbf{w} \leftarrow \mathbf{w} + \Delta \mathbf{w}_t$
  end
end

two-pixel images $(-1, -1)$ and $(+1, +1)$ and the other contains the two-pixel images $(-1, +1)$ and $(+1, -1)$. It follows that a linear network cannot separate the 64-dimensional space into two regions such that one region contains the class $C_1 = (F, H)$ and other contains $C_2 = (L, L')$. In other words, there is no linear decision boundary that can separate the class C_1 from C_2. Therefore, as a matter of principle, a perceptron cannot classify F and H into class C_1 and L and L' into class C_2.

3.5. Summary

Historically, the ups and downs of the perceptron represent a microcosm of neural network history. Initially there is much excitement, as the neural network is compared to the human brain. Then there is disappointment, as the practical limitations of the neural network are gradually realised. Then, after a neural network winter lasting several years, a new neural network is invented, along with much excitement as the neural network is once again compared to the human brain. It is as hard to deny the truth of this pattern as it is to deny that, eventually, there will come a time when there will be no more winters.

Chapter 4

The Backpropagation Algorithm

Until recently, learning in multilayered networks was an unsolved problem and considered by some impossible.
T Sejnowski and C Rosenberg, 1986.

4.1. Introduction

The backpropagation algorithm or *backprop* was brought to prominence by Rumelhart, Hinton, and Williams (1986).

It might seem obvious that the performance of a perceptron could be improved by increasing the number of layers of units. The problem is knowing how to train such a *multi-layer perceptron*. If we used a method based on gradient descent then this would involve the derivative of the perceptron unit activation function. However, because the perceptron unit activation function is a step function, its derivative is infinite. Another strategy would be to increase the number of layers in a linear associative network, where each unit has a linear activation function. However, just as the composite input/output function of a linear associative network with two layers is linear (see Chapter 2), the composite function of a linear associative network with many layers is also linear; adding layers adds no functionality.

A compromise would be to add extra layers with units that have activation functions that lie somewhere between the step function of a perceptron and the linear activation function of a linear associative network. One such compromise is represented by a *sigmoidal* (S-shaped) activation function, often referred to as a semi-linear activation function (Figure 4.1). A typical sigmoidal activation function is

$$y = f(u) = (1 + e^{-u})^{-1}, \qquad (4.1)$$

where u is the total input to a unit. The derivative of this activation function is

$$\frac{dy}{du} = y(1 - y), \qquad (4.2)$$

as shown in Figure 4.1. Unlike a step function, a sigmoidal activation function has a finite derivative for all input values. Additionally, in contrast to a network of linear units, the overall input/output function computed by a network with three (or more) layers of sigmoidal units cannot be computed by any network with just two layers of sigmoidal units; so adding layers here does add functionality.

In historical terms, the compromise represented by a sigmoidal activation function was not deduced in the straightforward manner suggested above, but it is the solution implicit in backpropagation networks. Moreover, backpropagation networks only became well known after an interlude of several years, during which Hopfield nets and Boltzmann machines dominated the field. Even though there was a considerable interval between perceptrons and the development of backpropagation networks, the learning algorithms they employ are qualitatively similar. For this reason, backpropagation will be described before we consider Hopfield nets and Boltzmann machines.

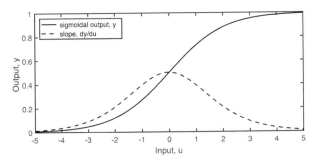

Figure 4.1. Sigmoidal activation function (solid curve, Equation 4.1) and its derivative (dashed curve, Equation 4.2, not drawn to scale).

4.2. The Backpropagation Algorithm

The backpropagation algorithm or *backprop* comprises two phases: 1) a forward phase, in which the states of units are propagated from the input layer to the output layer; and 2) a backward phase, in which error terms are propagated backwards from the output layer to the input layer.

Notation. A backprop network has three layers of units, as in Figure 4.2. We represent the output or state of the ith unit in the input layer as x_i, the state of the jth unit in the hidden layer as z_j, and the state of the kth unit in the output layer as y_k; the numbers of units in these layers are I, J and K, respectively. The total input to a unit in the input, hidden and output layers is represented by u_i, u_j and u_k, respectively. Because the activation function of each input unit is an identity function, the state of the input layer is the same as the current input (training) vector.

Forward Propagation of Inputs. Each of the $t = 1, \ldots, T$ associations comprises an input vector $\mathbf{x}_{it} = (x_{11}, \ldots, x_{It})$ and a target output y_{kt}. For the tth association, the total input to the jth hidden unit is a weighted sum of the I unit states in the input layer:

$$u_{jt} = \sum_{i=1}^{I} w_{ij}\, x_{it} - b_j, \qquad (4.3)$$

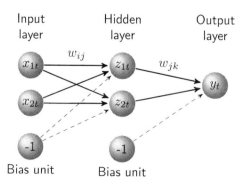

Figure 4.2. A 2-2-1 network showing how bias weights can be implemented by adding a bias unit that connects to the hidden and output layers with a fixed state of -1.

where w_{ij} is the weight connecting the ith input unit to the jth hidden unit, and b_j is the bias of the jth hidden unit. Equation 4.3 can be written more succinctly if we treat the bias as if it came from an extra *bias unit* that has a constant output of -1, with corresponding weight $w_{I+1,j} = b_j$:

$$u_{jt} = \sum_{i=1}^{I+1} w_{ij}\, x_{it}. \tag{4.4}$$

The activation function of units in the input and output layers is usually the identity function (Figure 2.3), whereas the activation functions f_j of units in the hidden layer are sigmoidal,

$$z_{jt} = f_j(u_{jt}) = (1 + e^{-u_{jt}})^{-1}, \tag{4.5}$$

as shown in Figure 4.1. Similarly, the kth output unit (our network only has one) has a total input of

$$u_{kt} = \sum_{j=1}^{J+1} w_{jk}\, z_{jt}, \tag{4.6}$$

where w_{jk} is the weight connecting the jth hidden unit to the kth output unit; the state of the kth output unit is therefore $y_{kt} = f_k(u_{kt})$, where the output layer activation function is usually the identity function, $f_k(u_{kt}) = u_{kt}$. In summary, the state of each output unit is

$$y_{kt} = f_k \left(\sum_{j=1}^{J+1} w_{jk}\, f_j \left(\sum_{i=1}^{I+1} w_{ij}\, x_{it} \right) \right). \tag{4.7}$$

Given a target state y_t for the tth association, the error is $E_t = (y_t - \mathsf{y}_t)^2$. Considered over T associations, the error function is usually the same quadratic function as in Chapter 2 (Equation 2.27):

$$E = \sum_{t=1}^{T} E_t = \frac{1}{2} \sum_{t=1}^{T} (y_{kt} - \mathsf{y}_{kt})^2. \tag{4.8}$$

Backward Propagation of Errors. The rule for adapting weights in a network with three layers of units is identical to the rule for the two-layer network described in Chapter 2, and therefore involves the gradient of E with respect to each weight in the network. From Chapter 2, we know how to calculate this gradient for the weights connecting to output units, so this section is really about how to calculate the gradient of E for the weights connecting to hidden units. In fact, the advent of *automatic gradient* software tools (e.g. autograd[141]) has made the explicit calculation of derivatives for backpropagation redundant; but it is always a good idea to know exactly what such automatic tools calculate in practice.

There is a kind of anti-symmetry between the calculation of unit states and the adaptive change in weight values. We have seen how the input to an output unit is a weighted sum of states of units in the previous hidden layer, and that the input to a hidden unit is a weighted sum of states of units in the previous input layer. When adapting weights, rather than working from the input layer to the output layer, we work backwards from the output layer to the input layer. To achieve this, we define a *delta term* for each unit. Specifically, we shall see that the changes in weight between an input unit and a hidden unit depend on the delta term of the hidden unit, and the delta term of the hidden unit is a weighted sum of delta terms from units in the output layer. We can express this formally as follows.

For the tth association, the change in the weight between the jth hidden unit and the kth output unit is

$$\Delta w_{jkt} = -\epsilon \frac{\partial E_t}{\partial w_{jk}}, \tag{4.9}$$

where ϵ is the learning rate and where the gradient of E_t can be expressed using the chain rule as

$$\frac{\partial E_t}{\partial w_{jk}} = \frac{\partial E_t}{\partial u_{kt}} \frac{\partial u_{kt}}{\partial w_{jk}}. \tag{4.10}$$

Here u_{kt} is the input to the kth output unit for the tth association.

It will prove useful to define the delta term of the kth output unit as the first term on the right of Equation 4.10, which is the derivative of E with respect to the input to that unit:

$$\delta_{kt} = \frac{\partial E_t}{\partial u_{kt}}. \qquad (4.11)$$

Given Equation 4.6, the second term on the right of Equation 4.10 is

$$\frac{\partial u_{kt}}{\partial w_{jk}} = z_{jt}, \qquad (4.12)$$

so we can write Equation 4.9 as

$$\Delta w_{jkt} = -\epsilon \, \delta_{kt} \, z_{jt}. \qquad (4.13)$$

This is a general recipe for updating weights in a backprop network. The only problem lies in calculating the delta terms of hidden layers. Fortunately, just as the state of each unit in the output layer is calculated by propagating unit states forward from the input layer, so the delta term of each unit in the hidden layer can be calculated by propagating delta values backward from the output layer. To do this, we first need to evaluate the delta term of each output unit.

The Delta Term of an Output Unit. For each output unit, we can use the chain rule to express the delta term in Equation 4.11 as

$$\delta_{kt} = \frac{\partial E_t}{\partial y_{kt}} \frac{dy_{kt}}{du_{kt}}, \qquad (4.14)$$

where

$$\frac{\partial E_t}{\partial y_{kt}} = (y_t - \mathsf{y}_t), \qquad \frac{dy_{kt}}{du_{kt}} = 1, \qquad (4.15)$$

because for output units $y_{kt} = u_{kt}$. So Equation 4.14 can be written as

$$\delta_{kt} = (y_{kt} - \mathsf{y}_{kt}). \qquad (4.16)$$

When considered over all training vectors, the gradient of E is

$$\frac{\partial E}{\partial w_{jk}} = \sum_{t=1}^{T} \delta_{kt} \, z_{jt}, \qquad (4.17)$$

so the change in w_{jk} is

$$\Delta w_{jk} = -\epsilon \sum_{t=1}^{T} (y_{kt} - \mathsf{y}_{kt})\, z_{jt}. \qquad (4.18)$$

The Delta Term of a Hidden Unit. For a weight w_{ij} between the ith input unit and the jth hidden unit, the gradient with respect to E_t can be obtained using the chain rule:

$$\frac{\partial E_t}{\partial w_{ij}} = \frac{\partial E_t}{\partial u_{jt}} \frac{\partial u_{jt}}{\partial w_{ij}}. \qquad (4.19)$$

Just as the input to each output unit depends on every hidden unit state, so the delta term of each hidden unit depends on the delta term of every output unit (see Figure 4.3). We can recognise the first term

---

Backprop (Short Version)
    initialise network weights **w** to random values
    set learning to true
    while *learning* **do**
        set vector of gradients ∇E to zero
        foreach *association from $t = 1$ to T* **do**
            set input unit states $\mathbf{x}_{it}$ to tth training vector
            get state of output units $\mathbf{y}_{kt}$
            get delta term δ_{kt} for each output unit
            use output delta terms to get hidden unit delta terms
            use delta terms to get vector of weight gradients ∇E_t
            accumulate gradient $\nabla E \leftarrow \nabla E + \nabla E_t$
        end
        get weight change $\Delta \mathbf{w} = -\epsilon \nabla E$
        update weights $\mathbf{w} \leftarrow \mathbf{w} + \Delta \mathbf{w}$
        if $|\nabla E| \approx 0$ **then**
            set learning to false
        end
    end

4 The Backpropagation Algorithm

on the right of Equation 4.19 as the delta term of the jth hidden unit,

$$\delta_{jt} = \frac{\partial E_t}{\partial u_{jt}}, \tag{4.20}$$

which we evaluate below. The final term of Equation 4.19 evaluates to

$$\frac{\partial u_{jt}}{\partial w_{ij}} = x_{it}, \tag{4.21}$$

so that

$$\frac{\partial E_t}{\partial w_{ij}} = \delta_{jt} x_{it}, \tag{4.22}$$

which fits the general recipe defined in Equation 4.13. The hidden unit delta term can be evaluated using the chain rule:

$$\delta_{jt} = \frac{\partial E_t}{\partial z_{jt}} \frac{dz_{jt}}{du_{jt}}. \tag{4.23}$$

Because the error E_t includes all output units, and because the state z_{jt} of the jth hidden unit affects all output unit states, it follows that z_{jt} must contribute to the error of every output unit. The extent to which the error of each output unit depends on each hidden unit state z_{jt} clearly depends on the value of z_{jt}. Accordingly, we proceed by evaluating the first term on the right of Equation 4.23 as

$$\frac{\partial E_t}{\partial z_{jt}} = \sum_{k=1}^{K} \frac{\partial E_t}{\partial u_{kt}} \frac{\partial u_{kt}}{\partial z_{jt}}. \tag{4.24}$$

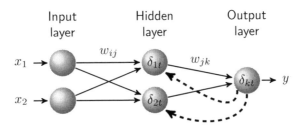

Figure 4.3. Backward propagation of delta term δ_{kt} of the output unit through connection weights in a 2-2-1 network. Bias unit not shown.

We can recognise the delta term $\delta_{kt} = \partial E_t / \partial u_{kt}$ of each output unit, and $\partial u_{kt} / \partial z_{jt} = w_{jk}$ so that

$$\frac{\partial E_t}{\partial z_{jt}} = \sum_{k=1}^{K} \delta_{kt}\, w_{jk}. \tag{4.25}$$

Substituting Equations 4.24 and 4.25 into Equation 4.23 yields

$$\delta_{jt} = \frac{dz_{jt}}{du_{jt}} \sum_{k=1}^{K} \delta_{kt}\, w_{jk}. \tag{4.26}$$

Now we can see that the delta term of a hidden unit is proportional to a weighted sum of the delta terms of units in the output layer.

Using Equation 4.2, which gives $dz_{jt}/du_{jt} = z_{jt}(1 - z_{jt})$, the delta term of a hidden unit is

$$\delta_{jt} = z_{jt}(1 - z_{jt}) \sum_{k=1}^{K} \delta_{kt}\, w_{jk}, \tag{4.27}$$

and so Equation 4.22 can be written as

$$\frac{\partial E_t}{\partial w_{ij}} = \left(z_{jt}\,(1 - z_{jt}) \sum_{k=1}^{K} \delta_{kt}\, w_{jk} \right) x_{it}. \tag{4.28}$$

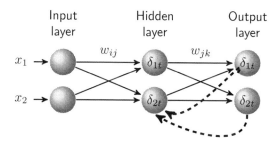

Figure 4.4. Backward propagation of delta terms of output units through connection weights in a 2-2-2 network. Note that the delta terms of *all* output units contribute to the delta term of *each* hidden unit.

For all T associations, the gradient of E with respect to w_{ij} is

$$\frac{\partial E}{\partial w_{ij}} = \sum_{t=1}^{T} \delta_{jt} x_{it} \qquad (4.29)$$

so that

$$\Delta w_{ij} = -\epsilon \sum_{t=1}^{T} \delta_{jt} x_{it}. \qquad (4.30)$$

At this point, we have obtained an expression for the weight change applied to every weight in the neural network.

Weights as Vectors. For practical purposes, we define the $I + 1$ weights (including bias) between the input layer and the jth hidden unit as a weight vector

$$\mathbf{w}_j^{\text{hid}} = (w_{j1}, \ldots, w_{jI}, w_{j,I+1}), \qquad (4.31)$$

and collect the weights to all hidden units in the hidden layer weight vector

$$\mathbf{w}^{\text{hid}} = (\mathbf{w}_1^{\text{hid}}, \ldots, \mathbf{w}_J^{\text{hid}}), \qquad (4.32)$$

which consists of $N^{\text{hid}} = (I + 1) \times J$ weights. Similarly, we define the $J + 1$ weights from the hidden layer to the kth output unit as

$$\mathbf{w}_k^{\text{opt}} = (w_{k1}, \ldots, w_{kJ}, w_{k,J+1}), \qquad (4.33)$$

and the entire set of weights to all output units as

$$\mathbf{w}^{\text{opt}} = (\mathbf{w}_1^{\text{opt}}, \ldots, \mathbf{w}_K^{\text{opt}}), \qquad (4.34)$$

which consists of $N^{\text{opt}} = (J + 1) \times K$ weights. We then concatenate the weights of the hidden and output units into a single vector

$$\mathbf{w} = (\mathbf{w}^{\text{hid}}, \mathbf{w}^{\text{opt}}) = (w_1, \ldots, w_N), \qquad (4.35)$$

which consists of $N = N^{\text{hid}} + N^{\text{opt}}$ weights.

The Vector Gradient. We can then write the gradient with respect to $\mathbf{w}$ as a vector (which is analogous to Equation 2.31),

$$\nabla E = \left(\frac{\partial E}{\partial w_1}, \ldots, \frac{\partial E}{\partial w_N} \right). \tag{4.36}$$

The change in the weight vector in the direction of steepest descent is

$$\Delta \mathbf{w} = -\epsilon \, \nabla E, \tag{4.37}$$

The Backpropagation Algorithm (Long Version)
initialise network weight vector $\mathbf{w}$ to random values
set learning to true
while *learning* **do**
    set recorder of weight gradient vector ∇E to zero
    foreach *association from $t = 1$ to T* **do**

        Forward pass for tth association:
        set input unit states $\mathbf{x}$ to tth training vector $\mathbf{x}_t$
        get state of output units $\mathbf{y}_t$

        Backward pass for tth association:
        calculate delta term δ_{kt} for each output unit
        calculate gradient for each output weight
        $\nabla E_{jkt} = \delta_{kt} z_{jt}$
        store ∇E_{jkt} in one element of ∇E_t

        use δ_{kt} of all output units to calculate δ_{jt} of each hidden unit
        calculate gradient for each hidden weight $\nabla E_{ijt} = \delta_{jt} z_{it}$
        store ∇E_{ijt} in one element of ∇E_t

        accumulate gradient $\nabla E \leftarrow \nabla E + \nabla E_t$
    end

    calculate weight changes: $\Delta \mathbf{w} = -\epsilon \nabla E$
    update weights $\mathbf{w} \leftarrow \mathbf{w} + \Delta \mathbf{w}$
    if $|\nabla E| \approx 0$ **then**
        set learning to false
    end
end

---

and the rule for changing the weight vector is

$$\mathbf{w}_{new} \quad = \quad \mathbf{w}_{old} + \Delta \mathbf{w}. \qquad (4.38)$$

Solving XOR With Backprop. We can use backprop to solve the XOR problem using the 2-2-1 neural network shown in Figures 4.5 and 4.6. If we set the activation function of the hidden and output units to be sigmoidal, then the XOR problem is solved in under 40 learning iterations, as shown in Figure 4.6. However, the final weights produced by backprop can be inscrutable. Accordingly, using input values and target outputs of 0 or 1, idealised weights are shown in Figure 4.5.

4.3. Why Use Sigmoidal Hidden Units?

A general lesson from the XOR example above is that the input and output layers do not need to have sigmoidal activation functions. The underlying reason for this involves a remarkable theorem of Cybenko (1989), which states that one layer of nonlinear hidden units is sufficient to approximate any mapping from input to output units (where units in the input and output layers have linear activation functions). It follows that any nonlinear activation function that the input and output units could have can be absorbed into the nonlinear mapping provided by the hidden layer.

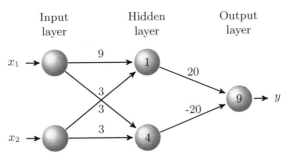

Figure 4.5. Solving the XOR problem. Each unit is labelled with a bias weight, which gets subtracted from its input. Binary vectors of the XOR problem are assumed to consist of 0s and 1s, and the hidden and output units have sigmoidal activation functions.

The only problem is that Cybenko's theorem does not state how many hidden units are required to learn a given set of associations, nor how long it should take for the network to learn those associations. For a problem like XOR, it is not hard to discover by trial and error that two hidden units suffice. However, for more complex problems, the correct number of hidden units is not known.

4.4. Generalisation and Over-fitting

How do we recognise the number 5? Clearly, we were not born with that ability, so we had to learn it. But in order to learn to recognise a 5, we had to be exposed to many examples. Additionally, so that we do not confuse a 5 with any other character, we had to be exposed to examples of characters that are not 5, especially characters that are similar to a 5 (e.g. S). So, we not only learn to recognise 5, but we also learn to recognise S as not 5. In other words, we learn to *discriminate* between a 5 and all other characters. However, we also recognise general handwritten characters, even though we have not seen those particular examples before; so we are able to *generalise* beyond the examples we have learned. This ability to generalise represents a problem at the core of all learning, both within and beyond neural networks.

To see how generalisation can fail, we examine a simple example in detail. Suppose the training data consist of the six associations indicated by the dashed line in Figure 4.7a. This sounds almost trivial,

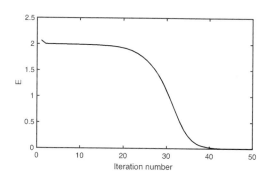

Figure 4.6. The error function E during training on the XOR problem.

but it displays all of the fundamental problems confronting any system
that learns from examples.

The network has one input unit, one output unit, and N^h hidden
units, where N^h will be varied as an experiment. If the network has
a large number of hidden units then it can learn a wide variety of
mappings from input to output. For simplicity, let's call the input-to-
output mapping a function $y = F(x)$, where the precise nature of this
function depends on the values of the weights $\mathbf{w}$ that connect input
units to hidden units and hidden units to output units.

If we had access to a large number of associations in the training
data, then it is probable that the network would adjust its weights so
that the network mapping function F is a good approximation to the
required function F^* (i.e. $F \approx F^*$). But in practice it is rarely the case
that the number of associations in the training set is sufficiently large
to guarantee that $F \approx F^*$.

For this simple example, we can visualise the entire network function
F by probing the network with a range of input values between -1 and
$+1$ and then recording the corresponding output values. For a network
with three hidden units, after training the network function F maps
each training input to its target value, and the network function is
smooth, as in Figure 4.7a. However, as the number of hidden units is
increased, the network function F can adopt increasingly complicated

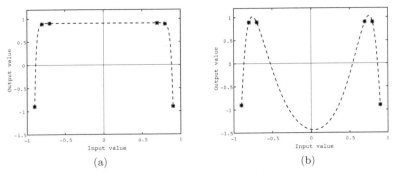

(a)   (b)

Figure 4.7. Over-fitting. Network function $y = F(x)$ (dashed line) with three
hidden units (a) and four hidden units (b). Training data are shown as six
asterisks. The network function in (a) seems about right, but over-fitting
occurs in (b).

forms, as in Figure 4.7b. For example, with four hidden units, an input of $x = 0.1$ yields an output of about $y = -1.4$, which is definitely not what was intended. The network with four hidden units does map each training input to its target value, but inputs at intermediate values get mapped to outputs that are frankly bizarre. This is a classic case of *over-fitting*, which amounts to paying too much attention to the details of the data whilst ignoring the underlying trend. In this example, over-fitting was reduced by increasing the training set so that it includes inputs with values close to zero.

A robust method for reducing over-fitting is *early stopping*. This consists of splitting the data into three sets: a training set (90% of the data), a validation set (5%), and a test set (5%). The validation set acts like a proxy test set during training, so the network is trained on the training set while the performance error is simultaneously monitored on the validation set (Figure 4.8). Once the performance error on the validation set begins to increase, over-fitting is probably occurring, so training is stopped. In theory, performance on the test set should be similar to performance on the validation set. Empirical experiments using large data sets suggest that generalisation improves in proportion to the logarithm of the number of training items in the data set (Sun et al., 2017). In other words, there are diminishing generalisation returns as the size of the training set is increased.

More generally, we can assume that the data are samples from a function that is fairly smooth, where smoothness can be measured in

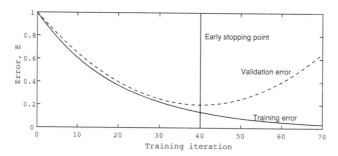

Figure 4.8. Schematic example of early stopping. While learning a training set, the error on a separate validation set is monitored to gauge generalisation performance. Training is stopped when the validation error stops decreasing. Generalisation is measured by performance on the test set.

terms of curvature. The process of constraining function approximation to conform to such generic assumptions falls under a general class of *regularisation methods*, which includes *pruning* weights based on Bayesian principles[137], and *dropout* (see Section 9.5).

4.5. Vanishing Gradients

Early attempts to train networks with many hidden layers encountered the problem of *extreme gradients* — that is, gradients that became larger or smaller with each successive layer. These are known as the *exploding gradient* and *vanishing gradient* problems, respectively. In practice, the exploding gradient problem is more relevant to temporal backprop networks (see Section 4.8). The vanishing gradient problem occurs because the gradient of the error function E with respect to the weights shrinks rapidly for layers further away from the output layer. This matters because the weight changes applied to each layer are proportional to this gradient, so almost no learning occurs in the layers closest to the input layer.

As an example of vanishing gradients, consider a network with two hidden layers, as in Figure 4.9. Application of the chain rule means that the gradient of E_t with respect to the weights of units in the output layer involves the derivative

$$\frac{\partial E_t}{\partial w_{jk}} = \frac{\partial E_t}{\partial y_{kt}} \left[\frac{dy_{kt}}{du_{kt}} \right] \frac{\partial u_{kt}}{\partial w_{jk}}. \tag{4.39}$$

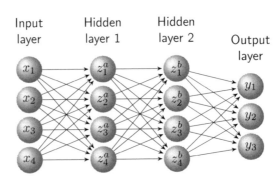

Figure 4.9. A backprop neural network with two hidden layers, indicated by superscripts a and b.

If the output units have sigmoidal activation functions then the problem is immediately apparent. The term in square brackets is the gradient of the sigmoidal activation function, which is

$$f'(u_k) = y_k \left(1 - y_k\right). \tag{4.40}$$

From this and Figure 4.1 we can see that the gradient has a maximum value when $y_k = 0.5$, but it approaches zero as $y_k \to 0$ or 1.

One reason for taking the activation function of the output layer to be the identity function is to reduce the vanishing gradient problem. If $y_k = f(u_k) = u_k$ then the derivative of the activation function is $f'(u_k) = 1$, so

$$\frac{\partial E_t}{\partial w_{jk}} = \left(y_{kt} - \mathsf{y}_{kt}\right) z_{jt}^b, \tag{4.41}$$

where y_k is the target value for the kth output unit. But even this does not overcome the vanishing gradient problem, because the only way for a network to implement a nonlinear input/output function is for its hidden units to have nonlinear activation functions (see Section 2.2). For clarity, we omit the t subscript from the equations below. For weights that project to units in hidden layer 2 (with state z_j^b), the gradient is

$$\frac{\partial E}{\partial w_{mj}} = \frac{\partial E}{\partial y_k} \left[\frac{dy_k}{du_k}\right] \left(\frac{\partial u_k}{\partial z_j^b} \left[\frac{dz_j^b}{du_j}\right] \frac{\partial u_j}{\partial w_{mj}}\right), \tag{4.42}$$

where we have ignored the summation over units in the output layer (see Equation 4.24). Finally, for weights that project to units in hidden layer 1 (with state z_m^a), the gradient is

$$\frac{\partial E}{\partial w_{im}} = \left(\frac{\partial E}{\partial y_k}\left[\frac{dy_k}{du_k}\right]\right)\left(\frac{\partial u_k}{\partial z_j^b}\left[\frac{dz_j^b}{du_j}\right]\right)\frac{\partial u_j}{\partial z_m^a}\left[\frac{dz_m^a}{du_m}\right]\frac{\partial u_m}{\partial w_{im}}, \tag{4.43}$$

where $\partial u_k / \partial z_j^b = w_{jk}$ and $\partial u_j / \partial z_m^a = w_{mj}$, so that

$$\frac{\partial E}{\partial w_{im}} = \frac{\partial E}{\partial y_k}\left[\frac{dy_k}{du_k}\right] w_{jk}\left[\frac{dz_j^b}{du_j}\right] w_{mj}\left[\frac{dz_m^a}{du_m}\right]\frac{\partial u_m}{\partial w_{im}}, \tag{4.44}$$

53

where we have ignored the summation over units in hidden layer 2.

Notice that each term in square brackets is the gradient of an activation function, and it gets multiplied by the activation function gradient from the previous term (layer). This means that the gradient of E_t for the first hidden layer involves the products of activation function gradients from all layers closer to the output layer. Because the weight change between the jth and kth units is proportional to the gradient $\partial E_t / \partial w_{jk}$ (see Equation 4.37), it follows that as we consider layers closer to the input, the gradients of E_t shrink, and so too do the weight changes. Consequently, almost all of the changes in weights made during training tend to be concentrated close to the output layer. This, in turn, means that almost all the learning takes place close to the output layer.

A partial solution is to use the *cross-entropy* error function

$$E_t^{\text{cross}} \;=\; \sum_{k=1}^{K} \mathsf{y}_{kt} \log \frac{1}{y_{kt}} + (1 - \mathsf{y}_{kt}) \log \frac{1}{(1 - y_{kt})}. \qquad (4.45)$$

Using a sigmoidal activation function, it can be shown that the gradient of the cross-entropy function with respect to weights connecting to the output layer is the same as Equation 4.41. Thus, there is an equivalence between using 1) a linear output layer activation function with a quadratic error function, and 2) a sigmoidal activation function with a cross-entropy error function. However, even option 2) does not eliminate the vanishing gradient problem, because hidden unit layers still rely on gradients with the same form as in Equation 4.40.

Aside from any other considerations, if the network weights are initialised with large values then any unit with a sigmoidal activation function will tend to be saturated (i.e. close to zero or one). This means that the derivative of the unit activation function, and therefore the derivative of E with respect to that unit's input weights, will be close to zero. This problem can be ameliorated using *batch normalization*[53].

A different approach is to initialise the weights so that they are close to a minimum of E, and then use backprop to optimise the weights. This can be achieved either by *pre-training* the layers one by one (Chapter 7), or by pre-training using a denoising autoencoder

(Section 9.9) as in Glorot and Bengio (2010). Indeed, it seems odd to call such pre-training a form of weight initialisation; and, in practice, pre-training may account for most of the learning effort, with backprop providing some fine-tuning. Additionally, principled weight initialisation can have substantial benefits, as demonstrated in Glorot and Bengio (2010). However, precisely how much advantage can be gained from pre-training versus principled weight initialisation remains an open research question.

4.6. Speeding Up Backprop

Trying to find the optimal network weights by taking one small step at a time is a robust, but notoriously inefficient, method. Fortunately, the problem of minimising a function E with respect to a set of parameters $\mathbf{w}$ belongs to a class of optimisation problems for which a suite of standard methods exist.

Gradient descent methods have to contend with three fundamental problems. First, the direction of steepest descent does not necessarily point directly at the minimum, so the path to the minimum can be fairly circuitous as it follows the twists and turns of the steepest descent path (Figure 4.10).

Second, and probably more importantly, the magnitude of the gradient of any function decreases as the function's minimum is approached. Because the step size of the weight change is proportional to the magnitude of the gradient, successive step sizes decrease as the distance to the minimum decreases. Thus, in principle, the minimum can only be reached after an infinite number of steps (this is analogous to Zeno's paradox).

Third, error surfaces can contain long shallow valleys, which have very small gradients along the length of the valley and very large gradients on the valley walls. Because the change in a weight is proportional to its gradient, a learning rate that is large enough to make progress along the valley floor can effectively eject the weight vector from the valley altogether. Conversely, a learning rate that is small enough to prevent ejection can yield glacial progress along the valley floor.

These problems can be alleviated to some extent by using *second-order methods*[88]. Such methods depend on estimating the local curvature of the function (as opposed to its gradient) and using this to jump to the estimated minimum. The curvature is simply the gradient of the gradient, and in the case of two parameters it is defined by a 2×2 matrix of second derivatives, known as a *Hessian matrix*. More generally, a problem with n parameters defines a function whose curvature is given by an $n \times n$ Hessian matrix. Second-order methods such as the *Broyden–Fletcher–Goldfarb–Shanno* (BFGS) algorithm and the simpler *conjugate gradient* technique are beyond the scope of this book; suffice it to say that second-order methods and simple gradient descent arrive at the same solution for estimated parameter values, but second-order methods tend to reach this solution sooner. A practical introduction to these methods can be found in Press et al. (1989).

Several methods exist for speeding up learning without estimating the Hessian, and one of the earliest to be introduced involved a *momentum term*. This is based on the simple heuristic that if a series of consecutive steps $\Delta\mathbf{w}$ lead in approximately the same direction in $\mathbf{w}$, then the minimum of E probably lies in that direction, so it is a good idea to take bigger steps in that direction. More formally, the current weight update is a linear combination of the current gradient ∇E_t and the previous weight update $\Delta\mathbf{w}_{t-1}$:

$$\Delta\mathbf{w}_t \leftarrow \alpha\Delta\mathbf{w}_{t-1} + \epsilon\nabla E_t, \qquad (4.46)$$

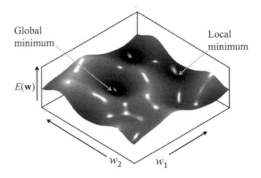

Figure 4.10. Schematic diagram of local and global minima in the error function $E(\mathbf{w})$ for a network with just two weights.

where α is a parameter that controls the amount of momentum and ϵ is the learning rate parameter. The value of α is typically initialised to between 0.5 and 0.9. For example, this ought to work well if **w** is at the bottom of a long shallow valley where the gradient (and therefore the step size) along the valley floor is small. However, like all heuristic methods, there are likely to be regions of the error surface where using momentum is not such a good idea (e.g. heading down the side of a long shallow valley). Despite these caveats, the use of a momentum term remains a popular method for speeding up backprop and deep learning. More recent non-Hessian methods for speeding up learning include Adagrad, Adadelta, RMSprop, and Adam[134].

4.7. Local and Global Mimima

Given an initial set of weights **w** and an error function $E(\mathbf{w})$, gradient descent adjusts the weight values to move downhill, towards the nearest minimum in E. If E has only one minimum then moving towards the nearest minimum is a good strategy. However, E can have many minima, some of which are quite shallow, so they represent poor solutions (see Figures 4.10 and 4.11). The deepest minimum of E is known as the *global minimum*, and the other minima are *local minima*.

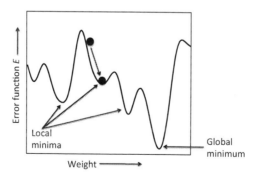

Figure 4.11. Local and global minima in a cross-section of the error function $E(\mathbf{w})$. At a given initial weight, $E(\mathbf{w})$ may be high, as represented by the black disc. Gradient-based methods always head downhill, but because they can only move downwards, the final weight often corresponds to a local minimum.

A potential disadvantage of gradient-based methods is that they head for the nearest minimum, which is usually not the global minimum.

This means that the different gradient-based search methods described above yield the same solution (i.e. the same final weight values). Thus, the only difference between these search methods is the speed with which solutions are obtained, and not the nature of those solutions. An important consideration is *time complexity*, which is the rate at which the time required to find a solution increases with the number of parameters (weights). In short, the time complexities of a range of different gradient-based methods (including second-order methods) seem to be similar[71].

We should note that learning the optimal weights of a neural network belongs to a class of problems known as *NP-complete*[6]. For such problems, the time required to find the optimal weights increases disproportionately (e.g. exponentially) with the number of weights, *regardless of the method used for training*.

However, finding the *optimal* weights may not matter in practice. During the 1980s, it gradually became apparent that neural networks do not seem to suffer from the effects of local minima. It now seems clear that the reason for this is related to the nature of the neural network error surfaces, which typically have very high dimensionalities (equal to the number of weights). This matters because it can be shown that neural network error surfaces are qualitatively similar to the high-

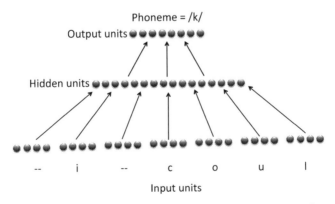

Figure 4.12. The NETtalk neural network used a sliding window of text at its input units, and each output unit represented a different phoneme. Successive phoneme outputs were fed into a speech synthesizer.

dimensional energy landscapes of physical systems called *spin-glasses*, which form the foundations of statistical physics (Solla, Sorkin, and White, 1986). Theoretical analyses suggest that not only do such surfaces have many equally deep local minima, but most of these minima are almost as deep as the global minimum (e.g. Lister 1993; Gallagher, Downs, and Wood, 1998; Choromanska et al., 2014), even for deep networks (Du et al., 2018).

4.8. Temporal Backprop

A natural extension of using neural networks to recognise static inputs (e.g. images) is the recognition of sequences[72] (e.g. speech). However, time has an intangible quality that makes it difficult to operationalise in neural networks. Unlike for a spatial image, where a unit's weights harvest data from a particular image region, it is not obvious how a network could harvest data from a particular point in time. Consequently, we begin with networks capable of taking account of events in the recent past.

The most obvious method for processing a temporal sequence in a neural network is to represent a series of events as a one-dimensional spatial array. For example, a speech signal can be represented as an array of signal values, and values over the most recent few seconds are presented to the input units of a neural network as a sliding window.

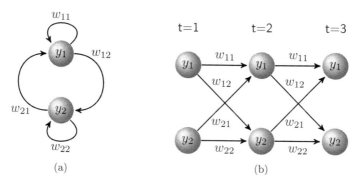

Figure 4.13. The recurrent network of two units in (a) can be unfolded to yield the equivalent feedforward network in (b). The recurrent weights (w_{11} and w_{22}) in (a) are represented as the duplicated feedforward weights in (b). Here, the recurrent network is considered over three time steps.

This is essentially the strategy adopted for the NETtalk network shown in Figure 4.12 and described in Section 4.9.

Sejnowski and Rosenberg (1987) used a network called *NETtalk* to learn the mapping between text and the basic elements of speech, called phonemes. A sliding window of seven consecutive characters was scanned along written text, and the network generated a phoneme code, which allowed a speech generator to produce audible speech. The network architecture comprised 7×29 inputs, 80 hidden units, and 26 output units, with one output unit per phoneme, as shown in Figure 4.12. The network was trained on 1024 words, for which it attained 95% accuracy. The ability of this network to generalise beyond the (relatively small) training set was tested by using new text as input, which yielded an accuracy of 78%.

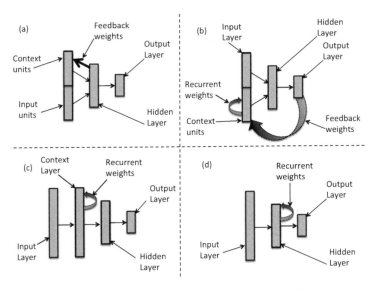

Figure 4.14. Temporal backprop network architectures. (a) A set of context units holds a copy of the hidden unit states from the previous time step using fixed feedback weights (Elman, 1990). (b) A set of context units holds information about the output units as a decaying trace of activity using fixed feedback and recurrent weights (Jordan, 1986). (c) Recurrent connections from an extra layer of hidden units ensure that units in the second hidden layer are modulated by previous inputs using learned recurrent weights (Mozer, 1993). (d) Recurrent connections from the hidden units ensure that the hidden unit states are modulated by previous inputs using learned recurrent weights (Stone, 1989).

However, because temporal sequences are usually generated by dynamical systems, it makes sense to model them using a *recurrent backprop network* that also behaves like a dynamical system, as in Figure 4.13a. Temporal networks can be represented as equivalent multi-layer networks by *unfolding*, as in Figure 4.13b. Unfolding involves reduplicating the entire network for each time step under consideration, which yields a series of networks in which contiguous networks represent network states at consecutive time steps. Thus, a change in the network state over time is represented as a change from one reduplicated network to the next.

Several variants of the basic backprop network attempt to do this by adding feedback connections between the output layer and special *context units* in the input layer [54], or from the hidden layer to context units in the input layer [19], or within the hidden layer [116], as shown in Figure 4.14. These connections ensure that the input to a unit depends not only on the current input vector from the environment, but also on previous inputs. Thus, the feedback connections implement a form of short-term memory that allows the current input to be interpreted in the context of recent inputs. More generally, the motivation for adding these feedback connections is to allow the network to learn the intrinsic dynamics of a sequence of input and output vectors. Williams and Zipser (1989) provide a backprop rule for online learning of sequences. However, most of the different varieties of recurrent backprop networks described above are special cases of a general network proposed by Pearlmutter (1988). These early temporal backprop networks have now evolved into temporal deep learning networks (Section 9.12).

Note that the vanishing gradient problem described in Section 4.5 can be particularly acute for temporal backprop networks, because the unfolding process portrayed in Figure 4.13 can yield an extremely large number of hidden layers. However, if the feedback connections are set to fixed values (i.e. they do not learn), then the problem of vanishing gradients is avoided (e.g. Elman, 1990; Jordan, 1986; Hochreiter and Schmidhuber, 1997). Finally, Schaffer et al. (2006) proved that recurrent networks can approximate dynamical systems to arbitrary precision.

4.9. Early Backprop Achievements

Backprop is widely recognised as the work-horse of modern neural networks, but its promise was apparent from its earliest days. The achievement of NETtalk has already been described in Section 4.8. An early pattern recognition application involved using underwater sonar signals to discriminate between rocks and metal cylinders, on which a performance of 90% was achieved (Gorman and Sejnowski, 1988). The idea of driverless cars is now commonplace, but one of the first attempts to use a backprop network for this task involved learning to steer a car using only a sequence of images as training data (Pomerleau, 1989). In the domain of games, Tesauro (1995) used a backprop network in combination with a *reinforcement learning algorithm* to beat the best human players at backgammon (Chapter 10).

One of the first successful attempts to train networks to recognise handwritten digits was by LeCun et al. (1989). When applied to the problem of recognising ZIP codes, an accuracy of 99% was achieved. Interestingly, their network had three layers of hidden units and used a form of weight sharing that would nowadays be recognised as implementing a type of convolutional network (Chapter 9).

4.10. Summary

Even though backprop networks came to prominence in the 1980s, their initial promise only began to be realised around 2015, probably due to a combination of faster computers, more training data, and architectural modifications. Whatever the exact reason, there is little doubt that backprop remains a key factor in the success of modern neural networks.

Chapter 5

Hopfield Nets

The ability of large collections of neurons to perform "computational" tasks may in part be a spontaneous collective consequence of having a large number of interacting simple neurons.
JJ Hopfield, 1982.

5.1. Introduction

Historically, the Hopfield net preceded the backprop networks described in the previous chapter. The Hopfield net is important because it harnesses the mathematical machinery of a branch of physics called *statistical mechanics*, which enabled learning to be interpreted in terms of *energy functions*. Hopfield nets led directly to *Boltzmann machines* (Chapter 6), which represent an important stepping stone to modern deep learning systems. Today, Hopfield nets and Boltzmann machines are collectively classified as *energy-based networks* (EBN).

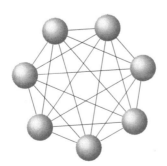

Figure 5.1. A Hopfield network with seven units and $(7 \times 7 - 7)/2 = 21$ weights (bias unit and thresholds not shown).

5.2. The Hopfield Net

A Hopfield net consists of K binary units with *symmetric, bidirectional* connection weights between them, which means that each unit is connected to all other units (Figure 5.1). In its original incarnation (Hopfield, 1982), each unit was binary and could have state $y = 0$ or $y = 1$, but it simplifies notation if we use $y = -1$ and $y = +1$ instead. The total input u_j to a unit depends on the states of all other units:

$$u_j = \sum_{i=1}^{K} w_{ij}\, y_i - \theta_j, \qquad (5.1)$$

where w_{ij} is the weight of the connection between the ith and jth units, and θ_j is the threshold of the jth unit. Note that there is no connection from a unit to itself, so if $i = j$ then $w_{ij} = 0$.

To simplify notation, we can pretend that the threshold is equal to a weight w_{ij} from an extra (bias) unit with index $i = K + 1$ that is always in state -1, so that

$$u_j = \sum_{i=1}^{K+1} w_{ij}\, y_i. \qquad (5.2)$$

For convenience, we assume $\theta = 0$ below, so we can ignore the bias unit. Units in a Hopfield net have the same activation functions as perceptron units, shown in Figure 3.3:

$$f(u_j) = \begin{cases} -1 & \text{if } u_j \leq 0, \\ +1 & \text{if } u_j > 0, \end{cases} \qquad (5.3)$$

so that the state of a unit is

$$y_j = f\left(\sum_{i=1}^{K} w_{ij}\, y_i\right). \qquad (5.4)$$

In order for the network to settle into a stable state, it is vital that unit states are updated asynchronously (i.e. one at a time) and that they are updated in random order.

5.3. Learning One Network State

The states of K units can be represented as a column vector

$$\mathbf{y} \;=\; (y_1,\ldots,y_K)^{\mathsf{T}}. \tag{5.5}$$

Suppose we wish the network to memorise a particular set of values, represented by the binary column vector

$$\mathbf{x} \;=\; (x_1,\ldots,x_K)^{\mathsf{T}}. \tag{5.6}$$

If we can find a set of weights such that the network state $\mathbf{y}$ matches the training vector $\mathbf{x}$, then $\mathbf{x}$ is a stable state of the network. In other words, if we can set the weights so that the state of each unit is

$$x_j \;=\; f\!\left(\sum_{i=1}^{K} w_{ij}\, y_i\right), \tag{5.7}$$

then, according to Equation 5.4, no further state changes will occur and the network will stay in the state $\mathbf{y} = \mathbf{x}$. In other words, if Equation 5.7 holds true, then $\mathbf{y} = \mathbf{x}$ is a stable state of the network.

To set the weights correctly, all we need to do is use the learning rule

$$w_{ij} \;=\; x_i\, x_j. \tag{5.8}$$

To see this, substitute Equation 5.8 into Equation 5.4 to get

$$y_j \;=\; f\!\left(\sum_{i=1}^{K} x_i\, x_j\, y_i\right). \tag{5.9}$$

If $y_i = x_i$ then $x_i y_i = +1$ (because $+1 \times +1 = +1$ and $-1 \times -1 = +1$), so

$$y_j = f\!\left(\sum_{i=1}^{K} x_j\right) = x_j. \tag{5.10}$$

Thus the learning rule in Equation 5.8 ensures that the learned state $\mathbf{y} = \mathbf{x}$ is a stable state.

For example, if the required state of unit U_j is $y_j = +1$ and if $y_i = -1$, then given that $w_{ij} = x_i x_j = -1$, the input to U_j contributed by U_i is $w_{ij} y_i = -1 \times -1 = +1$. Similarly, if $y_i = +1$, then since $w_{ij} = x_i x_j = +1$, the input contributed by U_i is $w_{ij} y_i = +1 \times +1 = +1$. Thus, irrespective of the state y_i, the learning rule (Equation 5.8) ensures that the weight connecting unit i to unit j pushes the state of y_j towards its required state; and the step activation function means that inputs above zero yield $y_j = +1$, while inputs below zero yield $y_j = -1$.

For T training vectors, we sum the weights for each training vector:

$$w_{ij} = \epsilon \sum_{t=1}^{T} x_{it}\, x_{jt}, \tag{5.11}$$

where $\epsilon = 1/T$ is a learning rate parameter. It can be shown that the learned states are stable in most cases[36]. We should note that if a learned state is $\mathbf{y}$ then its complementary state $\mathbf{y}' = \mathbf{y} \times (-1)$ is also stable. Note that the learning rule in Equation 5.8 can be implemented as the *outer product* (see Appendix C) $W = \mathbf{x}\mathbf{x}^\mathsf{T}$, which is a $K \times K$ matrix in which the (i, j)th entry is w_{ij}.

5.4. Content Addressable Memory

We can understand how a Hopfield net implements content addressable memory by examining the network in Figure 5.1. This network has $K = 7$ units, and we can represent the collective state of the network as a vector $\mathbf{y} = (y_1, \ldots, y_7)^\mathsf{T}$. Suppose this network has learned a vector of $+1$s, $\mathbf{x} = (+1, +1, +1, +1, +1, +1, +1)^\mathsf{T}$. If we change the

---

Hopfield Net: Learning

initialise network weights W to zero
foreach *training vector from $t = 1$ to T* **do**
   | find weights for the vector $\mathbf{x}_t$: $W_t = \mathbf{x}_t \mathbf{x}_t^\mathsf{T}$
   | update weights $W \leftarrow W + W_t$
end

state of the seventh element in **x** then this defines a corrupted vector **x**′ = $(+1, +1, +1, +1, +1, +1, -1)^\mathsf{T}$, so that the initial network state is **y** = **x**′. Note that each unit receives input from six units (i.e. all units excluding itself). Now six units have the uncorrupted (i.e. memorised) state, and one unit is corrupted. The settling process defined in Equation 5.4 means that unit U_7 receives a total input that will switch it from a corrupted state $y_7 = -1$ to an uncorrupted state $y_7 = +1$. Thus, if it so happens that the unit chosen to be updated before any other is U_7, then the learned state is recalled almost immediately, so that **y** = **x**. But what if the unit chosen to be updated before any other is not U_7?

In this case, the contribution from U_7 to the six other units will push them towards corrupted states. However, even though each of the six units $U_1, \ldots, U_6$ receives corrupted input from U_7, they also receive uncorrupted inputs from five other units. For example, U_1 receives uncorrupted input from five units, $U_2, \ldots, U_6$. Thus, to all intents and purposes, the effect of U_7's corrupted state y_7 on the other six units $U_1, \ldots, U_6$ will be out-voted by the effects of the majority of (five)

Hopfield Net: Recall

Recall vector x from corrupted vector x′
set network state to **y** = **x**′
while *stable = false* **do**
    set stable to true (can be reset in loop below)
    reset the set of unit indices to $J = \{1, \ldots, K\}$
    foreach k *from* 1 *to number of units* K **do**
        choose unit index j from J without replacement
        find input to unit j: $u_j = \sum_i w_{ij} y_i$
        note current state as $y_{\text{last}} = y_j$
        get state of unit j: $y_j = f(u_j)$
        if $y_j \neq y_{\text{last}}$ **then**
           set stable to false
        end
    end
end

uncorrupted unit states. This majority voting effect is quite literal, so that content addressable memory works provided more than half of the unit states are set to a state that has been learned previously.

5.5. Tolerance to Damage

Hopfield nets can tolerate damage to their connection weights. Just as a corrupted unit state pushes all other unit states towards incorrect states, so a corrupted weight can push one pair of units towards incorrect states. However, just as the effect of a corrupted unit state can be out-voted by the collective effect of uncorrupted unit states, so the effect of a corrupted weight can be compensated for by the presence of uncorrupted weights. Both content addressable memory and tolerance to damage yield results like that shown in Figure 5.2.

5.6. The Energy Function

The state update rule (Equation 5.4) ensures that the state of the net 'rolls' downhill on an *energy landscape* or *energy function*. This is hard to visualise for the binary units used here, but if the unit states are continuous then the energy landscape can be represented as in Figure 4.10 (with unit state along each horizontal axis). The energy landscape consists of many minima, some of which correspond to learned vectors. In effect, setting the weights to particular values

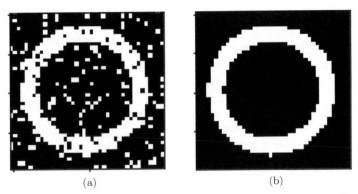

(a)   (b)

Figure 5.2. (a) Input image. (b) Recalled image, which is identical to the image learned. Reproduced with permission from Tom Stafford.

defines an energy landscape. Ideally, the process of learning defines an energy landscape in which the largest minima correspond to learned vectors. If the network state is initialised in a state that corresponds to the side of a *basin of attraction*, then the state update rule guarantees that the network state will end up in a stable state that corresponds to the bottom of this basin. We will not consider the continuous version of the Hopfield net here (Hopfield, 1984); suffice it to say that the continuous version has all of the key properties that the binary Hopfield net has. Indeed, the binary Hopfield net is really a special case of the continuous Hopfield net.

Given a set of weight values, the height of the energy function is defined for every possible set of unit states by the formula

$$E(\mathbf{y}) = -\sum_{i=1}^{K} \sum_{j=i+1}^{K} w_{ij}\, y_i\, y_j. \tag{5.12}$$

Note that the energy contributed by unit U_i is

$$E_i = -y_i \sum_{j=1}^{K} w_{ij} y_j \tag{5.13}$$

and that the total energy is the sum of these unit energies,

$$E(\mathbf{y}) = \sum_{i=1}^{K} E_i. \tag{5.14}$$

For a given pair of units, their contribution to the global energy E is only minimised if their states are mutually consistent. Recall that $w_{ij} = x_i x_j$ here. If x_i and x_j have been learned and if the units U_i and U_j are in their learned states (i.e. $y_i = x_i$ and $y_j = x_j$), then the energy contributed by this pair of units is

$$E_{ij} = -w_{ij} y_i y_j \tag{5.15}$$
$$= -x_i x_j y_i y_j \tag{5.16}$$
$$= -y_i^2 y_j^2 \tag{5.17}$$
$$= -1. \tag{5.18}$$

On the other hand, if unit U_j is in a learned state $(y_j = x_j)$ but U_i is not $(y'_i \neq x_i)$, then

$$
\begin{aligned}
E'_{ij} &= -w_{ij} y'_i y_j & (5.19) \\
&= -x_i x_j y'_i y_j & (5.20) \\
&= -(x_i y'_i) y_j^2 & (5.21) \\
&= +1. & (5.22)
\end{aligned}
$$

Thus, learned unit states yield lower energy values than other states.

The defining property of the Hopfield net energy function is that its value always decreases (or stays the same) as the network evolves according to its dynamics (Equation 5.4). This, in turn, means that the system converges to a stable state. The energy function is derived from statistical mechanics, where it is called the *Hamiltonian*; in optimisation theory it is called a *Lyapunov function*.

5.7. Summary

Hopfield nets were almost entirely responsible for ending a neural network winter. By identifying the states of neurons with the states of elements in a physical system, the whole mathematical framework of statistical mechanics, constructed piece by piece over the previous century, could be harnessed for learning in artificial neural networks. Hopfield's epiphany heralded a step-change in the perception of neural networks, which had been viewed with considerable scepticism by the more traditional members of the artificial intelligence community. Probably because Hopfield nets were formulated within the ultra-respectable framework of statistical mechanics, neural networks attracted the attention of physicists and gradually gained some acceptance amongst more technically minded researchers in artificial intelligence. And even though Hopfield nets eventually proved to be of limited practical use, there is little doubt that they laid the foundations upon which the modern era of neural networks was built.

Chapter 6

Boltzmann Machines

By studying a simple and idealized machine that is in the same general class of computational device as the brain, we can gain insight into the principles that underlie biological computation.
G Hinton, and T Sejnowski, and D Ackley, 1984.

6.1. Introduction

Introduced by Ackley, Hinton, and Sejnowski in 1985, the Boltzmann machine is important because it can be interpreted as a *generative model*. This is based on the insight that a neural network should be capable of generating unit states that have the same statistical structure as its inputs. A fundamental assumption of generative models is that the correct interpretation of input data can only be achieved if a network has learned the underlying statistical structure of those data.

Learning in generative models can be considered an (extremely loose) analogy to dreaming in humans. If a human grew up in a forest, it is likely that their dreams would contain trees and animals rather than cars and TVs. The ability of the human to generate (dream) data that exist in their environment can be taken as evidence that they have learned a model of that environment. In a similar manner, if a network can be shown to generate data that are similar to its 'environment', then it may be inferred that the network has learned about that environment.

6.2. Learning in Generative Models

A Boltzmann machine is essentially a Hopfield net, but with the addition of *hidden units*, as shown in Figure 6.1. Units that receive inputs from the environment (i.e. from the training set) are called *visible units*, whereas hidden units receive inputs only from visible units. Visible and hidden units are binary, with states that are either 0 or 1.

Learning consists of finding weights that force the visible units of the network to accurately mirror the states of those units when they are exposed to the physical environment. Thus, the problem is to find a set of weights which generates visible unit states that are similar to vectors in the training set, which is derived from the environment.

The strategy for solving this problem is implemented as two nested loops, where the inner loop is used to gather statistics that are then used to adjust the weights in the outer loop, as shown in Figure 6.2. Specifically, the inner loop functions with a fixed set of weights and has two components, commonly called the *wake* and *sleep* components. The wake inner loop component is used to estimate the correlation between the states of connected units (i.e. how often both are on) when the visible units are *clamped* (i.e. fixed) to each of the vectors in the training set. The sleep inner loop component is used to estimate

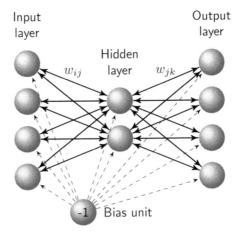

Figure 6.1. A 4-2-4 autoencoder architecture, with bias unit. All units within each layer are also connected to each other (not shown). The bias unit has a fixed state of $y = -1$. The input and output units are visible units.

the correlation between the states of connected units when the visible units are unclamped. Both inner loop components involve *simulated annealing* (described below), which is used to settle the network so that it attains thermal equilibrium before correlations are measured.

In the outer loop, for each pair of connected units, the difference between their clamped and unclamped correlations is used to adjust the weight between them. Specifically, the weight is adjusted to reduce the difference in clamped and unclamped correlations. Ideally, when learning is complete, the states of visible units in the unclamped network will be similar to the states of visible units when the network is clamped to vectors in the training set.

The reason this works is because all connections are symmetric. Therefore, the hidden unit states induced by training vectors are

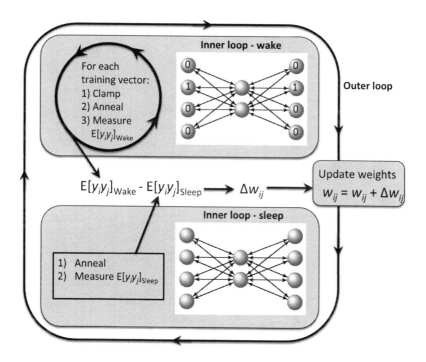

Figure 6.2. Learning in a Boltzmann machine comprises two nested loops. On each iteration of the inner loop, the correlation between unit states y_i and y_j is measured under two conditions: 1) when visible units are clamped to training vectors, which yields $\mathbb{E}[y_i y_j]_{\text{Wake}}$; and 2) when visible units are unclamped, which yields $\mathbb{E}[y_i y_j]_{\text{Sleep}}$. On each iteration of the outer loop, the weights are adjusted so that after learning, $\mathbb{E}[y_i y_j]_{\text{Wake}} \approx \mathbb{E}[y_i y_j]_{\text{Sleep}}$.

precisely the hidden unit states most likely to generate states resembling the training vectors when the visible units are unclamped. This procedure is described in more detail in the following sections.

6.3. The Boltzmann Machine Energy Function

The state of each unit is either $y_j = 0$ or $y_j = 1$, and is updated using a stochastic update rule. The probability P that the state of unit U_j will be set to $y_j = 1$ is a sigmoidal function of the unit's input u_j:

$$P = (1 + e^{-\beta u_j})^{-1}, \tag{6.1}$$

where $\beta = 1/T$; here T is a temperature parameter that determines the steepness of the activation function, as shown in Figure 6.3. Temperature plays a vital role in finding stable states of the network. The total input u_j to the unit U_j is a weighted sum of the unit states connected to U_j:

$$u_j = \sum_{i=1}^{K+1} w_{ij} y_i, \tag{6.2}$$

where K is the total number of units in the network. Note that $w_{ij} = 0$ if units U_i and U_j are not connected or if $i = j$ (i.e. each unit has no

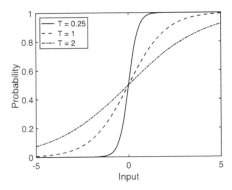

Figure 6.3.   The sigmoidal activation function used to determine the probability that a unit's state is $y = 1$ (Equation 6.1). As the temperature $T = 1/\beta$ increases, decisions regarding y become increasingly noisy.

connection to itself). A bias term is implemented with an extra $(K+1)$th bias unit, as explained in Section 5.2 and shown in Figure 6.1.

The states of the K network units are represented as a vector $\mathbf{y} = (y_1, \ldots, y_K)$. The Boltzmann machine has the same energy function as the Hopfield net in Equation 5.12,

$$E(\mathbf{y}) \quad = \quad -\sum_{i=1}^{K}\sum_{j=i+1}^{K} w_{ij} y_i y_j. \tag{6.3}$$

For simplicity, we have ignored the $(K+1)$th weight normally associated with the bias unit. The probability $p(\mathbf{y})$ that a Boltzmann machine adopts a state $\mathbf{y}$ is defined in terms of a *Boltzmann distribution*,

$$p(\mathbf{y}) \quad = \quad \frac{1}{Z} e^{-\beta E(\mathbf{y})}, \tag{6.4}$$

as shown in Figure 6.4. The term Z is the *partition function*

$$Z \quad = \quad \sum_{k=1}^{2^K} e^{-\beta E(\mathbf{y}_k)}, \tag{6.5}$$

where the sum is taken over all 2^K possible combinations of binary unit states of the entire network. The partition function ensures that values

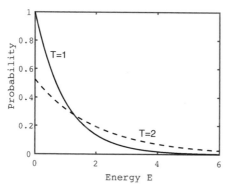

Figure 6.4. The Boltzmann distribution at temperatures $T = 1$ and $T = 2$. As the energy associated with a state increases, the probability of observing that state decreases exponentially, as defined in Equation 6.4. High-energy states become more probable at high temperatures.

of $p(\mathbf{y})$ sum to unity. Unless K is small, calculating Z is impractical; it is therefore estimated using *simulated annealing*, as described below.

Equation 6.4 is borrowed from *statistical mechanics*. It states that, once the network has reached *thermal equilibrium* at temperature $T = 1/\beta$, the probability that the network is in state $\mathbf{y}$ falls exponentially as the energy associated with that state increases. In other words, almost all states observed at thermal equilibrium are low-energy states. From a practical perspective, the temperature term T allows us to find low-energy states using simulated annealing. Note that we have used T to denote both the number of training vectors and temperature, but the different meanings can be disambiguated below because we will express temperature through the parameter $\beta = 1/T$.

6.4. Simulated Annealing

If white-hot iron is allowed to cool slowly then the atomic structure forms a low-energy, stable matrix. Conversely, if iron is cooled quickly by quenching it in cold water, then the atomic structure forms small islands of stability but the overall structure is disorganised, resulting in a brittle metal.

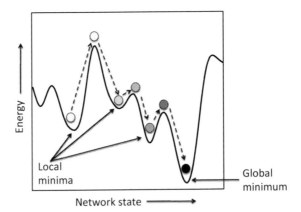

Figure 6.5. Simulated annealing. The network state is represented as a disc, and the colour of the disc represents temperature (white = hot, black = cool). At high temperatures, the network often chooses states that increase energy, allowing escape from shallow minima to deep minima. As temperature decreases, the network is more likely to choose states that decrease energy.

By analogy, if the temperature term in a Boltzmann machine is reduced slowly, this encourages the formation of low-energy stable states. More precisely, at low temperatures, Equation 6.1 dictates that a unit's state will be chosen so that it almost always decreases energy. In contrast, at high temperatures, the decision regarding a unit's state is very noisy, so its chosen state frequently increases energy. This may sound like a bad idea, but increasing energy can allow the state to escape from local minima in the energy function, as shown in Figure 6.5. If the temperature is decreased gradually, then the state can hop between successively lower local minima, so that it almost certainly arrives at the global minimum [22]. Formally, simulated annealing is a type of *Markov chain Monte Carlo* (MCMC) method.

6.5. Learning by Sculpting Distributions

We can decompose the network of K unit states $\mathbf{y}$ into a vector of H hidden unit states $\mathbf{h} = (y_1, \ldots, y_H)$ and a vector of V visible unit states $\mathbf{v} = (y_{H+1}, \ldots, y_{H+V})$, where $\mathbf{v}$ includes both input and output

---

Simulated Annealing

foreach *temperature* $T = T_{\max}$ *to* $T_{\min}$ **do**
    set $\beta = 1/T$
    foreach *settling iteration* $s = 1$ *to* S *iterations* **do**
        foreach *unclamped unit index from* $k = 1$ *to* K **do**
            choose unit U_j without replacement
            find input to U_j: $u = \sum_i w_{ij} y_i$
            get probability $P_j = 1/(1 + e^{-u\beta})$ that $y_i = 1$
            generate random number r between 0 and 1
            if $P > r$ then set $y_j = 1$, else set $y_j = 0$
        end
        settling iteration now complete
    end
    assume thermal equilibrium reached at current temperature
end
network is now in thermal equilibrium at a low temperature

---

unit states, so that $\mathbf{y} = (\mathbf{h}, \mathbf{v})$. Using these definitions, we can express formally how a network can generate visible unit states that match those from the environment: for each training vector $\mathbf{v}_t$, modify the weights so that the joint distribution $p(\mathbf{h}, \mathbf{v}_t)$ of the network units when the visible units are clamped to a training vector $\mathbf{v}_t$ is the same as the joint distribution $p(\mathbf{h}, \mathbf{v})$ when the visible units are free to vary.

6.6. Learning in Boltzmann Machines

We wish to learn the set of T training vectors

$$\{\mathbf{v}\} \quad = \quad (\mathbf{v}_1, \dots, \mathbf{v}_T). \tag{6.6}$$

In essence, if the network weights are adjusted so that the probability distribution $p_{\mathrm{s}}(\mathbf{v})$ of visible unit states *generated by the network* matches the probability distribution $p_{\mathrm{w}}(\mathbf{v})$ of the training vectors, then the network can be said to have learned the training vectors. The subscripts 's' and 'w' indicate distributions that correspond to the *sleep* and *wake* phases (respectively) of learning.

Accordingly, the learning rule for Boltzmann machines is obtained by forcing the distribution $p_{\mathrm{s}}(\mathbf{v})$ of visible unit states generated by the network when the visible units are unclamped to be similar to the distribution $p_{\mathrm{w}}(\mathbf{v})$ of visible unit states when the visible units are clamped to the training set.

So, considered over all visible unit states when unclamped, we would like the probability of each state to be the same as when the visible units are clamped. The extent to which this is not true is measured using the *Kullback–Leibler divergence* (KL) between $p_{\mathrm{s}}(\mathbf{v})$ and $p_{\mathrm{w}}(\mathbf{v})$:

$$G \quad = \quad \sum_{v=1}^{2^V} p_{\mathrm{w}}(\mathbf{v}_v) \log \frac{p_{\mathrm{w}}(\mathbf{v}_v)}{p_{\mathrm{s}}(\mathbf{v}_v)} \tag{6.7}$$

$$= \quad \sum_{v=1}^{2^V} p_{\mathrm{w}}(\mathbf{v}_v) \log p_{\mathrm{w}}(\mathbf{v}_v) - \sum_{v=1}^{2^V} p_{\mathrm{w}}(\mathbf{v}_v) \log p_{\mathrm{s}}(\mathbf{v}_v), \tag{6.8}$$

where each summation is over all 2^V combinations of visible unit states.

Note that G achieves its minimum value of zero when $p_w(\mathbf{v}) = p_s(\mathbf{v})$. The distribution of training vectors $p_w(\mathbf{v})$ is fixed by the environment, so the first term on the right is constant. Therefore, instead of minimising G we can minimise the second term, the *cross-entropy*

$$J = \sum_{v=1}^{2^V} p_w(\mathbf{v}_v) \log \frac{1}{p_s(\mathbf{v}_v)}. \tag{6.9}$$

If the number T of training vectors is large, then the number n_v of occurrences of the training vector $\mathbf{v}_v$ is approximately $p_w(\mathbf{v}_v) \times T$, so that

$$p_w(\mathbf{v}_v) \approx n_v/T. \tag{6.10}$$

Substituting Equation 6.10 into Equation 6.9 yields

$$J \approx \frac{1}{T} \sum_{v=1}^{2^V} n_v \log \frac{1}{p_s(\mathbf{v}_v)}. \tag{6.11}$$

Given that each vector $\mathbf{v}_v$ occurs n_v times in the training set, J can be estimated by summing over the T vectors in the training set:

$$J \approx \frac{1}{T} \sum_{t=1}^{T} \log \frac{1}{p_s(\mathbf{v}_t)}. \tag{6.12}$$

In practice, we ignore the factor of $1/T$ because it has no effect on the weight values $\mathbf{w}$ that minimise J. Finally, rather than minimising J, we can choose to maximise $-J \times T$ (and to drop the approximation symbol), which defines

$$L(\mathbf{w}) = \sum_{t=1}^{T} \log p_s(\mathbf{v}_t), \tag{6.13}$$

where $L(\mathbf{w})$ is standard notation for the *log likelihood* of $\mathbf{w}$, because (as we shall see in the next section) that is what it is.

6.7. Learning by Maximising Likelihood

We are primarily interested in the set of training vectors $\{\mathbf{v}\}$, defined over the visible units. The Boltzmann machine energy function was defined in Equation 6.3, which can be written more succinctly as

$$E_t = -\sum_{i,j} w_{ij} y_i y_j. \tag{6.14}$$

As a reminder, the probability that the network is in the state $\mathbf{y}$ is

$$p(\mathbf{y}) = \frac{1}{Z} e^{-\beta E(\mathbf{y})}, \tag{6.15}$$

where

$$Z = \sum_{v,h} e^{-\beta E(\mathbf{h}_h, \mathbf{v}_v)}. \tag{6.16}$$

Throughout this section, the subscript v indexes the 2^V combinations of binary visible unit states, and the subscript h indexes the 2^H combinations of binary hidden unit states. Given that $p(\mathbf{y}) = p(\mathbf{h}, \mathbf{v}_t)$, the probability of observing the visible unit state $\mathbf{v}_t$ can be found by marginalising over the hidden unit states:

$$p_s(\mathbf{v}_t) = \sum_{h=1}^{2^H} p(\mathbf{h}_h, \mathbf{v}_t). \tag{6.17}$$

Assuming that all T training vectors are mutually independent, the probability of the training set $\{\mathbf{v}\}$ given the weight vector $\mathbf{w}$ is

$$p_s(\{\mathbf{v}\}|\mathbf{w}) = \prod_{t=1}^{T} p_s(\mathbf{v}_t), \tag{6.18}$$

$$= \prod_{t=1}^{T} \sum_{h=1}^{2^H} p(\mathbf{h}_h, \mathbf{v}_t), \tag{6.19}$$

which is called the *likelihood* of the weight vector $\mathbf{w}$. Because the logarithm is a monotonic function, the weight values that maximise the likelihood also maximise the logarithm of the likelihood, so it does not matter whether we choose to maximise the likelihood or the log likelihood. In practice, it is usually easier to maximise the log likelihood

$$L(\mathbf{w}) = \log p_s(\{\mathbf{v}\}|\mathbf{w}) \tag{6.20}$$

$$= \sum_{t=1}^{T} \log p_s(\mathbf{v}_t), \tag{6.21}$$

which (as promised) tallies with Equation 6.13. Thus, in the process of learning weights that maximise $L(\mathbf{w})$, we are performing *maximum likelihood estimation* (see Appendix D). Substituting Equation 6.17 into Equation 6.21 gives

$$L(\mathbf{w}) = \sum_{t} \log \sum_{h} p(\mathbf{h}_h, \mathbf{v}_t), \tag{6.22}$$

where (from Equation 6.15)

$$p(\mathbf{h}, \mathbf{v}_t) = \frac{1}{Z} e^{-\beta E(\mathbf{h}, \mathbf{v}_t)}. \tag{6.23}$$

Substituting Equation 6.23 into Equation 6.22 yields

$$L(\mathbf{w}) = \sum_{t} \log \left(\frac{1}{Z} \sum_{h} e^{-\beta E(\mathbf{h}_h, \mathbf{v}_t)} \right) \tag{6.24}$$

$$= \sum_{t} \log \left(\sum_{h} e^{-\beta E(\mathbf{h}_h, \mathbf{v}_t)} \right) - \sum_{t} \log Z. \tag{6.25}$$

Substituting Equation 6.16 into Equation 6.25 then gives

$$L(\mathbf{w}) = \sum_{t} \log \sum_{h} e^{-\beta E(\mathbf{h}_h, \mathbf{v}_t)} - \sum_{t} \log \sum_{v,h} e^{-\beta E(\mathbf{h}_h, \mathbf{v}_v)}. \tag{6.26}$$

Using Equation 6.14, this can be rewritten as

$$L(\mathbf{w}) = \sum_{t} \log \overbrace{\sum_{h} \exp\left(\beta \sum_{i,j} w_{ij} y_i y_j \right)}^{\text{Wake}} - \sum_{t} \log \overbrace{\sum_{v,h} \exp\left(\beta \sum_{i,j} w_{ij} y_i y_j \right)}^{\text{Sleep}}. \tag{6.27}$$

However, the transition from Equation 6.26 to Equation 6.27 should be interpreted with care. Specifically, comparison of Equations 6.26 and

Boltzmann Machine Learning Algorithm

initialise network weights **w** to random values
set learning to true

while *learning* **do**

set $\mathbb{E}[y_i y_j]_{\text{Wake}} = 0$
set $\mathbb{E}[y_i y_j]_{\text{Sleep}} = 0$

collate statistics of clamped network
set correlation $\mathbb{E}[y_i y_j]_{\text{Wake}} = 0$
foreach *association from $t = 1$ to T* **do**
clamp visible unit states to $\mathbf{v}_t = \mathbf{x}_t$
anneal non-clamped unit states
iterate to estimate correlation $\mathbb{E}_t[y_i y_j]_{\text{Wake}}$
update correlation:
$\mathbb{E}[y_i y_j]_{\text{Wake}} \leftarrow \mathbb{E}[y_i y_j]_{\text{Wake}} + \mathbb{E}_t[y_i y_j]_{\text{Wake}}$
end

collate statistics of unclamped network
anneal network state
iterate at equilibrium to estimate correlation $\mathbb{E}[y_i y_j]_{\text{Sleep}}$

update weights
weight change: $\Delta w_{ij} = \epsilon \beta \left(\mathbb{E}[y_i y_j]_{\text{Wake}} - \mathbb{E}[y_i y_j]_{\text{Sleep}} \right)$
update weights: $w_{ij} \leftarrow w_{ij} + \Delta w_{ij}$

if $|\Delta \mathbf{w}| \approx 0$ **then**
set learning to false
end

end

Boltzmann Machine Recall

Recall output given an input x
clamp input unit states to **x**
anneal to find hidden and output unit states

6.27 implies that all visible unit states in the sum marked with 'Wake' are set to an element of the current training vector. In contrast, all unit states in the sum marked with 'Sleep' are independent of the training vectors. The terms wake and sleep are in common usage, by analogy with the waking and sleeping states of brains.

In order to maximise the log likelihood using gradient ascent, we need an expression for the derivative of $L(\mathbf{w})$ with respect to the weights. It can be shown that the derivative for a single weight w_{ij} is

$$\frac{\partial L(\mathbf{w})}{\partial w_{ij}} = \beta \sum_t \mathbb{E}_t[y_i y_j]_{\text{Wake}} - \beta \sum_t \mathbb{E}_t[y_i y_j]_{\text{Sleep}} \qquad (6.28)$$

$$= \beta\,(\,\mathbb{E}[y_i y_j]_{\text{Wake}} - \mathbb{E}[y_i y_j]_{\text{Sleep}}\,). \qquad (6.29)$$

where $\mathbb{E}[\cdot]$ represents *expected value* (see Glossary). The two terms on the right are often called the *wake* and *sleep* terms. The wake term refers to the co-occurrence of the states y_i and y_j weighted by the probability of those states when the visible units are clamped to a vector $\mathbf{v}_t$ from the training set. In contrast, the sleep term refers to the co-occurrence of the states y_i and y_j under the probability distribution $p(\mathbf{h}_h, \mathbf{v}_v)$ in which hidden and visible units are free to vary. The learning rule is therefore

$$\Delta w_{ij} = \epsilon\beta\big(\mathbb{E}[y_i y_j]_{\text{Wake}} - \mathbb{E}[y_i y_j]_{\text{Sleep}}\big). \qquad (6.30)$$

This can be used to perform gradient ascent using simulated annealing, as follows. For each of a sequence of temperatures from high to low, clamp each of the T training vectors to the visible units. Then repeatedly update the hidden unit states to find low-energy states at the lowest temperature, and then estimate the correlations $\mathbb{E}[y_i y_j]_{\text{Wake}}$ between all connected units. Next, unclamp the visible units and, for each of a sequence of temperatures from high to low, repeatedly sample the hidden and visible unit states to find low-energy states at the lowest temperature, and then estimate the correlations $\mathbb{E}[y_i y_j]_{\text{Sleep}}$ between all connected units. Finally, use these correlations to adjust all weights in the direction of the gradient of $L(\mathbf{w})$ with respect to $\mathbf{w}$, as defined in Equation 6.30.

6.8. Autoencoder Networks

The main ideas implicit in the Boltzmann machine can be exemplified with the *autoencoder* architecture, shown in Figure 6.1. Training consists of associating each input vector with itself, so the input and output layers have the same number of units. However, because the hidden layer has fewer units than the input layer, the states of the units in the hidden layer represent a compressed version of the input. In terms of *information theory*[123], the hidden units should represent the same amount of information as the input units. For example, the autoencoder in Figure 6.1 was trained to associate each of four binary vectors with itself: $(0001) \to (0001)$, $(0010) \to (0010)$, $(0100) \to (0100)$, and $(1000) \to (1000)$. After training, each input vector induces one of four unique states (codes) in the two hidden units (i.e. 00, 01, 10, or 11), which allows the input vector to be reproduced at the output layer[1].

The autoencoder is important for three main reasons. First, it is one of the first demonstrations of a network finding a code (implicit in the states of the hidden units) to represent its inputs. Second, even though Boltzmann machines have fallen out of favour, the general idea of forcing a network to compress its input into a hidden layer with minimal loss of information has re-emerged several times, and is now a fundamental part of neural network methodology using the backprop algorithm. Third, the development of *variational autoencoders*[2;60] promises to provide a more efficient method for training autoencoder networks (see Chapter 8).

6.9. Summary

Boltzmann machines represent an important transition between Hopfield nets and backprop networks. The statistical mechanics framework introduced by Hopfield nets allowed Boltzmann machines to learn interesting toy problems, but their slow learning rate effectively barred application to more realistic problems. As we shall see in the next chapter, a relatively small modification yielded the *restricted Boltzmann machine*, which learned more quickly and performed well on real-world problems such as handwritten digit recognition.

Chapter 7

Deep RBMs

All of this will lead to theories of computation which are much less rigidly of an all-or-none nature ... this new system of formal logic will move closer to another discipline which has been little linked in the past with logic. This is thermodynamics primarily in the form it was received from Boltzmann.

J von Neumann, 1958.

7.1. Introduction

The only difference between a Boltzmann machine and a *restricted Boltzmann machine* (RBM) is that there are no connections within each layer of an RBM, as in Figure 7.1. This modification allows a series of RBMs to be joined together to make a deep or *stacked RBM*, as in Figure 7.4.

In general, a deep neural network has more than one hidden layer. The reason for having multiple hidden layers is that the first hidden layer combines visible unit states to represent low-level features (e.g. edges) in the visible input layer, and the second hidden layer combines hidden unit states in the first hidden layer to represent higher-order features (e.g. extended lines). If this process of cumulative abstraction can be achieved over many layers, then units in the final hidden layer should represent features that are essentially whole objects. Extracting increasingly high-order features through successive layers is analogous to the processing thought to occur in the human visual system. For many years, this represented the holy grail for neural networks.

However, this plausible-sounding objective raises two questions. First, in principle, does a deep neural network have sufficient power to represent or *express* high-order features? Second, in practice, can these high-order features be learned?

The question regarding representational power or *expressibility* has been addressed in Le Roux and Bengio (2008), where it was proved that Boltzmann machines can approximate any discrete distribution to arbitrary accuracy (this also applies to RBMs). Additionally, it can be shown that each additional hidden layer increases the probability of generating the training set. Specifically, each additional layer can (given certain mild conditions[45]) increase the maximum value of the log likelihood function (Equation 6.21). The empirical finding that deep networks are useful in practice is underpinned by Eldan and Shamir (2015), who proved that increasing the depth of networks (i.e. number of layers) is exponentially more valuable than increasing the width of network layers (i.e. number of units per layer). We can therefore be reasonably confident that deep neural networks have sufficient representational power to solve most problems.

Regarding the question of whether high-order features can be learned by a deep neural network, no formal proofs exist, and so we must rely on empirical evidence. To date, the evidence seems to suggest that it

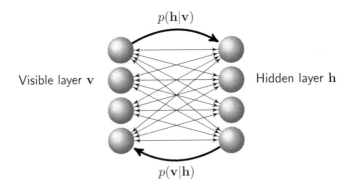

$$p(\mathbf{h}|\mathbf{v})$$

Visible layer **v**   Hidden layer **h**

$$p(\mathbf{v}|\mathbf{h})$$

Figure 7.1. A restricted Boltzmann machine (RBM) with four input units and four hidden units. Because there are no connections within each layer, the state of each unit in the hidden layer depends only on the states of units in the visible layer, and vice versa. This makes the conditional probability distributions $p(\mathbf{h}|\mathbf{v})$ and $p(\mathbf{v}|\mathbf{h})$ (thick curved arrows) easy to estimate.

is possible to train a network with hundreds of hidden layers, where deeper layers represent higher-order features (see Chapter 9). The idea of using more than one hidden layer in a neural network is not new, but in order to get such a network to learn, the problem of vanishing gradients (see Section 4.5) had to be overcome or circumvented.

7.2. Restricted Boltzmann Machines

RBMs were originally called *harmoniums*, and were first introduced by Paul Smolensky in 1986. As stated above, the only difference between a Boltzmann machine and an RBM is that there are no connections within each layer of an RBM, as shown in Figure 7.1. However, the implications of this relatively small difference are substantial. Specifically, whereas simulated annealing in a Boltzmann machine takes a long time because each individual unit state must be updated multiple times to reach equilibrium at a given temperature, the restricted connectivity in an RBM means that all of the units in each layer can be updated simultaneously. Therefore, for two connected layers, collecting co-occurrence statistics consists of alternately updating all of the units in each layer, which provides large savings. In practice, the savings are even larger, because the extensive sampling involved in simulated annealing of Boltzmann machines is replaced with a minimal sampling procedure called *contrastive divergence* in RBMs.

RBMs can be concatenated to form a stacked RBM, as in Figure 7.4. Each RBM in a stacked RBM consists of a visible input and a hidden layer. The novelty of this approach is that a new RBM is added after the previous RBM has finished learning. In effect, each new RBM adopts the previous RBM's hidden layer as its input layer[41].

7.3. Training Restricted Boltzmann Machines

The lack of connections within each layer means that the states of all units in the hidden layer do not depend on each other, but they do depend on the states of units in the visible layer. Consequently, the state of each hidden unit is independent of the states of the other hidden units, given the states of the visible units. In other words, the state of each hidden unit is *conditionally independent* of the states of the other hidden units. As an example, consider the simple RBM in Figure 7.2 with $V = 4$ visible unit states,

$$\mathbf{v} \;=\; (v_1, v_2, v_3, v_4), \tag{7.1}$$

and $H = 4$ hidden unit states,

$$\mathbf{h} \;=\; (h_1, h_2, h_3, h_4). \tag{7.2}$$

Conditional independence means that the conditional probability $p(\mathbf{h}|\mathbf{v})$ of the hidden unit states is the product of individual hidden state conditional probabilities:

$$p(\mathbf{h}|\mathbf{v}) \;=\; p(h_1|\mathbf{v})p(h_2|\mathbf{v})p(h_3|\mathbf{v})p(h_4|\mathbf{v}) \tag{7.3}$$

$$=\; \prod_{j=1}^{H} p(h_j|\mathbf{v}). \tag{7.4}$$

Similarly, the states of the visible units are conditionally independent of each other, given the states of the hidden units, and so

$$p(\mathbf{v}|\mathbf{h}) \;=\; p(v_1|\mathbf{h})p(v_2|\mathbf{h})p(v_3|\mathbf{h})p(v_4|\mathbf{h}) \tag{7.5}$$

$$=\; \prod_{i=1}^{V} p(v_i|\mathbf{h}). \tag{7.6}$$

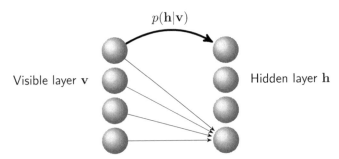

Figure 7.2. Thin lines show connections between input units and one hidden unit. The thick curve represents the conditional distribution $p(\mathbf{h}|\mathbf{v})$ of all hidden unit states given the visible unit states.

In essence, this conditional independence means that unit states can be sampled without having to iteratively update unit states for long periods. For consistency with the published literature, we have adopted notation similar to Hinton and Salakhutdinov's (2006).

The Wake Training Phase: Assuming that the training data consists of real-valued V-element training vectors $\mathbf{x}_1, \ldots, \mathbf{x}_T$, vector elements are first normalised so that the value of each element is between 0 and 1. Given a normalised training vector $\mathbf{x}_t$, the visible unit states are set to $\mathbf{v}_t = \mathbf{x}_t$, and each element of $\mathbf{v}_t$ is then treated as a probability P. The input to each binary hidden unit is

$$u_{jt} = \sum_{i=1}^{V+1} w_{ij} v_{it}, \qquad (7.7)$$

where the $(V+1)$th unit represents a bias unit with a constant state of -1. If the input to a unit is u then the probability P that the unit is on is given by the sigmoidal activation function in Equation 6.1 (repeated here with $\beta = 1$):

$$P = (1 + e^{-u})^{-1}. \qquad (7.8)$$

In general, if the probability that a unit is on is P, then its state is decided as follows. First, generate a random number r between 0 and 1; then, if $r < P$ set the unit's state to one, else set it to zero.

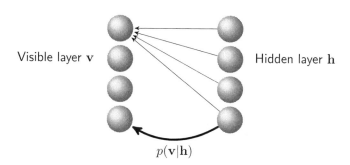

$$p(\mathbf{v}|\mathbf{h})$$

Figure 7.3. Thin lines show connections between hidden units and one visible unit. The thick curve represents the conditional distribution $p(\mathbf{v}|\mathbf{h})$ of all visible unit states given the hidden unit states.

The correlation between the ith visible unit's state and the jth hidden unit's state is estimated as

$$\mathbb{E}[v_i P_j]_{\text{Wake}} \approx \frac{1}{T}\sum_{t=1}^{T} v_{it}\, P_{jt}. \tag{7.9}$$

If this were a Boltzmann machine then we would let the network settle by sampling unit states at a series of decreasing temperatures before estimating the correlations between the states of connected units. However, Hinton et al. used heuristic arguments (based on conditional independence) to justify sampling unit states over a small number of updates. For the wake phase above, just one update is used (as above),

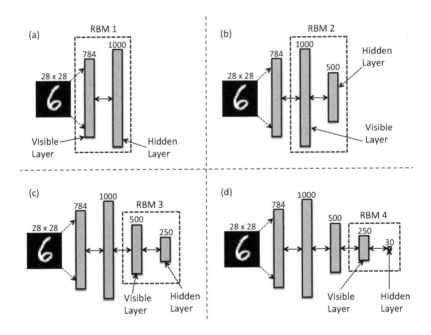

Figure 7.4. Incremental pre-training of a stacked RBM for the DAN in Figure 7.5. The number above each layer is the number of units it contains. (a) The 28×28 pixels in the image of a digit are copied to 784 ($= 28 \times 28$) units in the visible layer of the first RBM, which has 1000 units in its hidden layer. Contrastive divergence is used to train this RBM (labelled RBM 1). (b) After RBM 1 has been trained, its hidden units act as the visible units of RBM 2, which has 500 hidden units. (c) Similarly, RBM 3 has 500 visible units and 250 hidden units. (d) Finally, RBM 4 has 250 visible units and 30 hidden units.

and for the sleep phase, a small number N_{CD} of updates is required. The resultant method is called *contrastive divergence*.

The Sleep Training Phase: The state of each hidden unit is chosen in the same way as in the wake phase (i.e. Equations 7.7 and 7.8), but the state of each visible unit is decided as follows. Given sampled binary states for the hidden units, the input to the ith visible unit is

$$u_{it} = \sum_{j=1}^{H+1} w_{ij} h_{jt}, \qquad (7.10)$$

where the $(H+1)$th unit refers to a bias unit with a constant state of -1, and the probability P_{it} that the visible unit is on is given by Equation 7.8. Then the correlation between the ith visible unit's state and the jth hidden unit's state is estimated as

$$\mathbb{E}[P_i P_j]_{\text{Sleep}} \approx \frac{1}{T} \sum_{t=1}^{T} P_{it}^{N_{CD}} P_{jt}^{N_{CD}}, \qquad (7.11)$$

where the superscript N_{CD} indicates probabilities are associated with the final contrastive divergence iteration (see text box overleaf).

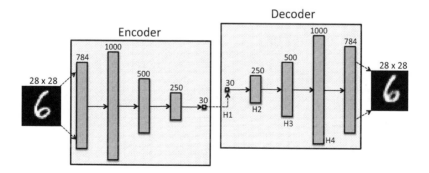

Figure 7.5. The deep autoencoder network (DAN) used for digit recognition in Hinton and Salakhutdinov (2006). After pre-training, the encoder network in Figure 7.4d is duplicated and flipped to generate the decoder network. Fine-tuning using backprop is applied to the DAN. Solid arrows depict connections, which are bidirectional during RBM pre-training and directional during fine-tuning. The dashed arrow indicates copied states.

Given a learning rate ϵ, the RBM learning rule is

$$\Delta w_{ij} = \epsilon \big(\mathbb{E}[v_i P_j]_{\text{Wake}} - \mathbb{E}[P_i P_j]_{\text{Sleep}} \big).$$ (7.12)

In the first publications involving stacked RBMs, a series of RBMs were arranged to form a *deep autoencoder network* (DAN, described in the next section) and a *deep belief network* (DBN). A DBN (Hinton, Osindero, and Teh, 2006) consists of a stacked RBM in which connections between layers are directional, except for the connections between the two final hidden layers (i.e. those furthest from the visible layer). The bidirectional connections in these final layers act as an associative memory. The success of RBMs was probably inspired by the development of multi-layer *deep Boltzmann machines*[43;99] (DBM). A theoretical analysis of contrastive divergence can be found in Larochelle et al. (2009).

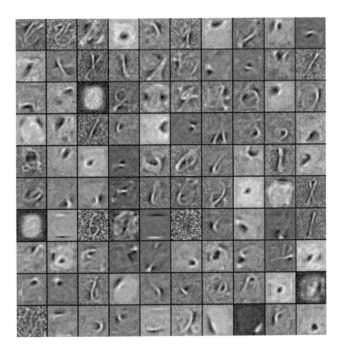

Figure 7.6. Features from a restricted Boltzmann machine trained on the MNIST data set of digits (Figure 7.7). Each image is composed of the weight values of a hidden unit in the first hidden layer. Reproduced with permission from the LISA laboratory, University of Montreal.

7.4. Deep Autoencoder Networks

In order to understand the minutiae of a landmark deep learning network, we explore the deep autoencoder network (DAN) developed by Hinton and Salakhutdinov (2006) in some detail. The overall training procedure consists of incrementally pre-training a series of stacked RBMs using contrastive divergence (Figure 7.4), and then fine-tuning the network weights using the backprop algorithm (Figure 7.5)

Pre-Training an RBM on Digits

foreach *learning iteration* **do**
    foreach *training vector* $\mathbf{x}_t$ *from* $t = 1$ *to* T **do**

        get data for clamped correlations $\mathbb{E}[v_i P_j]_{\text{Wake}}$
        set each visible unit state v_i to input value x_i
        use $\mathbf{v}_t$ to calculate input u_{jt} to each hidden unit
        calculate probability P_{jt} that hidden unit is on (Eq. 7.8)
        record wake products $v_{it} P_{jt}$ between connected units

        get data for unclamped correlations $\mathbb{E}[P_i P_j]_{\text{Sleep}}$
        initially use hidden state probabilities P_{jt} from above
        foreach $k = 1$ *to* N_{CD} *samples* **do**

            sample binary hidden states $\rightarrow \mathbf{h}_t^k$
            use $\mathbf{h}_t^k$ to calculate input u_{it}^k to each visible unit
            probability that ith visible unit is on is P_{it}^k (Eq. 7.8)

            sample binary visible states $\rightarrow \mathbf{v}_t^k$
            use $\mathbf{v}_t^k$ to calculate input u_{jt}^k to each hidden unit
            probability that jth hidden unit is on is P_{jt}^k (Eq. 7.8)

            record sleep products $P_{it}^k P_{jt}^k$ between connected units
        end

    end

    calculate $\mathbb{E}[v_i P_j]_{\text{Wake}}$ (Equation 7.9)
    calculate $\mathbb{E}[P_i P_j]_{\text{Sleep}}$ (Equation 7.11)
    update weights (Equation 7.12)
end

---

described in Chapter 4. Crucially, it can be shown that training an autoencoder to minimise reconstruction error maximises the lower bound on the mutual information between the input and the hidden unit states[133]. Hinton and Salakhutdinov (2006) used several different architectures and data sets, but we will concentrate on their results regarding digit recognition here.

The data were grey-level handwritten single digits between 0 and 9 from the MNIST data set. Each image consisted of $28 \times 28 = 784$ pixels, and each pixel was normalised to have a value between 0 and 1. The network was trained using 60,000 images and tested on a different set of 10,000 images. Learning proceeded as follows.

First, an RBM with 784 input units and 1,000 hidden units learned the training set of 60,000 images using contrastive divergence; this is labelled as RBM 1 in Figure 7.4a. After training RBM 1, its hidden layer is then used as the input (visible) layer to another RBM, labelled as RBM 2 in Figure 7.4b, which has its own hidden layer of 500 units. This process of training and then adding new hidden layers is repeated several times, resulting in the *encoder network* shown in Figure 7.4d.

However, contrastive divergence pre-training is imperfect, so the network weights are fine-tuned using the backprop algorithm. Because backprop is a form of supervised learning, both input and output (target) vectors are required, as was the case for the autoencoder described in Section 6.8. Here, this is achieved by duplicating the encoder network in a head-to-toe manner, as shown in Figure 7.5. Another adjustment is needed because all units in a backprop network have real-valued states. Accordingly, during backprop fine-tuning, each

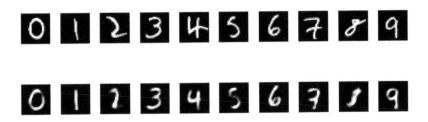

Figure 7.7. Results from the deep autoencoder network in Figure 7.5. Top: Examples of training images. Bottom: Autoencoder outputs. MATLAB code obtained from www.cs.toronto.edu/~hinton/MatlabForSciencePaper.html and modified by Peter Dunne.

binary RBM unit is treated as if it has a real-valued state equal to the probability P of being on (Equation 7.8).

For this network, both the input and the output training vectors are identical, and the network's task is to learn to map each input image to the output layer. Hidden unit characteristics are shown in Figure 7.6, and results obtained using Hinton and Salakhutdinov's code are shown in Figure 7.7.

Notice that if the RBMs had learned perfectly during pre-training, then all of the information in each image would be represented in the middle layer, and therefore no backprop fine-tuning would be required. Conversely, if the DAN had been trained using only backprop (i.e. without pre-training), then there would be very little gradient and therefore very little learning, as reported by Hinton and Salakhutdinov (2006). Specifically, they state that, 'without pre-training, the very deep autoencoder always reconstructs the average of the training data, even after prolonged fine-tuning'. Alternatively, stacked RBMs can be fine-tuned using a version of the 'wake–sleep' algorithm[42].

The fact that the input images are reproduced at the output layer suggests that most of the information implicit in the input is represented in the middle hidden layer. However, in order to measure the ability of a network to classify each image as a single digit, some further modification is required. Accordingly, an encoder network with

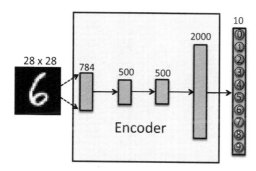

Figure 7.8. Classifying images using the network described in Hinton and Salakhutdinov (2006). After the 784-500-500-2000 encoder had been pre-trained with contrastive divergence, an output layer with 10 units was added, and then backprop was used to associate one output unit with each digit. The misclassification rate on the test set of 10,000 images was 1.2%.

four layers was trained on 60,000 images, where the numbers of units in the successive layers were 784, 500, 500 and 2000. The 2000 units in the final layer had sigmoidal activation functions, so the unit states were between 0 and 1. After pre-training, a layer of 10 classification units was connected to the hidden layer of 2000 units, as in Figure 7.8. Each classification unit had a state defined by the *softmax function*

$$y_i = \frac{e^{u_i}}{\sum_{j=1}^{10} e^{u_j}}, \tag{7.13}$$

where u_i is the total input to unit U_i. The softmax function is a generalisation of the sigmoidal activation function for more than two alternatives. The entire network was then trained using backprop by replacing stochastic binary states with deterministic real-valued probabilities, using the cross-entropy error function (Equation 4.45). The misclassification rate on a test set of 10,000 images was 1.2% (the test set was not part of the training set of 60,000 images). Hinton and Salakhutdinov stated that the best result on this data set obtained using only conventional backprop was 1.6%.

We should note that LeCun et al. (1998) had achieved an error rate of 0.95% on the MNIST test data set using a convolutional backprop network (see Chapter 9). Additionally, Ciresan et al. (2010) used backprop only to achieve a misclassification rate of 0.35% on the MNIST test data set used by Hinton and Salakhutdinov (2006), with a network configuration of 2500-2000-1500-1000-500-10. This suggests that Hinton and Salakhutdinov's pre-training effectively acted as a proxy for the extended data sets and faster processor speeds involved in Ciresan et al.'s later study.

7.5. Summary

Restricted Boltzmann machines and their role in deep autoencoders were instrumental in demonstrating the utility of neural networks for solving practical problems. The autoencoder architecture, with and without the use of RBMs, continues to have a substantial influence on neural network research[2;132].

Chapter 8

Variational Autoencoders

*When one understands the causes, all vanished images can easily be
found again in the brain through the impression of the cause.*
R Descartes, 1859.

8.1. Introduction

The main objective of a variational autoencoder is to squeeze high-
dimensional data (e.g. images) through a low-dimensional information
bottleneck. By definition, the bottleneck is narrow, which forces it to
extract as much information as possible about the data (Kingma and
Welling, 2014; Rezende et al., 2014; Alemi et al., 2017). A variational
autoencoder consists of two modules, an encoder and a decoder, as

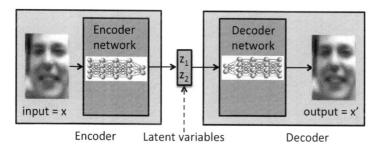

Figure 8.1.   Simplified schematic of a variational autoencoder, which
comprises an encoder and a decoder. The encoder maps each input image $\mathbf{x}$
to several output unit states (z_1 and z_2), which can be assumed to be equal
to the latent variables for now. The outputs of the encoder act as inputs to
the decoder, which produces an approximation $\mathbf{x}'$ of the input image. All
faces in this chapter are reproduced from Kingma (2017) with permission.

shown in Figure 8.1. The encoder is a neural network that transforms each input image into a vector of unit states in its output layer, which represents the values of the latent variables in the input image. The decoder uses the states of units in the encoder output layer as its input, and attempts to generate an output that is a reconstruction the encoder's input image. Variational autoencoders do not seem to suffer from the problem of over-fitting, probably because the training method includes a regularisation term.

Variational autoencoders represent a synthesis of ideas immanent in generative models such as Boltzmann machine autoencoders (Section 6.8), RBM deep autoencoder networks (Section 7.4), denoising autoencoders[133], and the *information bottleneck* (Tishby et al., 2000), which have their roots in the idea of *analysis by synthesis* (Selfridge, 1958). Unlike Boltzmann machines, which rely only on computationally intensive *Gibbs sampling*, variational autoencoders employ fast variational methods. For readers unfamiliar with these terms, Gibbs sampling provides unbiased estimates of the network weights (but those estimates have high variance), whereas variational methods provide biased estimates that have low variance. In essence, this is the nature of the trade-off between sampling and variational methods. The method described here is based on Kingma and Welling (2014), and a more detailed account of different methods for learning in variational autoencoders can be found in Kim et al. (2018).

8.2. Why Favour Independent Features?

Consider the image of a child in a hat in Figure 8.2a. How could this image be described as efficiently as possible? An extravagantly lengthy description would be the set of values of all $512 \times 512 = 262,144$ pixels in the image, which, by definition, provides enough information to allow the image to be reconstructed. A more efficient description would be 'a child in a hat sitting at a table', but this description does not provide enough information for the image to be reconstructed. Ideally, we would like a compromise between these levels of description that would allow the image to be reconstructed almost exactly. Even though the grey-level of every pixel in the image can take one out of 256 values, each grey-level is the result of a small number of underlying physical parameters, such as brightness or the orientations of local contrast edges. Crucially, if the values of these physical parameters were known, then they could be used to reconstruct the image almost exactly. These physical parameters are the *latent variables* of the image; they are called latent because they cannot usually be observed directly in the image.

Implicit in every pixel of an image is a range of different, statistically independent physical quantities, such as texture and contrast (Figure 8.2a). Given that we wish to represent inputs with many different quantities or features, it makes sense to encode inputs so that each unit in the encoder output represents a feature that is independent of the features represented by other output units. But features can appear in many combinations in the physical world. For example, if each pixel is associated with $n=7$ physical features (e.g. line colour, motion speed, motion direction, orientation, contrast, width, brightness) and if each feature can adopt $k=10$ possible values (e.g. red, green, blue . . .), then each pixel effectively represents one out of $N=k^n=10^7$ (10 million) possible combinations of features. Of course, physical features are merely implicit in an image, and it is the job of any vision system worthy of the name to make those features explicit.

Now consider just $n = 3$ features, where each feature can take one out of $k = 4$ possible values. In this case, we can represent the $N = k^n = 4^3 = 64$ different combinations of feature values in a 3D feature space,

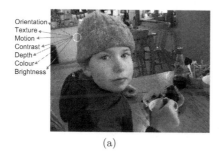

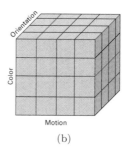

(a)   (b)

Figure 8.2. (a) Each point in an image represents many physical parameters. (b) Three-dimensional table of hypothetical populations of neurons, each sensitive to a particular combination of colour, motion, and orientation. Reproduced with permission from Stone (2012) and Teleri Stone.

where each feature is represented by a different dimension, and each combination of feature values corresponds to one of 64 small cubes, as in Figure 8.2b. Clearly, if each combination is represented by an encoder output unit then $N = 64$ units would be required. On the other hand, if each feature is represented by one unit, and if each unit can adopt $k = 4$ different states (one state per feature value), then only $n = 3$ units are required. This is why it is more efficient for a network to represent each independent feature with a single unit, rather than dedicating one unit to each possible combination of feature values.

In fact, the notion of a feature would ideally be defined as a physical property that is independent of other physical properties. For example, the size of an object is independent of its shape, and the orientation of an object is independent of its colour; so representing objects in terms of size, shape, orientation, and colour would give an efficient representation. Indeed, if a network tries to find an efficient representation, it should end up with different units being dedicated to distinct independent physical properties. Given that the only independent physical properties are features like size, colour, and orientation, we should be unsurprised to find that each unit represents a different, independent feature. The main point is that efficient representation demands that different independent features should be represented by different units.

If a neural network could encode the image in terms of independent features or latent variables, then the resultant description of the image would be the compromise referred to above. Such a description would have a Goldilocks length — not too long and not too short — known as a *minimal description length*. In summary, the answer to the question 'Why favour independent features?' is that independent features provide an efficient coding of images in terms of familiar independent physical parameters like orientation, colour, and speed.

8.3. Overview of Variational Autoencoders

The main problem solved by variational autoencoders is learning which physical latent variables describe the images in a training set. In practice, these physical latent variables are usually only implicit in the states of the encoder output units, but we will treat these output unit states as if they were physical latent variables for now.

The method used to learn is intimately related to a measure of how well latent variables have been extracted. Specifically, if a variational autoencoder has extracted the latent variables of a particular image, then we would expect that the image could be reconstructed based only on the values of these latent variables. In other words, if an image is mapped to its latent variables, then the values of these variables should be sufficient to produce an accurate rendition of the image.

Before we explore the details of the variational autoencoder, let's consider what we would expect under ideal conditions. In a perfect world, we want the variational autoencoder to extract the underlying latent variables implicit in an image. For example, given the input image of a child wearing a hat, the encoder output units of the variational autoencoder should have states that explicitly represent the colour, texture, and position of the hat in the image. Because the number of latent variables is small in relation to the number of pixels in a typical image, we expect that only a relatively small number of units will be required to represent the latent variables. In practice, this number can be as high as 100, but in order to visualise the latent variables, we can force the network to use just two latent variables, which are represented as two units in the encoder output layer.

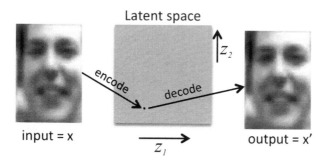

Figure 8.3. An input image $\mathbf{x}$ corresponds to one location $\mathbf{z} = (z_1, z_2)$ in a latent space of two variables z_1 and z_2. In this example, z_1 indicates the left–right head orientation, whereas z_2 indicates facial expression, as shown in Figure 8.4. The values of these two variables can then be used to recover an approximation $\mathbf{x}'$ to the input image.

Consider Figure 8.3, depicting an example used to train a variational autoencoder on images in which facial expression and head orientation varied from image to image. The number of hidden units in the input layer of the decoder was artificially restricted to two, which effectively forced the network to extract just two latent variables. The reason for restricting the number of decoder input units to two is that it enables us to visualise the nature of the latent variables being used by the variational autoencoder to reproduce the encoder input images at the decoder output layer. Because there are just two decoder input units, the states of these units, $\mathbf{z} = (z_1, z_2)$, can be represented as points in a two-dimensional coordinate system. For example, if we fix the values of the decoder input units to be $\mathbf{z} = (0.2, 0.1)$ then we can observe the

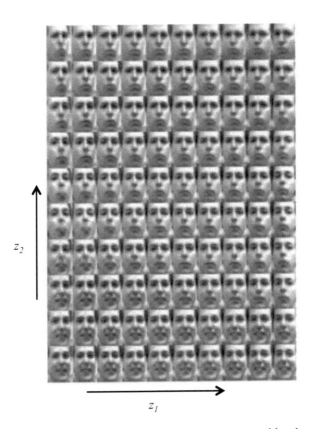

z_2

z_1

Figure 8.4. Embeddings of faces in two dimensions generated by the decoder. Head orientation varies from left to right, whereas facial expression varies along the vertical direction. From Kingma (2017) with permission.

image $\mathbf{x}'$ associated with this point as the output of the decoder when it is given the input $\mathbf{z}$. If our coordinate system has a range between 0 and 1 along each axis, then we can place $\mathbf{x}'$ at the location $\mathbf{z}$ used to generate $\mathbf{x}'$. Of course, this exercise can be repeated for uniformly spaced intervals along the z_1 and z_2 axes, which defines a regular grid of m locations $\mathbf{z}_1, \ldots, \mathbf{z}_m$, such that each location corresponds to a unique decoder output. When presented with a vector $\mathbf{z}_i$, the decoder output image is placed at the location $\mathbf{z}_i = (z_{1i}, z_{2i})$, as in Figure 8.4. The result is a visual representation of the *embedding* of the input image into two latent variables.

8.4. Latent Variables and Manifolds

We already know that the value of a two-element vector $\mathbf{z} = (z_1, z_2)$ can be plotted as a point on a plane (Figure 8.3). Similarly, an image of 10×10 pixels defines a vector $\mathbf{x} = (x_1, \ldots, x_{100})$, which specifies a point in 100-dimensional space, denoted by $\mathbb{R}^{100}$. If we consider a large number of images of faces, say, we would not expect the corresponding points to be scattered at random in $\mathbb{R}^{100}$. In fact, the majority of these images will occupy a relatively small volume in $\mathbb{R}^{100}$ (see Section 8.6).

Suppose we restrict the images by including only photographs of a single face, but taken at different angles and with expressions that

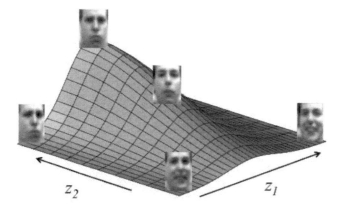

Figure 8.5. Schematic example of a two-dimensional curved manifold. Each point $\mathbf{z} = (z_1, z_2)$ on the manifold corresponds to the values of two latent variables, $z_1 =$ head orientation and $z_2 =$ facial expression.

vary between sad and happy (e.g. Figure 8.4). In this case, we have effectively defined a set of images that can be described with the values of just two variables, $z_1 =$ orientation and $z_2 =$ expression. If we consider the images formed by varying head orientation, then they define a smooth trajectory through $\mathbb{R}^{100}$. Because the relationship between head orientation and image pixel values is nonlinear, this smooth trajectory is a curved line in $\mathbb{R}^{100}$. Similarly, if we consider the images formed by varying facial expression, then they define a different smooth curve through $\mathbb{R}^{100}$. Taken together, varying head orientation and facial expression defines a two-dimensional curved surface, or *manifold*, in $\mathbb{R}^{100}$, as shown in Figure 8.5. Note that this is not a vague analogy, but a precise account of how a population of images of 10×10 pixels represented in terms of two variables defines a two-dimensional manifold in $\mathbb{R}^{100}$.

8.5. Key Quantities

It is common practice in the literature to refer to the states of decoder input units as latent variables. For consistency, we follow that practice here, but we make a distinction between the *latent variables* $\mathbf{z}$ represented by decoder input states and *physical latent variables* such as colour and speed. The status of each variable is specified in parentheses (e.g. known, unknown, learned).

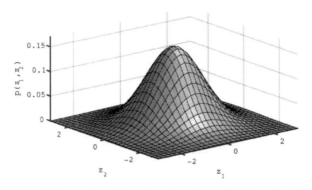

Figure 8.6. Multivariate Gaussian function with $J = 2$. The height at $\mathbf{z} = (z_1, z_2)$ is $p(\mathbf{z})$, obtained by replacing $(\mathbf{x} - \mathbf{x}')$ with $\mathbf{z}$ in Equation 8.29.

$\mathbf{x}_t$ Encoder input vector (e.g. image). The set of T training vectors is represented as $\{\mathbf{x}\} = \{\mathbf{x}_1, \ldots, \mathbf{x}_T\}$ or simply $\mathbf{x}$ here. (Known.)

$p(\mathbf{x}_t)$ The *marginal likelihood* or *model evidence* of the image $\mathbf{x}_t$. When considered over all images, $p(\mathbf{x})$ is the probability distribution of the data to be learned. (Unknown; learned during training.)

J Number of latent variables, which are represented by $2J$ units: J means and J standard deviations (see below). (Known; specified before training.)

$\boldsymbol{\mu}_t$ Vector of J encoder output unit states (means) from $2J$ encoder output units. (Unknown; learned during training.)

Σ_t Covariance matrix of the J-dimensional (posterior) Gaussian distribution with mean and standard deviation specified by the $2J$ encoder output states. Σ_t is diagonal, which encourages different units to represent independent physical quantities and allows Σ_t to be represented as a vector $\boldsymbol{\sigma}_t^2 = (\sigma_{1t}^2, \ldots, \sigma_{Jt}^2)$. (Unknown; learned during training.)

$\mathbf{z}_{it}$ The ith sample from the Gaussian distribution defined by states $\boldsymbol{\mu}_t$ and $\boldsymbol{\sigma}_t$ of the $2J$ encoder output units, $\mathbf{z}_{it} \sim \mathcal{N}(\boldsymbol{\mu}_t, \boldsymbol{\sigma}_t^2)$, referred to as latent variables. (Unknown; learned during training.)

$p(\mathbf{z})$ The prior distribution of the latent variables, implemented as a J-dimensional Gaussian distribution with zero mean and unit variance (i.e. $\mathcal{N}(\mathbf{0}, \Sigma^{\mathrm{prior}})$). A distribution with $J = 2$ is shown in Figure 8.6. (Known; specified before training.)

$\mathbf{x}_t'$ Decoder output image. (Unknown; learned during training.)

$q(\mathbf{z}|\mathbf{x}_t)$ Variational distribution of the latent variables used as decoder input vectors, where $\mathbf{z} \sim \mathcal{N}(\boldsymbol{\mu}_t, \boldsymbol{\sigma}_t^2)$. (Unknown; parametric form, i.e. Gaussian, specified before training; $\boldsymbol{\mu}_t$ and $\boldsymbol{\sigma}_t$ values learned during training.)

$p(\mathbf{z}|\mathbf{x}_t)$ Posterior distribution of latent variables. (Unknown; estimated during training as $q(\mathbf{z}|\mathbf{x}_t) = \mathcal{N}(\boldsymbol{\mu}_t, \boldsymbol{\sigma}_t^2)$, where $\boldsymbol{\mu}_t$ and $\boldsymbol{\sigma}_t$ are encoder output states.)

$p(\mathbf{x}_t|\mathbf{z})$ Conditional distribution of decoder output vectors, where the probability density of $\mathbf{x}_t$ given $\mathbf{z}$ is determined by the decoder. (Unknown; learned during training.)

8.6. How Variational Autoencoders Work

As stated earlier, a variational autoencoder consists of two modules, an encoder and a decoder. The data are a set of T images $\{\mathbf{x}\} = \{\mathbf{x}_1, \ldots, \mathbf{x}_T\}$. The encoder maps each input $\mathbf{x}_t$ to a layer of $2J$ encoder output units, which represent the values of a small number J of latent variables.

The reason each latent variable is represented by two encoder output units is that each pair of encoder output units represents the mean μ and standard deviation σ of a Gaussian distribution, as shown in Figure 8.7. Thus, each encoder output state consists of two J-element vectors $\boldsymbol{\mu} = (\mu_1, \ldots, \mu_J)$ and $\boldsymbol{\sigma} = (\sigma_1, \ldots, \sigma_J)$. For now, we restrict our attention to the encoder output units that represent the means $\boldsymbol{\mu}$.

In practice, we rarely get to see the J physical latent variables represented by the encoder output states, because the state of each encoder output unit is a mixture of several physical latent variables, unless special measures are taken during training (e.g. Figure 8.4). For example, the state of an encoder output unit might represent a combination of contrast and the curvature of lines in the input image. However, the important point is that values of key physical latent variables are encoded in the collective states of the encoder output

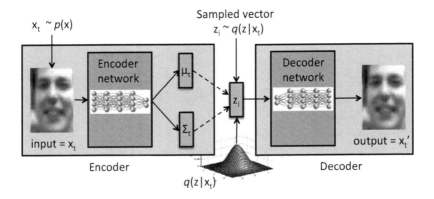

Figure 8.7. Each encoder input $\mathbf{x}_t$ yields an encoder output represented as J means $\boldsymbol{\mu}_t = (\mu_{1t}, \ldots, \mu_{Jt})$ and J standard deviations $\boldsymbol{\sigma}_t = (\sigma_{1t}, \ldots, \sigma_{Jt})$ of a Gaussian distribution $\mathcal{N}(\boldsymbol{\mu}_t, \boldsymbol{\sigma}_t^2)$ ($\boldsymbol{\sigma}_t^2$ denotes the vector of diagonal elements of a $J \times J$ diagonal covariance matrix Σ_t). The decoder input is a sample $\mathbf{z}_i$ from $\mathcal{N}(\boldsymbol{\mu}_t, \boldsymbol{\sigma}_t^2)$, which yields a decoder output $\mathbf{x}_t'$.

units. Ideally, after training, the decoder maps each sampled value of the encoder output state $\mathbf{z} \sim \mathcal{N}(\boldsymbol{\mu}, \boldsymbol{\sigma}^2)$ to a decoder output $\mathbf{x}'_t$, such that $\mathbf{x}'_t \approx \mathbf{x}_t$. Thus, the combined effect of the encoder and decoder is to map each encoder input $\mathbf{x}_t$ to a similar decoder output $\mathbf{x}'_t$.

Mapping Latent Variables to Images. As a toy example, consider a set of images where each image $\mathbf{x}_t = (x_{1t}, x_{2t})$ consists of two pixels, as in Figure 3.2. This is an unusual example because the number $(J = 2)$ of latent variables equals the number of elements in each input vector (image). Because each image has two pixels, it can be plotted as a point on the plane, as in Figure 8.8.

For simplicity we consider just two classes, C_A (e.g. images of A) and C_B (e.g. images of B), of inputs with distributions $p(\mathbf{x}_A)$ and $p(\mathbf{x}_B)$, respectively. Now, if an instance $\mathbf{x}_1$ is chosen from C_A, it yields an encoder output consisting of means $\boldsymbol{\mu}_1 = (\mu_1, \mu_2)$ and standard deviations $\boldsymbol{\sigma}_1 = (\sigma_1, \sigma_2)$, which are the elements of the diagonal covariance matrix Σ_1. These outputs define the Gaussian distribution $q(\mathbf{z}|\mathbf{x}_1) = \mathcal{N}(\boldsymbol{\mu}_1, \Sigma_1)$ shown in the box on the left of Figure 8.8. Given a sample $\mathbf{z}_t$ drawn from $q(\mathbf{z}|\mathbf{x}_1)$, the decoder maps it to a point $\mathbf{x}'_1$. When considered over all points in $q(\mathbf{z}|\mathbf{x}_1)$, the decoder

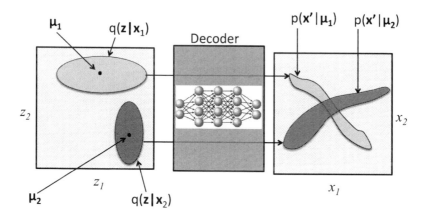

Figure 8.8. Decoding two classes C_A and C_B, with distributions $p(\mathbf{x}_A)$ and $p(\mathbf{x}_B)$ (not shown). If a typical item $\mathbf{x}_1$ in C_A is presented to the encoder then its output $(\boldsymbol{\mu}_1, \Sigma_1)$ defines the Gaussian distribution $q(\mathbf{z}|\mathbf{x}_1) = \mathcal{N}(\boldsymbol{\mu}_1, \Sigma_1)$. After training, the decoder maps $q(\mathbf{z}|\mathbf{x}_1)$ to a distribution $p(\mathbf{x}'|\boldsymbol{\mu}_1)$, which should be similar to $p(\mathbf{x}_A)$; similarly, we would like $p(\mathbf{x}'|\boldsymbol{\mu}_2) \approx p(\mathbf{x}_B)$.

maps this entire distribution to the distribution $p(\mathbf{x}'|\mathbf{z}(\boldsymbol{\mu}_1))$, which is labelled as $p(\mathbf{x}'|\boldsymbol{\mu}_1)$ in the box on the right of Figure 8.8. After training, the encoder should map each input vector $\mathbf{x}$ from class C_A to a point $\mathbf{x}'$ close to $\boldsymbol{\mu}_1$, so that $p(\mathbf{x}'|\boldsymbol{\mu}_1)$ is roughly the same as the distribution $p(\mathbf{x}_A)$ of vectors in class C_A. Similarly, we should have $p(\mathbf{x}'|\boldsymbol{\mu}_2) \approx p(\mathbf{x}_B)$ for vectors in class C_B.

Naming Distributions. Ideally, the inputs to the decoder would have a *posterior distribution* $p(\mathbf{z}|\mathbf{x}_t)$ such that the $\mathbf{z}$ values reflect the underlying latent variables of the input image $\mathbf{x}_t$. The process of using the input image $\mathbf{x}_t$ to estimate $p(\mathbf{z}|\mathbf{x}_t)$ is called *inference*. The posterior distribution is often written as $p(\mathbf{z}|\mathbf{x})$, where $\mathbf{x}$ implicitly refers to the set of all possible values of the inputs $\mathbf{x}_t$. The reason we write $\mathbf{x}_t$ here is to emphasize which quantities are given (i.e. the single image $\mathbf{x}_t$) and which are inferred (i.e. the distribution $p(\mathbf{z}|\mathbf{x}_t)$).

Using Bayes' theorem (Appendix E), the posterior can be written as

$$p(\mathbf{z}|\mathbf{x}_t) \;=\; \frac{p(\mathbf{x}_t|\mathbf{z})p(\mathbf{z})}{p(\mathbf{x}_t)}, \tag{8.1}$$

where $p(\mathbf{x}_t|\mathbf{z})$ is the *likelihood*, $p(\mathbf{z})$ is the *prior distribution*, and $p(\mathbf{x}_t)$ is the *marginal likelihood* or *model evidence*. The difficulty in evaluating the posterior distribution lies with the marginal likelihood.

Why Evaluating the Marginal Likelihood $p(\mathbf{x}_t)$ is Hard. In principle, we could estimate $p(\mathbf{x}_t)$ using a uniform sampling of N points $\{\mathbf{z}_1, \ldots, \mathbf{z}_N\}$ on a grid of $\mathbf{z}$ values, so that

$$p(\mathbf{x}_t) \;\approx\; \sum_{i=1}^{N} p(\mathbf{x}_t|\mathbf{z}_i)p(\mathbf{z}_i). \tag{8.2}$$

However, even though we know how to evaluate every term in this sum, the sum itself is intractable. For example, if each of J variables $\mathbf{z}=(z_1, \ldots, z_J)$ is sampled at n uniformly spaced points then the number of samples will be $N=n^J$, which becomes impractical as J increases. Worse, almost all values $\mathbf{z}_i$ have a density $p(\mathbf{z}_i)\approx 0$, as explained next.

We assume that each vector $\mathbf{z}$ is drawn from a multivariate Gaussian distribution, $\mathbf{z} \sim \mathcal{N}(\boldsymbol{\mu}, \boldsymbol{\sigma}^2)$, where $\boldsymbol{\mu} = (\mu_1, \ldots, \mu_J)$ and $\boldsymbol{\sigma} =$

$(\sigma_1, \ldots, \sigma_J)$. If all the σ_j values are the same, this defines a spherical distribution. For large values of J, it can be shown[5] that almost all Gaussian vectors $\mathbf{z}$ are located within the *typical set*[75], an extremely thin spherical shell at distance $r \approx \sigma\sqrt{J}$ from $\boldsymbol{\mu}$. Therefore, the volume of the typical set is less than the volume v of a J-dimensional hypersphere with radius r. For large values of J, it can be shown that $v \propto (1/\sqrt{J})$, so that $v \to 0$ as $J \to \infty$. Therefore, the space in which $\mathbf{z}$ resides is almost entirely empty, except near the surface of a vanishingly small hypersphere. If the covariance matrix Σ is not diagonal, then this hypersphere becomes a hyperellipsoid, but the same reasoning regarding the typical set applies. Thus, if we try to estimate $p(\mathbf{x}_t)$ (Equation 8.2) by randomly sampling $\mathbf{z}$, this is doomed to failure because $p(\mathbf{z}) \approx 0$ for almost all values of $\mathbf{z}$. More generally, random sampling is ineffective because the volume occupied by a probability distribution shrinks rapidly as the number J of dimensions increases, a phenomenon called *concentration of measure*.

Competing Objectives. The main goal of the variational autoencoder is to train a network to minimise the difference between the (known) estimate of the posterior $q(\mathbf{z}|\mathbf{x}_t)$ and the true (but unknown) posterior $p(\mathbf{z}|\mathbf{x}_t)$. This is achieved by (simultaneously) training two interdependent networks: 1) an encoder network, which minimises the difference between $q(\mathbf{z}|\mathbf{x}_t)$ and an assumed (known) prior distribution $p(\mathbf{z})$; and 2) a decoder network, which uses $\mathbf{z}$ to minimise the difference between its output $\mathbf{x}'_t$ and the original input $\mathbf{x}_t$.

We wish to find parameter values $\mathbf{w}$ (i.e. weights) such that (roughly speaking) the probability distribution of decoder outputs $p(\mathbf{x}|\mathbf{z}_t)$ is maximised, subject to the constraint that $q(\mathbf{z}|\mathbf{x}_t) \approx p(\mathbf{z}|\mathbf{x}_t)$. The autoencoder is summarised as

$$\mathbf{x}_t \xrightarrow[\text{encoder}]{q(\mathbf{z}|\mathbf{x}_t)} \mathbf{z}_t \xrightarrow[\text{decoder}]{p(\mathbf{x}|\mathbf{z}_t)} \mathbf{x}'_t. \tag{8.3}$$

Thus, the autoencoder has two competing objectives. First, the decoder, given an input $\mathbf{z}_t$ from the encoder, tries to generate an output $\mathbf{x}'_t$ similar to $\mathbf{x}_t$. Second, the encoder tries to generate outputs which yield decoder inputs $\mathbf{z}_t$ such that the encoder output distribution $q(\mathbf{z}|\mathbf{x}_t)$ is similar to the (unknown) posterior distribution $p(\mathbf{z}|\mathbf{x}_t)$.

To understand the source of these competing objectives, we express the model evidence as a marginal distribution. Specifically, the model evidence $p(\mathbf{x}_t)$ can be expressed as the marginal distribution of the joint distribution $p(\mathbf{x}, \mathbf{z})$ at $\mathbf{x} = \mathbf{x}_t$. Since $p(\mathbf{x}_t, \mathbf{z}) = p(\mathbf{x}_t|\mathbf{z})p(\mathbf{z})$,

$$p(\mathbf{x}_t) \quad = \quad \int_{\mathbf{z}} p(\mathbf{x}_t|\mathbf{z})p(\mathbf{z}) \, d\mathbf{z}. \tag{8.4}$$

To learn the correct weights, we need to know how to evaluate $p(\mathbf{x}_t)$.

8.7. The Evidence Lower Bound

Consider a variational autoencoder with weights that have been initialised with random values. When presented with a training vector $\mathbf{x}_t$, the encoder produces outputs that yield decoder inputs $\mathbf{z}$ with a distribution $q(\mathbf{z}|\mathbf{x}_t)$. However, as explained above, the resultant decoder outputs have vanishingly small probabilities $p(\mathbf{x}_t|\mathbf{z})$. Consequently, we need to adjust the weights so that the decoder yields outputs $\mathbf{x}'_t \approx \mathbf{x}_t$. To this end, imagine an *ideal encoder* that implements $p(\mathbf{z}|\mathbf{x}_t)$ (the true posterior) rather than the distribution $q(\mathbf{z}|\mathbf{x}_t)$ of decoder inputs provided by the encoder. If we knew $p(\mathbf{z}|\mathbf{x}_t)$ then the

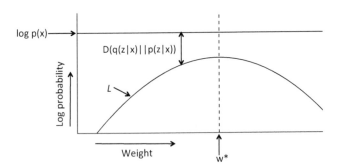

Figure 8.9. The lower bound L of $\log p(\mathbf{x})$ can be maximised by varying the encoder weights $\mathbf{w}$ to decrease the Kullback–Leibler divergence $D(q(\mathbf{z}|\mathbf{x})\|p(\mathbf{z}|\mathbf{x}))$ between the variational distribution $q(\mathbf{z}|\mathbf{x})$ and the posterior distribution $p(\mathbf{z}|\mathbf{x})$. The graph shows a cross-section through $D(q(\mathbf{z}|\mathbf{x})\|p(\mathbf{z}|\mathbf{x}))$ for a single weight. The optimal weight is labelled as w^*.

dissimilarity between $q(\mathbf{z}|\mathbf{x}_t)$ and $p(\mathbf{z}|\mathbf{x}_t)$ could be measured by the Kullback–Leibler divergence

$$D(q(\mathbf{z}|\mathbf{x}_t)\|p(\mathbf{z}|\mathbf{x}_t)) \quad = \quad \int_z q(\mathbf{z}|\mathbf{x}_t) \log \frac{q(\mathbf{z}|\mathbf{x}_t)}{p(\mathbf{z}|\mathbf{x}_t)} \, d\mathbf{z}, \qquad (8.5)$$

where $D \geq 0$, with $D = 0$ if and only if $q(\mathbf{z}|\mathbf{x}_t) = p(\mathbf{z}|\mathbf{x}_t)$. Given a sample of $\mathbf{z}$ values, the Kullback–Leibler divergence is estimated as

$$D(q(\mathbf{z}|\mathbf{x}_t)\|p(\mathbf{z}|\mathbf{x}_t)) \quad = \quad \sum_i q(\mathbf{z}_i|\mathbf{x}_t) \log \frac{q(\mathbf{z}_i|\mathbf{x}_t)}{p(\mathbf{z}_i|\mathbf{x}_t)}. \qquad (8.6)$$

Next, we will use the Kullback–Leibler divergence to derive two expressions for a key quantity called the *evidence lower bound* (ELBO). The form of the first expression (Equation 8.19) makes it obvious that we wish to minimise it, though it is not obvious how to do so. The second expression for the ELBO (Equation 8.28) can be minimised, but it is less obvious that we would want to do so — apart from the fact it is also an expression for the ELBO.

The First ELBO Expression. Because

$$p(\mathbf{z}, \mathbf{x}_t) \quad = \quad p(\mathbf{x}_t|\mathbf{z})p(\mathbf{z}), \qquad (8.7)$$

Bayes' theorem (Equation 8.1) can be written $p(\mathbf{z}|\mathbf{x}_t) = p(\mathbf{z}, \mathbf{x}_t)/p(\mathbf{x}_t)$, and taking logarithms gives

$$\log p(\mathbf{z}|\mathbf{x}_t) \quad = \quad \log p(\mathbf{z}, \mathbf{x}_t) - \log p(\mathbf{x}_t). \qquad (8.8)$$

If we invert the log ratio in Equation 8.6 then we get

$$D(q(\mathbf{z}|\mathbf{x}_t)\|p(\mathbf{z}|\mathbf{x}_t)) \quad = \quad -\sum_i q(\mathbf{z}_i|\mathbf{x}_t) \log \frac{p(\mathbf{z}_i|\mathbf{x}_t)}{q(\mathbf{z}_i|\mathbf{x}_t)}. \qquad (8.9)$$

Substituting Equation 8.8 into Equation 8.9 yields

$$D(q(\mathbf{z}|\mathbf{x}_t)\|p(\mathbf{z}|\mathbf{x}_t)) = -\sum_i q(\mathbf{z}_i|\mathbf{x}_t) \left[\log \frac{p(\mathbf{z}_i, \mathbf{x}_t)}{q(\mathbf{z}_i|\mathbf{x}_t)} - \log p(\mathbf{x}_t) \right], (8.10)$$

and expanding the right-hand side yields

$$D(q(\mathbf{z}|\mathbf{x}_t)\|p(\mathbf{z}|\mathbf{x}_t)) = -\sum_i q(\mathbf{z}_i|\mathbf{x}_t) \log \frac{p(\mathbf{z}_i, \mathbf{x}_t)}{q(\mathbf{z}_i|\mathbf{x}_t)}$$

$$+ \sum_i q(\mathbf{z}_i|\mathbf{x}_t) \log p(\mathbf{x}_t). \qquad (8.11)$$

Since $\sum_i q(\mathbf{z}_i|\mathbf{x}_t) = 1$, the final term in Equation 8.11 is

$$\sum_i q(\mathbf{z}_i|\mathbf{x}_t) \log p(\mathbf{x}_t) = \log p(\mathbf{x}_t) \sum_i q(\mathbf{z}_i|\mathbf{x}_t) \qquad (8.12)$$

$$= \log p(\mathbf{x}_t). \qquad (8.13)$$

For convenience, we define the first summation on the right in Equation 8.11 as

$$\sum_i q(\mathbf{z}_i|\mathbf{x}_t) \log \frac{p(\mathbf{z}_i, \mathbf{x}_t)}{q(\mathbf{z}_i|\mathbf{x}_t)} = L_t. \qquad (8.14)$$

Therefore Equation 8.11 can be written as

$$D(q(\mathbf{z}|\mathbf{x}_t)\|p(\mathbf{z}|\mathbf{x}_t)) = -L_t + \log p(\mathbf{x}_t), \qquad (8.15)$$

and rearranging yields

$$L_t = \log p(\mathbf{x}_t) - D(q(\mathbf{z}|\mathbf{x}_t)\|p(\mathbf{z}|\mathbf{x}_t)). \qquad (8.16)$$

Because $D(q(\mathbf{z}|\mathbf{x}_t)\|p(\mathbf{z}|\mathbf{x}_t)) \geq 0$, it follows that L_t must be less than (or equal to) the log evidence $\log p(\mathbf{x}_t)$, so L_t defines a *lower bound* on $\log p(\mathbf{x}_t)$; this is why L_t is called the *evidence lower bound* (ELBO) or *variational lower bound*. The tightness of this bound depends on how well the variational distribution $q(\mathbf{z}|\mathbf{x}_t)$ approximates the posterior distribution $p(\mathbf{z}|\mathbf{x}_t)$. Clearly, if $q(\mathbf{z}|\mathbf{x}_t) \approx p(\mathbf{z}|\mathbf{x}_t)$ then D is close to zero and so the bound is tight, $L_t \approx \log p(\mathbf{x}_t)$. In this case, maximising L_t is almost as effective as maximising $\log p(\mathbf{x}_t)$, as shown in Figure 8.9.

When considered over the whole set of input vectors $\{\mathbf{x}\}$,

$$L = \sum_t L_t \tag{8.17}$$

$$= \log p(\{\mathbf{x}\}) - D(q(\mathbf{z}|\{\mathbf{x}\}) \| p(\mathbf{z}|\{\mathbf{x}\})). \tag{8.18}$$

For the sake of brevity, we will omit the set brackets $\{\}$ and write our first expression for the ELBO as

$$L = \log p(\mathbf{x}) - D(q(\mathbf{z}|\mathbf{x}) \| p(\mathbf{z}|\mathbf{x})). \tag{8.19}$$

The Second ELBO Expression. Substituting Equation 8.7 into Equation 8.14 gives

$$L_t = \sum_i q(\mathbf{z}_i|\mathbf{x}_t) \log \frac{p(\mathbf{x}_t|\mathbf{z}_i)p(\mathbf{z}_i)}{q(\mathbf{z}_i|\mathbf{x}_t)} \tag{8.20}$$

$$= \sum_i q(\mathbf{z}_i|\mathbf{x}_t) \left[\log p(\mathbf{x}_t|\mathbf{z}_i) + \log \frac{p(\mathbf{z}_i)}{q(\mathbf{z}_i|\mathbf{x}_t)} \right], \tag{8.21}$$

and expanding the brackets yields

$$L_t = \sum_i q(\mathbf{z}_i|\mathbf{x}_t) \log p(\mathbf{x}_t|\mathbf{z}_i) + \sum_i q(\mathbf{z}_i|\mathbf{x}_t) \log \frac{p(\mathbf{z}_i)}{q(\mathbf{z}_i|\mathbf{x}_t)}. \tag{8.22}$$

This equation is used to define two key quantities. First, we define

$$L_t^{\text{dec}} = \sum_i q(\mathbf{z}_i|\mathbf{x}_t) \log p(\mathbf{x}_t|\mathbf{z}_i) \tag{8.23}$$

$$= \mathbb{E}_{\mathbf{z} \sim q(\mathbf{z}|\mathbf{x}_t)}[\log p(\mathbf{x}_t|\mathbf{z})], \tag{8.24}$$

where $\mathbf{z} \sim q(\mathbf{z}|\mathbf{x}_t)$ means that $\mathbf{z}$ values are samples from the distribution $q(\mathbf{z}|\mathbf{x}_t)$. Thus, Equation 8.24 is the expected log likelihood given that $\mathbf{z}_i \sim q(\mathbf{z}|\mathbf{x}_t)$. Note that the mapping from the decoder input $\mathbf{z}_i$ to the decoder output $\mathbf{x}_t'$ is deterministic, so the weights $\mathbf{w}$ that maximise the likelihood $p(\mathbf{x}_t|\mathbf{z}(\mathbf{w}))$ also maximise the likelihood $p(\mathbf{x}_t|\mathbf{x}_t'(\mathbf{w}))$, where we have made the dependence on $\mathbf{w}$ explicit here. Using the second term in Equation 8.22 we define

$$L_t^{\mathrm{enc}} = \sum_i q(\mathbf{z}_i|\mathbf{x}_t) \log \frac{p(\mathbf{z}_i)}{q(\mathbf{z}_i|\mathbf{x}_t)} \qquad (8.25)$$

$$= -D(q(\mathbf{z}|\mathbf{x}_t)\|p(\mathbf{z})), \qquad (8.26)$$

which is minus the Kullback–Leibler divergence between the (known) variational distribution $q(\mathbf{z}|\mathbf{x}_t)$ and the prior distribution $p(\mathbf{z})$. Therefore, Equation 8.22 can be written as

$$L_t = L_t^{\mathrm{dec}} + L_t^{\mathrm{enc}} \qquad (8.27)$$

$$= \mathbb{E}_{\mathbf{z}\sim q(\mathbf{z}|\mathbf{x}_t)}[\log p(\mathbf{x}_t|\mathbf{z})] - \beta D(q(\mathbf{z}|\mathbf{x}_t)\|p(\mathbf{z})), \qquad (8.28)$$

where we have introduced the parameter β to vary the trade-off between decoder reconstruction and encoder inference[9;37] ($\beta = 1$ in Equation 8.22). When summed over T training vectors (Equation 8.17), we obtain our second expression for the ELBO.

It is important to note that the unknown posterior of the ideal encoder $p(\mathbf{z}|\mathbf{x})$ in Equation 8.19 has been replaced by the known prior $p(\mathbf{z})$ in Equation 8.28. Thus, the lower bound in Equation 8.19 can be evaluated, and maximised, from its equivalent Equation 8.28.

The quantity $\log p(\mathbf{x}_t|\mathbf{z})$ in Equation 8.28 is the log probability that the network generates the image $\mathbf{x}_t$ given a vector $\mathbf{z}$ derived stochastically from the encoder output. Because $\mathbf{x}_t$ is fixed, $p(\mathbf{x}_t|\mathbf{z})$ varies as a deterministic function of $\mathbf{z}$, and is called a *likelihood function*. Further, because $\mathbf{z}$ depends on the weights $\mathbf{w}$, the likelihood function is proportional to the likelihood of the weights. Thus, by adjusting the weights to maximise $\log p(\mathbf{x}_t|\mathbf{z})$, we are really performing *maximum likelihood estimation* of the weights (i.e. of $\log p(\mathbf{x}_t|\mathbf{w})$). However, we actually maximise a lower bound L, with L^{enc} acting as a constraint, so variational autoencoders perform a type of constrained or *penalised maximum likelihood estimation* of the weights.

8.8. An Alternative Derivation

For completeness, we derive Equation 8.28 using a different approach. This involves the pragmatic objective of reconstructing encoder inputs $\mathbf{x}$ as decoder outputs $\mathbf{x}'$. As above, the encoder output is used to generate decoder inputs $\mathbf{z}$, each of which yields a decoder output vector $\mathbf{x}'_t$. The overall performance is measured in terms of two components:

1. A reconstruction accuracy term, which is the similarity between the encoder input distribution $p(\mathbf{x})$ and the decoder output distribution $p(\mathbf{x}'|\mathbf{z})$.

2. A regularisation term, which is the difference between the distribution of decoder inputs $q(\mathbf{z}|\mathbf{x})$ and a pre-defined prior distribution $p(\mathbf{z})$.

The reconstruction accuracy is represented by L_t^{dec} (Equation 8.24), which is the expected log probability that the decoder generates the output $\mathbf{x}_t$ when the decoder's input $\mathbf{z}$ is derived from the encoder output. If $p(\mathbf{x}_t|\mathbf{z})$ is modelled as a Gaussian distribution then this expected log probability is the sum of squared differences between the encoder inputs $\mathbf{x}_t$ and the decoder outputs $\mathbf{x}'_t$ (see Equation 8.32). The regularisation term is represented by L_t^{enc}, the (negative) Kullback–Leibler divergence between the encoder output distribution $q(\mathbf{z}|\mathbf{x}_t)$ and the prior distribution $p(\mathbf{z})$ (Equation 8.26). Thus, L_t can be derived by considering a network that attempts to reconstruct the input image while simultaneously keeping the (latent variable) encoding of input images similar to a simple (i.e. Gaussian) distribution.

8.9. Maximising the Lower Bound

Knowing that L is a lower bound matters because, given that we wish to learn weights $\mathbf{w}$ that maximise the log likelihood $\log p(\mathbf{x}|\mathbf{z})$, we can instead maximise $\log p(\mathbf{x}|\mathbf{z})$ by gradient ascent on L (Equation 8.28). Maximising L might seem like a poor substitute for maximising $\log p(\mathbf{x}|\mathbf{z})$ itself. However, using Equation 8.28 to maximise L implicitly forces the variational (encoder output) distribution $q(\mathbf{z}|\mathbf{x})$ to be similar to the unknown posterior $p(\mathbf{z}|\mathbf{x})$, so that $D(q(\mathbf{z}|\mathbf{x})\|p(\mathbf{z}|\mathbf{x})) \approx 0$ in

Equation 8.19. Thus, as learning progresses, maximising the lower bound L can be almost as good as maximising $\log p(\mathbf{x}|\mathbf{z})$ itself.

The reconstruction accuracy is measured by the probability $p(\mathbf{x}_t|\mathbf{x}'_t)$ that the encoder input $\mathbf{x}_t$ is reconstructed at the decoder output, given the observed decoder output $\mathbf{x}'_t$. In general, given an n-dimensional vector $\mathbf{x}'_t$, the probability distribution of an n-dimensional Gaussian is

$$p(\mathbf{x}_t|\mathbf{x}'_t) \;=\; \frac{e^{-(\mathbf{x}_t-\mathbf{x}'_t)^\mathsf{T}\Sigma_\mathbf{x}^{-1}(\mathbf{x}_t-\mathbf{x}'_t)/2}}{((2\pi)^n \det(\Sigma_\mathbf{x}))^{1/2}}, \tag{8.29}$$

where $\Sigma_\mathbf{x}$ is an $n \times n$ covariance matrix, and $\det(\Sigma_\mathbf{x})$ is its determinant. A multivariate Gaussian distribution with $n = 2$ is shown in Figure 8.6, and a cross-section of it is shown in Figure 8.10 (see Appendix D). Because $\mathbf{x}'_t$ is a deterministic function of $\mathbf{z}$, this implies that $p(\mathbf{x}_t|\mathbf{x}'_t) = p(\mathbf{x}_t|\mathbf{z})$, and therefore

$$\log p(\mathbf{x}_t|\mathbf{z}) \;=\; \log p(\mathbf{x}_t|\mathbf{x}'_t). \tag{8.30}$$

Substituting Equation 8.29 into Equation 8.30 yields

$$\log p(\mathbf{x}_t|\mathbf{z}) = c - \tfrac{1}{2}(\mathbf{x}_t - \mathbf{x}'_t)^\mathsf{T}\Sigma_\mathbf{x}^{-1}(\mathbf{x}_t - \mathbf{x}'_t), \tag{8.31}$$

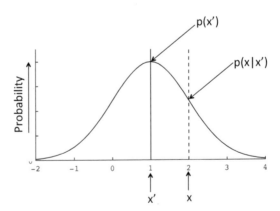

Figure 8.10.   Cross-section of a multivariate Gaussian function (Equation 8.29, Figure 8.6). If the decoder output is $\mathbf{x}'{=}1$ then the probability $p(\mathbf{x}|\mathbf{x}')$ that the output is the same as the encoder input $\mathbf{x}{=}2$ is a Gaussian function centred at $\mathbf{x}'$, so it is a Gaussian function of $|\mathbf{x} - \mathbf{x}'|$. See Appendix D.

where $c = -\log\left((2\pi)^n \det(\Sigma_{\mathbf{x}})\right)^{1/2}$. If we assume that $\Sigma_{\mathbf{x}}$ is proportional to the identity matrix I, so that it has identical diagonal elements $\sigma_{\mathbf{x}}^2$ (i.e. $\Sigma_{\mathbf{x}} = \sigma_{\mathbf{x}}^2 I$), then $\Sigma_{\mathbf{x}}^{-1} = I / \sigma_{\mathbf{x}}^2$ then

$$\log p(\mathbf{x}_t | \mathbf{z}) = c - \frac{1}{2\sigma_{\mathbf{x}}^2} |\mathbf{x}_t - \mathbf{x}_t'|^2, \tag{8.32}$$

which measures the similarity between the encoder input $\mathbf{x}_t$ and the decoder output $\mathbf{x}_t'$. Substituting Equation 8.32 into Equation 8.24, and assuming $\sigma_{\mathbf{x}}^2 = 1$,

$$L_t^{\text{dec}} = \mathbb{E}_{\mathbf{z} \sim q(\mathbf{z}|\mathbf{x}_t)}\left[c - \frac{1}{2}|\mathbf{x}_t - \mathbf{x}_t'|^2\right] \tag{8.33}$$

$$= c - \frac{1}{2} \times \mathbb{E}_{\mathbf{z} \sim q(\mathbf{z}|\mathbf{x}_t)}[|\mathbf{x}_t - \mathbf{x}_t'|^2]. \tag{8.34}$$

Given that the decoder input is $\mathbf{z} \sim q(\mathbf{z}|\mathbf{x}_t)$ and that each sampled value $\mathbf{z}_{it}$ produces a corresponding decoder output $\mathbf{x}_{it}'$, we can estimate the expectation above using N_z samples of $\mathbf{z}$, so that (for each input $\mathbf{x}_t$)

$$L_t^{\text{dec}} = c - \frac{1}{2N_z} \sum_{i=1}^{N_z} |\mathbf{x}_t - \mathbf{x}_{it}'|^2. \tag{8.35}$$

To use backprop with the encoder term in Equation 8.26, we need the *reparametrisation trick*. This allows us to use a sample $\eta \sim \mathcal{N}(0,1)$ to obtain a sample $z \sim \mathcal{N}(\mu_{jt}, \sigma_{jt}^2)$, where (μ_{jt}, σ_{jt}) is the state of the jth pair of encoder output units in response to the encoder input $\mathbf{x}_t$. Given a sample η, the corresponding sample z that would be obtained from $\mathcal{N}(\mu_{jt}, \sigma_{jt}^2)$ is $z = \mu_{jt} + \eta \sigma_{jt}$. When considered over all J pairs of encoder output units, this yields $\mathbf{z} \sim \mathcal{N}(\boldsymbol{\mu}_t, \Sigma_t)$. Assuming the $J \times J$ covariance matrix Σ_t is diagonal, the encoder regularisation term evaluates to[60]

$$L_t^{\text{enc}} = \frac{1}{2} \sum_{j=1}^{J} (1 + \log \sigma_{jt}^2 - \sigma_{jt}^2 - \mu_{jt}^2), \tag{8.36}$$

which attains its maximal value when $\boldsymbol{\mu}_t = \mathbf{0}$ and $\boldsymbol{\sigma}_t^2 = \mathbf{1}$, that is, when the estimate $q(\mathbf{z}|\mathbf{x}_t) = \mathcal{N}(\boldsymbol{\mu}_t, \Sigma_t)$ of the posterior distribution $p(\mathbf{z}|\mathbf{x}_t)$ equals the prior distribution $p(\mathbf{z}) = \mathcal{N}(\mathbf{0}, \mathbf{1})$. Therefore, L_t^{enc} measures the extent to which the estimated posterior distribution

$q(\mathbf{z}|\mathbf{x}_t)$ deviates from the prior distribution $p(\mathbf{z})$, where $q(\mathbf{z}|\mathbf{x}_t)$ is effectively implemented as the encoder.

Substituting Equations 8.35 and 8.36 into Equation 8.27 yields

$$L_t = c - \frac{1}{2N_z}\sum_{i=1}^{N_z}|\mathbf{x}_t - \mathbf{x}'_{it}|^2 + \frac{1}{2}\sum_{j=1}^{J}(1 + \log\sigma_{jt}^2 - \sigma_{jt}^2 - \mu_{jt}^2). \quad (8.37)$$

Training a Variational Autoencoder

set dimensionality J of latent space $\mathbf{z}$
initialise weight vector $\mathbf{w}$ to random values
set number N_z of $\mathbf{z}$ samples per input vector
set learning rate ϵ
foreach *learning iteration* **do**
    foreach *batch of T_{batch} training vectors* $\{\mathbf{x}\}$ **do**
        set $L = 0$ and gradient vector $\nabla L = 0$
        foreach *training vector* $\mathbf{x}_t$ *from $t = 1$ to T_{batch}* **do**

            Encoder
            given an input $\mathbf{x}_t$, the encoder outputs are $\boldsymbol{\mu}_t$ and $\boldsymbol{\sigma}_t$
            the encoder regularisation term is L_t^{enc} (Equation 8.36)

            Decoder
            set $L_t^{\text{dec}} = 0$
            foreach *sample i from 1 to N_z* **do**
                obtain sample $\mathbf{z}_{it}$ from $q(\mathbf{z}|\mathbf{x}_t) = \mathcal{N}(\boldsymbol{\mu}_t, \boldsymbol{\sigma}_t)$
                use $\mathbf{z}_{it}$ to obtain decoder output $\mathbf{x}'_{it}$
                reconstruction term: L_{it}^{dec} (from Equation 8.35)
                accumulate mean: $L_t^{\text{dec}} = L_t^{\text{dec}} + L_{it}^{\text{dec}}/(2N_z)$
            end
            Estimate L_t and its gradient
            $L_t = L_t^{\text{dec}} + L_t^{\text{enc}}$
            $\nabla L_t = \nabla L_t^{\text{dec}} + \nabla L_t^{\text{enc}}$
            accumulate L and gradient for this batch
            $L = L + L_t$
            $\nabla L = \nabla L + \nabla L_t$
        end
        Update weights
        $\mathbf{w} = \mathbf{w} + \epsilon\nabla L$
    end
end

In practice, gradient ascent with backprop is used to maximise $L = \sum_t L_t$ based on batches of inputs, as in Burda et al. (2015). The gradient of L with respect to the network weights is calculated using an automatic gradient tool such as autograd[141].

8.10. Conditional Variational Autoencoders

To force the decoder to produce images for a particular class of inputs, a variational autoencoder can be trained with an additional binary vector called a *one hot vector*. After training, the resultant *conditional variational autoencoder* can be used to generate images from a given class (Kingma et al., 2014). For example, given many images that contain the digits 0 to 9 (Figure 7.7), the class for the digit 3 would be represented as the one hot vector $\mathbf{c}_3 = (0001000000)$. During training, this hot vector is concatenated with every training vector $\mathbf{x}$ that is an image of the digit 3, and the resultant augmented vector $\mathbf{x}_3$ is used as input to the encoder; similarly, the hot vector $\mathbf{c}_3$ is concatenated with the decoder input $\mathbf{z}$ to produce a conditional latent vector $\mathbf{z}_3$.

After training, images that contain a 3 can be generated by using sampled vectors $\mathbf{z}_3$ as input to the decoder. In essence, the class-specific vector $\mathbf{z}_3$ forces the decoder to attend to a small region in the latent space (e.g. the region labelled $q(\mathbf{z}|\mathbf{x}_1)$ in Figure 8.8), just as if the decoder input had been produced by presenting the encoder with the image of a 3. Note that this requires the use of labelled data.

8.11. Applications

Variational autoencoders and related information bottleneck methods seem promising, but their ability to solve realistic tasks is still being explored. For example, after training on images of digits between 0 and 9, a small modification allows the hidden unit states to be used for classification, which yielded an impressive test error of 1.13% on the MNIST digit set (Alemi et al., 2017).

Using test images of objects with different sizes, positions, and orientations, Higgins et al. (2016) found that setting the regularisation parameter to $\beta = 4$ (Equation 8.28) was reasonably successful at forcing the hidden units to represent different physical parameters. Surprisingly, even though networks with $\beta = 1$ and $\beta = 4$ were equally good at reconstructing simple geometric objects (that were part of the training data), those with $\beta = 4$ performed substantially better on objects that were not part of the training data. This suggests that (as we might expect) forcing networks to represent independent physical parameters (e.g. position, orientation) in different hidden units yields networks that generalise well beyond their training data.

It is worth noting that results comparable to the embedding of faces in Figure 8.4 were obtained by combining variational autoencoders with generative adversarial networks (Larsen et al., 2015; see Section 9.11). However, training variational autoencoders tends to be more straightforward than training generative adversarial networks.

Variational autoencoders can generate molecules with pre-specified desirable physiological properties. Specifically, training a conditional variational autoencoder on molecules labelled with known properties allows novel molecules to be generated by treating a subset of the decoder input units as a one hot vector of desirable properties[27;69;86]. Variational autoencoders have also been used for speech recognition[50], and to recover images being viewed from electroencephalograph (EEG) data[56]. For a recent review, see Maaløe et al. (2019).

8.12. Summary

Variational autoencoders represent a step-change in neural network algorithms for three reasons. First, they provide a relatively efficient method for estimating latent variables. Second, because each input is mapped to itself, variational autoencoders do not require training data that have been labelled. Third, variational autoencoders provide a coherent theoretical framework that includes a principled method for separating the reconstruction error from the regularisation term.

Chapter 9

Deep Backprop Networks

Yann [LeCun] didn't slavishly try to duplicate the cortex. He tried many different variations, but the ones he converged onto were the ones that nature converged onto. This is an important observation. The convergence of nature and AI has a lot to teach us and there's much farther to go.
T Sejnowski, 2018.

9.1. Introduction

Modern neural networks depend on ideas and mathematical frameworks developed in the context of linear associative networks, Hopfield nets, and Boltzmann machines. However, almost without exception, neural networks are now essentially *deep backprop neural networks*.

By any standards, progress over the last thirty years, and especially over the last decade, has been extraordinary. This surge in progress began with LeCun's four-layer network LeNet1 (LeCun et al., 1989), which showed the potential of neural networks for classifying images of handwritten digits, and which eventually led to a 1,000-layer ResNet (He et al., 2016) for classifying objects from 1,000 different classes.

Such rapid progress means that neural networks are now commercially viable tools. The resultant influx of researchers employed by Google, Facebook, Amazon, and the like has further accelerated progress, so that new papers are now being published on a daily basis. It is, therefore, almost impossible to summarise all of the advances in deep neural networks at any given time. Accordingly, what follows is an account of the most important recent theoretical innovations.

9.2. Convolutional Neural Networks

Ever since computers were invented, scientists have tried to write programs that allowed computers to see. However (as discussed in Chapter 1), the word 'see' hides a multitude of skills, only some of which have been acquired by computers. It is noteworthy that almost all of the progress in building a seeing computer stems from advances in neural networks. This is particularly interesting from a neurophysiological perspective, because the only type of neural network that can definitely see is a biological neural network (i.e. a brain).

Accordingly, it should be unsurprising to learn that a major advance in getting artificial neural networks to see was achieved by copying key architectural features of the brain's visual system[121]. Probably the most important of these features is *convolution*, as used in *convolutional neural networks* (LeCun et al., 1989).

In order to understand convolutional neural networks, it is first necessary to understand convolution. Because convolutional neural networks are inspired by human vision, we begin with a brief account of image processing in the retina.

The retinal image is represented as the outputs of 126 million photoreceptors, each of which corresponds to a pixel in a digital image. The outputs of photoreceptors connect (via several neuronal layers within the retina) to *retinal ganglion cells*. Each retinal ganglion cell

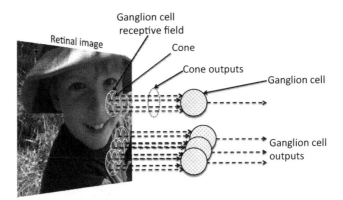

Figure 9.1. The retinal image activates photoreceptors, where each photoreceptor projects to one or more ganglion cells. Here, each ganglion cell receptive field has four photoreceptors.

collates the outputs from photoreceptors within a small area of the retina, which is the ganglion cell's *receptive field* (Figures 9.1 and 9.2). However, some photoreceptors have stronger connections than others, and the consequent differential weighting of photoreceptor outputs determines the structure of the ganglion cell's receptive field. In signal processing, these differential weightings define a *filter* or *kernel*.

The output of a ganglion cell can be calculated as a sum of products between weights and input values; so a ganglion cell acts like a filter. More generally, each hidden unit in a convolutional network acts as a filter **w** over a small region of the input image **x** (i.e. over a small region of the visible layer).

For example, the individual weights in the 3×3 two-dimensional filter shown in Figure 9.2 can be represented as

$$\mathbf{w} \;=\; \begin{pmatrix} w(-1,-1) & w(-1,0) & w(-1,+1) \\ w(0,-1) & w(0,0) & w(0,+1) \\ w(+1,-1) & w(+1,0) & w(+1,+1) \end{pmatrix}. \qquad (9.1)$$

To see how convolution works, consider a filter **w** centred at a point (a, b) in the image **x**, where a is location along the horizontal axis and b is location along the vertical axis. This filter gathers its inputs from the outputs of photoreceptors (pixels) that define the image **x**, and the effective connection strength between the filter and each pixel defines

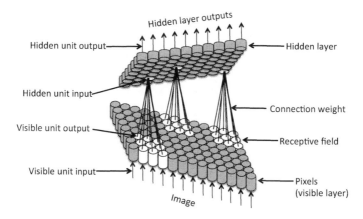

Figure 9.2. Each hidden unit (filter) receives inputs from a small region of the visible layer, which defines its receptive field.

the receptive field of the filter, as shown in Figure 9.2. The different connection strengths mean that the input to a hidden unit is a weighted average of pixel outputs within its receptive field:

$$\mathbf{v}(a,b) \;=\; \sum_{\alpha=-k}^{k} \sum_{\beta=-k}^{k} \mathbf{w}(\alpha,\beta)\,\mathbf{x}(a+\alpha,b+\beta), \tag{9.2}$$

where $k = 1$ for the filter in Equation 9.1. The value of k defines the outer limits of the receptive field, so that $\mathbf{w}$ has a total of $(2k+1)^2$ weights. If the image consists of a square array of $n = N \times N$ pixels, and if over each pixel we place the centre of one filter, then (using Equation 9.1) the array of filter inputs can be expressed using the *convolution operator* $*$ as $\mathbf{v} = \mathbf{w} * \mathbf{x}$, where $\mathbf{w}$ is a two-dimensional weight matrix of filter values, like Equation 9.1, and $\mathbf{x}$ represents the

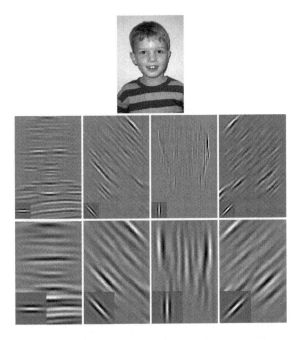

Figure 9.3. Examples of convolution. Each convolution image is obtained by using the filter shown in its lower left corner to convolve the top image. These (Gabor) filters are similar to filters found in the human visual system and in neural networks. Each filter acts like a feature detector, picking out a particular feature in the top image. Each convolution image corresponds to the activity within one feature map of a convolutional network.

image. The outputs of the filters define a new image, sometimes called the *convolution image*. Examples of convolution images are shown in Figures 9.3 and 9.4.

9.3. LeNet1

A landmark paper in the history of neural networks was published by LeCun et al. in 1989 and presented the network shown in Figure 9.5. This network combined several novel features, which allowed it to attain impressive performance in classifying handwritten (zip code) digits.

The network has a total of five layers: an input layer, three hidden layers, and an output layer. All units except those in the input layer have hyperbolic tangent (tanh) activation functions (the tanh function has a similar shape to the sigmoidal function shown in Figure 4.1, except that it has an output between -1 and $+1$). The input layer is a 16×16 array of units with linear activation functions.

The first hidden layer consists of 12 *feature maps*, where each feature map is an 8×8 array of hidden units. All units in a single feature map have the same 5×5 array of weights, which defines the receptive field of a single hidden unit in that feature map. Crucially, these weights are not pre-specified, but learned. Because all hidden units in each

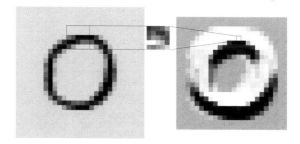

Figure 9.4. Left: Image of a zero, showing the 5×5 receptive field of a hidden unit. Middle: Weights within the 5×5 receptive field of a hidden unit. Right: Convolution image (hidden unit inputs). The lines show how the input to a hidden unit is obtained by multiplying each weight by the corresponding pixel within the unit's receptive field. All hidden units in one feature map have the same weights (middle), so their inputs can be represented as an image (right). For display purposes, the number of pixels and the number of hidden units are the same here, but there would usually be fewer hidden units than pixels, as in Figure 9.5. Reproduced with permission.

feature map have the same weights, this is known as *weight sharing*. Adjacent hidden units have overlapping receptive fields in the image, so each feature map effectively tiles the input image. Specifically, adjacent hidden units in a given feature map have receptive field centres separated by two pixels in the input image. The collection of outputs of units in a given feature map constitutes a convolution image, because it is the result of convolving the unit weights with the input image (and then passing each value through a unit activation function). Because there are many fewer hidden units than pixels, each feature map effectively *sub-samples* the image, producing an 8×8 feature map from a 16×16 image. In effect, each hidden unit acts like a ganglion cell in the retina.

There are two principal reasons for using feature maps. First, having shared weights reduces the number of free parameters (i.e. weights). Second, because all units in a feature map have the same weights, each feature map is able to detect a single feature in any part of the image. Notice that using 12 feature maps implicitly assumes that 12 types of localised features suffice for recognition of the digits.

The second hidden layer follows the same design as the first hidden layer, with 12 feature maps, each of which is an array of 4×4 units. This layer performs the same type of operation on the output of the

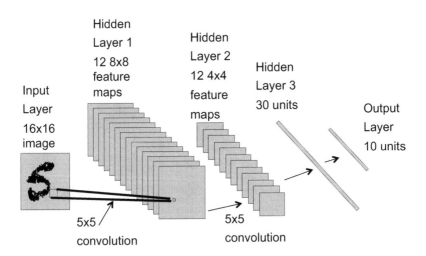

Figure 9.5. Schematic diagram of LeNet1.

first hidden layer as the first hidden layer performs on the input image. Each hidden unit has a 5×5 receptive field at the same location as for feature maps in the first hidden layer. The reason for this is that the second hidden layer should find combinations of the low-order features discovered by units in the first hidden layer. This cumulative 'features of features' strategy is analogous to processing in the human visual system. Even though all hidden units in a given feature map have the same weights, different units have unique biases. This bias reflects the frequency with which a given feature appears in the position occupied by that hidden unit's receptive field.

The third hidden layer consists of 30 units, each of which is fully connected to every unit in the second hidden layer. Finally, the output layer consists of 10 units, each of which is fully connected to every unit in the third hidden layer. In total, there are 1,256 units and 9,760 weights. The network was trained using backprop on 7,291 images in a training set, and tested on 2007 images in a test set. After 23 training iterations (each iteration involving 7,291 images), the training error was 0.14% and the error on the test set was 5%.

9.4. LeNet5

Almost a decade after LeNet1, LeNet5 was introduced in 1998. The main improvement over LeNet1 was the introduction of *pooling*. Pooling is a mechanism used to provide invariance with respect to a chosen image transformation. For example, if each of three hidden units responds to the image of a 5 but at different orientations, then another

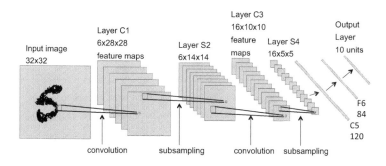

Figure 9.6. Schematic diagram of LeNet5.

unit that adopts the maximum state of the three units will behave as if it is an orientation-invariant detector of the digit 5. In LeNet5, pooling consists of taking the average output of four hidden units in the same feature map. This average is multiplied by an learned weight, added to an learned bias, and passed through a sigmoidal activation function.

LeNet5 consists of an input image of 32×32 pixels, plus seven layers. All units in layers 1 to 6 have sigmoidal activation functions. The first layer is labelled C1, where C stands for convolution. This layer consists of six feature maps, each of which is an array of 28×28 units. Each unit receives input from a 5×5 receptive field of the input image, and all units in the same feature map share the same set of 25 adjustable weights and the same bias weight. Because each feature map is dedicated to one feature, layer C1 can detect up to six different image features in any image location.

The second layer is labelled S2, where S stands for sub-sampling. This layer consists of six feature maps, each of which is an array of 14×14 units. Each unit in S2 receives input from a 2×2 receptive field in one feature map of C1. The input to each S2 unit is the average of the outputs from units in its receptive field, which is then multiplied by an adjustable weight and added to a adjustable bias; the unit's output is obtained by passing this through a sigmoidal function. Layer C3 consists of 16 feature maps, each of which is an array of 10×10 units. Each unit in layer C3 receives input from identical locations of between three and six 5×5 receptive fields in S2. All units in a single feature map of C3 have shared weights. Layer S4 consists of 16 feature maps, each of which is an array of 5×5 units. Each unit in S4 receives input from a 2×2 receptive field in one feature map of C3.

Layer C5 consists of 120 feature maps, each of which is a single unit. Each unit in C5 receives input from a 5×5 receptive field, with connectivity such that it effectively convolves all 16 feature maps of C3. Layer F6 has 84 units, each of which is connected to every unit in layer C5. All 10,164 weights between C5 and F6 are adjustable. Finally, the output layer consists of 10 *radial basis function* (RBF) units. Briefly, the output of an RBF unit is the Gaussian-weighted distance between the unit's weight vector and its 120-element input vector. The entire network contains 340,908 connections, but because some of these are shared, there are a total of 60,000 adjustable weights. The network was trained using backprop. The test error on the the MNIST digits (Section 7.4) was 0.95%.

9.5. AlexNet

In 2012 a deep convolutional neural network, now known as *AlexNet*, was published by Alex Krizhevsky, Sutskever, and Hinton. AlexNet was the first convolutional network to win the ImageNet Challenge. The network had seven hidden layers, plus max pooling layers, where the first few layers were convolutional. The authors claimed that a key contribution to AlexNet's success is the use of *rectified linear units* (ReLU, Figure 9.8) in every layer.

The images used to evaluate performance were from the standard ImageNet data set. The number of images in this set varies from year to year, but is never less than a million. In 2012, the training set consisted of 1.2 million 256 × 256 training images from 1,000 different classes, and a separate test set contained 100,000 images.

In order to increase the effective size of the training set, the network was trained on random 224 × 224 patches from the images, and on left–right reflections of the images. In order to reduce over-fitting, a technique called *dropout* was used. This means that half of the hidden units in a layer are randomly removed during each update of the weights. This dropout technique is remarkably effective, but the reasons for this remain unclear (Helmbold and Long, 2017).

Classification performance is often reported as a percentage based a 'top-n' threshold. After training, the probability that a given input

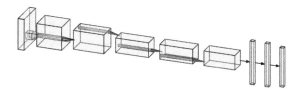

Figure 9.7. Schematic diagram of AlexNet. Reproduced with permission from http://alexlenail.me/NN-SVG/AlexNet.html.

belongs to each of 1,000 classes is computed. If inputs are classified as belonging to the top five classes 80% of the time, this is reported as a top-5 performance of 80%. A top-1 performance specifies how often the network classification is the correct class label. On the test data, AlexNet achieved a top-5 error of 17.0% and a top-1 error of 37.5%.

9.6. GoogLeNet

In 2014, Szegedy et al. introduced *GoogLeNet*. This uses a total of 22 layers, plus five pooling layers, in a complicated arrangement that includes all of the features (such as ReLU) of previous networks. The network's performance was tested in the 2014 ImageNet Challenge described above. It achieved a top-5 error of 6.67% on the test data, compared with 17% for AlexNet. An interesting aspect of this network is that it uses only about a twelfth of the number of weights as AlexNet while being significantly more accurate.

9.7. ResNet

In 2015 He et al. introduced the *residual network* (ResNet), a network with 152 layers, which is about 10 times more than networks used at that time. ResNet is notable because it was the first network to exceed human-level accuracy on the ImageNet Challenge, with a top-5 error rate of 3.75%.

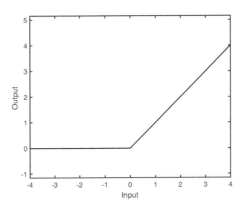

Figure 9.8. The rectified linear unit (ReLU) activation function.

The success of ResNet was due mainly to a single key innovation. Consider a network that is required to learn the mapping from its input $\mathbf{x}$ to its output $\mathbf{y}$, which defines a function $\mathbf{y} = H(\mathbf{x})$. Almost irrespective of the nature of the function H that the network is supposed to learn, it is usually easier to learn the identity function $\mathbf{y} = I(\mathbf{x})$, where $I(\mathbf{x}) = \mathbf{x}$. By extension, if learning I is easier than learning H, then learning $F \approx I$ should also be easier than learning H. This situation can be summarised as

$$\mathbf{x} \rightarrow I(\mathbf{x}) \quad \text{identity function (easy)}$$

$$\mathbf{x} \rightarrow H(\mathbf{x}) \quad \text{arbitrary function (hard)}$$

$$\mathbf{x} \rightarrow F(\mathbf{x}) = H(\mathbf{x}) - \mathbf{x} \quad \text{residual function (easier than } H).$$

Accordingly, rather than learning the function $\mathbf{y} = H(\mathbf{x})$, the network is trained on the *residual mapping* (Figure 9.9)

$$\mathbf{y} = F(\mathbf{x}) = H(\mathbf{x}) - \mathbf{x}. \tag{9.3}$$

It is usually an exaggeration to say that $F \approx I$, so the approximation should be interpreted very loosely. Recently, a 1,000-layer ResNet was tested on the CIFAR data set of 60,000 images with considerable success (He et al., 2016). By connecting every layer to every other layer, *DenseNets* (Huang, 2017) achieved even better performance than ResNet on the CIFAR data set.

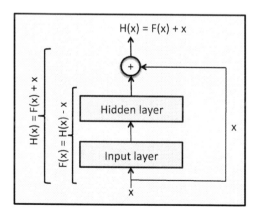

Figure 9.9. Schematic diagram of the ResNet architecture.

9.8. Ladder Autoencoder Networks

A practical problem for neural networks is that they require large amounts of *labelled data*, that is, data for which the class of each training vector is known. A major advantage of *ladder autoencoder networks* is that they can take advantage of unlabelled data to improve performance on relatively small amounts of labelled data.

Ladder networks were introduced by Rasmus et al. (2015). They combine supervised and unsupervised learning, and are therefore often called *semi-supervised networks*. The term ladder derives from their appearance, because corresponding layers in the encoder and decoder are connected to each other, as in Figure 9.10. Training is achieved using backprop. Results from using ladder networks are impressive, not only because they provide an accuracy of over 99% on the MNIST digit task (see Section 7.4), but also because this accuracy was achieved using merely 100 training images (10 training images per digit).

Conventional autoencoder networks attempt to reproduce their inputs at their output layer via a small number of hidden units (see Sections 6.8 and 7.4). The purpose of their architecture is to force the

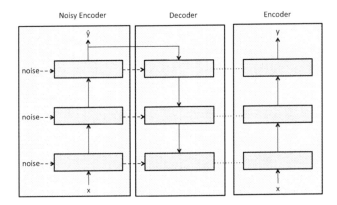

Figure 9.10. Ladder autoencoder network. The overall objective is to train the encoder. This is achieved by making a noisy version of the encoder and then forcing each layer in the decoder to reproduce the state of the corresponding encoder layer. In effect, the decoder attempts to denoise the noisy encoder states (dashed arrows) by comparing the decoder states to the encoder states (dotted lines). The error function combines this layer-wise denoising with learning labels implicit in the encoder output layer. Solid arrows represent adjustable weights.

network to preserve as much information as possible about the input vectors in the hidden units. Such networks are usually considered to be unsupervised, because the hidden unit states are not specified as part of the training set of vectors. However, a disadvantage of autoencoder networks is that they do not necessarily preserve the information required for discriminating between different classes of input vectors.

For example, an autoencoder network trained on images of handwritten digits cannot preserve all the information about its inputs in the hidden layer, so it must discard information about some image features. If the discarded information involves features that are important for discriminating between digits, this will inevitably reduce the ability of the network to classify images.

One way to deal with this problem is to force the hidden layers of the autoencoder network to preserve information relevant to the task of discriminating between images. This can be achieved by using a network error function that embodies a combination of two different constraints: *image reconstruction* and *image discrimination*. Image

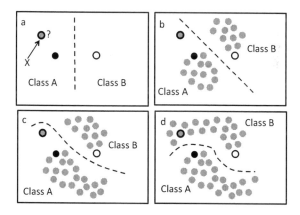

Figure 9.11. Combining supervised and unsupervised learning to reduce the number of labelled items required. (a) Given two labelled data points that belong to the classes A (black disc) and B (white disc), how should a third unlabelled data point X be classified? Given its proximity to the data point in class A, X would be classified as class A. (b) As more unlabelled data become available, clusters emerge, but X continues to be classified as class A. (c) With even more data, it becomes less certain which class X belongs to. (d) Finally, the statistical structure of both classes becomes apparent, and classifying X as belonging to A becomes untenable. Inspired by Rinu Boney.

reconstruction is enforced by using a noisy version of each layer in the encoder as a training vector for the corresponding layer in the decoder. In effect, this forces the decoder to act as a denoising network for the encoder network (Figure 9.10). Image discrimination is enforced by using image labels, where each label is a vector clamped to the encoder output layer.

An important side-effect of the semi-supervised training used in ladder networks is that these networks can take advantage of unlabelled data (e.g. raw images) to improve discrimination performance on a relatively small amount of labelled data. The intuition behind this is that training vectors in different classes (e.g. images of 1s and 2s) usually reside in different clusters within the input space. By using supervised learning so that even one exemplar of each class maps to a different output vector (label), the network is more likely to map other unlabelled members of each class (cluster) to the correct output vector. A schematic account of how unsupervised learning can be used in conjunction with supervised learning is shown in Figure 9.11. Here, a point X is initially classified as belonging to class A, but after a large number of data points have been observed, the clustering of points strongly suggests that X actually belongs to class B.

As described above, the central idea that motivates ladder autoencoder networks is fairly straightforward, but the implementation of that idea is not. One of the most transparent accounts is given in Rasmus et al. (2015), and the following is based on their paper. The encoder has seven layers with 784, 1000, 500, 250, 250, 250, and 10 units, where the input layer receives an image of $28 \times 28 = 784$ pixels. The rectified linear unit (ReLU) activation function (Figure 9.8) is used for all hidden units, and the softmax activation function (Equation 7.13) is used for the encoder output layer.

As in Section 7.4, the decoder network has an architecture that is a mirror image of the encoder. However, there are three major modifications to the conventional autoencoder structure. First, the input to every unit in the decoder is a copy of the input to the corresponding unit in the encoder. Second, each layer in the noisy encoder has a direct *skip connection* to the corresponding layer of the decoder. The skip connections simply allow the states of corresponding layers in the noisy encoder and decoder to be compared; these connections are not adjustable weights. The skip connections across corresponding layers are used to adjust the weights between layers so that the encoder and decoder unit inputs can be made more similar to each other. In effect, the decoder attempts to adopt unit input values that are denoised estimates of the noisy input values in the noisy encoder. Third, encoder output units can be trained using either a) image labels or b) the encoder output, as determined by the current input image after it is propagated forwards through the encoder. In practice, encoder output units are trained using both a) and b). Training with labelled images forces the network to attend to image features that facilitate discrimination, while training with unlabelled images forces the network to discover clusters amongst the training vectors. Labelled and unlabelled training vectors are used as part of the same training set, so both types of training vectors are effectively used simultaneously. Rasmus et al. (2015) includes a number of innovations, which are evaluated in Pezeshki et al. (2015).

9.9. Denoising Autoencoders

Rather than being trained to map each input to an identical output, a denoising autoencoder is trained to map a corrupted version of its input to an uncorrupted version of that input. In other words, a denoising autoencoder is trained to remove the effects of noise from its inputs. Denoising autoencoders were introduced in the context of stacked autoencoders by Vincent et al. (2010).

The reason for corrupting inputs is because we wish networks to be robust with respect to noisy inputs. One way to achieve such robustness is to explicitly corrupt inputs in ways that mimic the natural variation of inputs. This general idea, referred to as *tangent prop*, had been proposed for training backprop networks by Simard, LeCun, and Denker as early as 1992. Vincent et al. experimented with several methods for corrupting inputs, including setting image pixels to zero, adding salt and pepper noise, and adding Gaussian noise to inputs. Crucially, they showed that training an autoencoder to minimise reconstruction error amounts to maximising a lower bound on the mutual information between its inputs and the learned autoencoder outputs. This interpretation foreshadowed the development of variational autoencoders (see Chapter 8).

9.10. Fooling Neural Networks

Neural networks are easily fooled, provided you know how to fool them. In an insightful paper Goodfellow et al. (2014) showed that neural networks can be severely hampered by making tiny, but very specific, changes to their inputs (Figure 9.12). Their line of reasoning applies to any network, but is best understood in terms of a linear associative network.

Consider a network with 784 input units and a single output unit. Each input vector is an image with 28×28 pixels, represented as a single 784-element vector $\mathbf{x} = (x_1, \ldots, x_{784})$. The output unit's state y is given by the inner product of $\mathbf{x}$ with the output unit's weight vector $\mathbf{w} = (w_1, \ldots, w_{784})$, so that $y = \mathbf{w} \cdot \mathbf{x}$. If we change $\mathbf{x}$ to $\mathbf{x}'$ by adding $\Delta \mathbf{x}$, the output will change by Δy to

$$y' = \mathbf{w} \cdot \mathbf{x} + \mathbf{w} \cdot \Delta \mathbf{x} \qquad (9.4)$$

$$= y + \Delta y. \qquad (9.5)$$

Notice that $\Delta \mathbf{x}$ defines a direction in the input space; the question is, which direction $\Delta \mathbf{x}$ will have most impact on y? To make this a fair comparison, the magnitude (vector length) $|\Delta \mathbf{x}|$ of $\Delta \mathbf{x}$ is kept constant.

Figure 9.12. Fooling a network. If an image (left) that is initially classified as a panda with 58% confidence is corrupted by a specific noise image (centre), then the resultant image (right) is classified as a gibbon with 99% confidence. With permission from Goodfellow et al. (2014).

Suppose we choose $\Delta\mathbf{x}$ to be the direction of steepest ascent in y,

$$\nabla_{\mathbf{x}}y = \left(\frac{\partial y}{\partial x_1}, \ldots, \frac{\partial y}{\partial x_{784}}\right) = (w_1, \ldots, w_{784}). \qquad (9.6)$$

By definition, a change in $\mathbf{x}$ in the direction $\nabla_{\mathbf{x}}y$ produces the largest possible change in y. We now construct an *adversarial image*

$$\mathbf{x}' = \mathbf{x} + \epsilon\nabla_{\mathbf{x}}y \qquad (9.7)$$

(where ϵ is a small constant), which is a modification to $\mathbf{x}$ that will alter y more than a change in any other direction.

Adversarial images are conventionally constructed by taking the derivative of the error function E with respect to $\mathbf{x}$, that is, $\mathbf{x}' = \mathbf{x} + \epsilon\nabla_{\mathbf{x}}E$, and the change is implemented as the *fast gradient sign method*, for which $\Delta\mathbf{w} = \epsilon\,\text{sign}(\nabla_{\mathbf{x}}E)$; this adversarial image is proportional to the image defined in Equation 9.7.

9.11. Generative Adversarial Networks

A generative adversarial network (GAN) consists of two separate networks, a *generator network* (G) and a *discriminator network* (D), as shown in Figure 9.13 (Goodfellow et al., 2014). The discriminator network is presented with images from the generator network or from a training set of images taken by a camera. On each trial, the generator network assigns a probability to its input image, according to how realistic the image appears to be. In a sense, these two networks are engaged in an arms race, in which the generator network gradually learns to produce realistic synthetic images, while the discriminator network simultaneously learns to differentiate between the generator network's images and images from the training set.

Goodfellow et al. conceptualise the problem faced by a GAN by considering images in the training set as being samples from an underlying distribution $p_x(\mathbf{x})$ of images $\mathbf{x}_1, \mathbf{x}_2, \ldots$ taken by a camera (i.e. images of scenes). Similarly, each image produced by the generator network is considered to be a sample from the generator's distribution $p_G(G(\mathbf{z}))$ of images $G(\mathbf{z}_1), G(\mathbf{z}_2), \ldots$. Here, for the generator network

G, an input image $\mathbf{z}$ is chosen from a prior probability distribution $p_{\mathbf{z}}(\mathbf{z})$ of noise images.

The distribution $p_G(G(\mathbf{z}))$ is the generator network's estimate of $p_x(\mathbf{x})$; of course, initially $p_G(G(\mathbf{z}))$ is nothing like $p_x(\mathbf{x})$. Ideally, after training, $p_G(G(\mathbf{z})) \approx p_x(\mathbf{x})$, so the generator network would produce images that are indistinguishable from images in the training set. Consequently, when confronted with an equal proportion of images from the generator network and from the training set, the discriminator network would have an accuracy of 50%.

Given an image $\mathbf{x}$, the discriminator network's output $D(\mathbf{x})$ is an estimate of the probability that $\mathbf{x}$ was chosen from the distribution of training images $p_x(\mathbf{x})$ (rather than from the generator network's distribution $p_G(\mathbf{x})$). Goodfellow et al. proved that the optimal discriminator network's output is the probability that $\mathbf{x}$ was chosen from $p_x(\mathbf{x})$:

$$D^*(\mathbf{x}) \quad = \quad \frac{p_x(\mathbf{x})}{p_x(\mathbf{x}) + p_G(\mathbf{x})}. \tag{9.8}$$

Within each training iteration, first the weights in the discriminator network are adjusted repeatedly, and then the weights in the generator network are adjusted once.

For the discriminator network, a sample $\{\mathbf{x}\}$ of m images is chosen, and a sample $\{\mathbf{z}\}$ of m noise images is chosen. The weights are adjusted

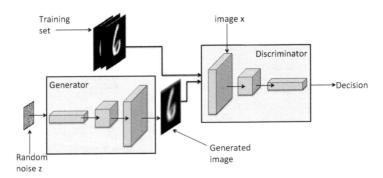

Figure 9.13. A generative adversarial network comprises two backprop networks. The discriminator network receives an image from the training set or the generator network. The output $D(\mathbf{x})$ of the discriminator network is the probability that the image $\mathbf{x}$ is from the training set.

so as to increase the probability that the discriminator network will increase its output (i.e. make $D(\mathbf{x})$ closer to 1) for members of $\{\mathbf{x}\}$ and decrease its output (i.e. make $D(\mathbf{x})$ closer to 0) for members of $\{\mathbf{z}\}$. These weight adjustments to the discriminator network are made using backprop by gradient ascent on the function

$$E_D \;=\; \frac{1}{m} \sum_{i=1}^{m} \Big[\log D(\mathbf{x}_i) + \log\big(1 - D(G(\mathbf{z}_i))\big)\Big]. \tag{9.9}$$

Notice that maximising E_D maximises $D(\mathbf{x}_i)$, which is the discriminator network's estimate of the probability that the image $\mathbf{x}_i$ belongs to the training set. Also, maximising $\log(1 - D(G(\mathbf{z}_i)))$ minimises $D(G(\mathbf{z}_i))$, which is the discriminator network's estimate of the probability that the image $G(\mathbf{z}_i)$ produced by the generator network belongs to the training set.

For the generator network, a sample $\{\mathbf{z}\}$ of m images is chosen, and weight adjustments are made by gradient descent on the function

$$E_G \;=\; \frac{1}{m} \sum_{i=1}^{m} \Big[\log\big(1 - D(G(\mathbf{z}_i))\big)\Big]. \tag{9.10}$$

Minimising $\log(1 - D(G(\mathbf{z}_i)))$ maximises $D(G(\mathbf{z}_i))$, which is the discriminator network's estimate of the probability that the image $G(\mathbf{z}_i)$ produced by the generator network belongs to the training set. In other words, the generator network weights are adjusted to increase the

Figure 9.14. Synthetic celebrities. These pictures were produced by a generative adversarial network that was trained on 30,000 images of celebrities. Reproduced with permission from Karras et al. (2018).

probability that the discriminator network will be fooled into classifying synthetic images $G(\mathbf{z}_i)$ as belonging to the training set $\{\mathbf{x}\}$.

Overall, maximising E_D while simultaneously minimising E_G defines an arms race in which the discriminator network becomes increasingly expert at differentiating between synthetic images and training set images, and the generator network becomes increasingly proficient at producing synthetic images that the discriminator network will classify as belonging to the training set. Recent research has extended the adversarial framework to autoencoders (Radford et al., 2015) and to high-resolution images of synthetic celebrities, as shown in Figure 9.14.

9.12. Temporal Deep Neural Networks

Following on from the review in Section 4.8, three key developments are described briefly here: *long short-term memory* (LSTM), *sequence-to-sequence learning*, and *temporal convolutional networks* (TCN).

Long Short-Term Memory. LSTM is essentially a sophisticated form of the temporal backprop networks described in Section 4.8. LSTM has two key innovations that allow it to retain information regarding recent inputs over substantial periods of time (Hochreiter and Schmidhuber, 1997; Gers, Schmidhuber, and Cummins, 2000). First, a *self-loop* implements a recurrent connection that retains information over a period of time determined by the recurrent weight value. Second, because the value of this recurrent weight is controlled by the state of a hidden unit, it can be adjusted dynamically according to the current context. LSTM networks have been used by Google for voice recognition since 2015.

Sequence-to-Sequence Learning. In 2014, the ability to translate text from one language to another was dramatically improved based on two papers published almost simultaneously (Sutskever, Vinyals, and Le; Cho et al.). The methods described in these papers also formed the basis of speech-to-text systems used in commercial applications, such as Siri, Cortana, and Alexa. Sequence-to-sequence learning consists of two coupled recurrent backprop neural networks, an encoder and a decoder. The encoder maps a sequence of inputs $\mathbf{x}=(x_1,\ldots,x_n)$ to a final state of its hidden units. If there are k hidden units then the encoder has effectively encoded a sequence of n inputs into a fixed-length k-element vector. In contrast, the decoder uses the k hidden unit states as a key to generate an output sequence $\mathbf{y}=(y_1,\ldots,y_m)$ where $m{\neq}n$.

Temporal Convolutional Networks. Both sequence-to-sequence learning and LSTM networks have become standard practice for processing temporal sequences, for example in voice recognition. However, a recent development may well displace LSTM as the primary sequential network. Specifically, temporal convolutional networks (TCN) seem to outperform LSTM networks across a range of temporal tasks (Elbayad, Besacier, and Verbeek, 2018; Bai et al., 2018).

Pixel Recurrent Neural Networks. Pixel recurrent neural networks (pixelRNNs) are generative models that utilise LSTM to model the long-range statistical structure of images (Oord, Kalchbrenner, and Kavukcuoglu, 2016). Strictly speaking, pixelRNNs are not temporal networks, but we mention them here because they make use of recurrent neural network architectures and methods.

9.13. Capsule Networks

Given a photograph of one or more objects, capsule networks attempt to extract the underlying physical parameters responsible for generating the image of each object (Sabour, Frosst, and Hinton, 2017). In this respect, they are similar to variational autoencoders and Boltzmann machines. Indeed, the central ideas behind these neural networks would be familiar to computer vision[31] and perceptual psychology researchers in the late 20th century, who developed a type of method known as *analysis by synthesis* (Selfridge, 1958). This posits that, in order to analyse an image, it is necessary to know how to generate or synthesise the image. Indeed, Hinton's own earliest papers reflect such an approach, containing ideas on instantiation parameters that are precursors to capsule networks[39;40;142].

A capsule network consists of three modules, called *conv1*, *primarycaps*, and *digitcaps*. Each element of conv1 detects a feature, and the conv1 output provides inputs to the primarycaps module. The primarycaps module acts like an inverse graphics generator, inasmuch as it attempts to estimate the values of local latent variables responsible for its inputs. The final module, digitcaps, has one capsule per digit class, and each capsule receives input from all the capsules in the primarycaps module. The key feature of the capsule network is the iterative adjustment of coupling coefficients between capsules in the primarycaps and digitcaps modules. In essence, each primarycaps capsule has a vector-valued output that represents a prediction for its own visual feature; this is not a prediction over time, but simply a prediction that the capsule's own feature is present in the image. For example, a feature might be a nose or an eye. Additionally, each primarycaps capsule specifies a particular feature with a particular set of instantiation (i.e. latent) parameter values; so, for example, the eye represented by a primarycaps capsule may have a particular orientation and position in the image. If enough primarycaps capsules make similar predictions regarding the values of the instantiation parameter values of different visual features, then (using an iterative routing procedure) the relevant digitcaps capsule becomes active. That digitcaps capsule then represents a combination of visual features, such as a face, which all share the instantiation parameter values that are consistent with a face. Even though it is early days for such a complex architecture, the performance of the capsule network is impressive when tested on the classic MNIST data set of digits.

9.14. Summary

Deep neural networks show super-human levels of performance. However, it has been noted that this is achieved only for certain types of tasks, such as object recognition. Additionally, a common criticism is that neural networks can learn those tasks only if they have access to enormous amounts of training data. Despite these reservations, neural networks are impressive within restricted domains, and have outstanding performance compared to their capabilities as little as ten years ago.

Chapter 10

Reinforcement Learning

Reinforcement learning is the best representative of the idea that an intelligent system must learn on its own, without supervision.
R Sutton, 2017.

10.1. Introduction

Animals choose actions that are rewarding, and avoid actions that are aversive. The feedback received from actions can be used to learn which actions are most rewarding, and the process of learning to maximise rewards on the basis of feedback is called *reinforcement learning.*

Just to give an idea of reinforcement learning's power, it has been used to train a neural network to play the game Go so well that world-class players have been beaten[108]. A more biologically relevant achievement is shown in Figure 1.2, which depicts a model glider that has learned to soar using reinforcement learning[28].

In essence, the problem confronting any learning system is that the consequences of each action often occur some time after the action has been executed. Meanwhile, many other actions would have been executed, so disentangling how much each action contributed to later rewards is a difficult problem. For example, if a rat eats a tainted food item then nausea usually follows several hours later, during which time it has probably eaten other items, so it is hard for the rat to know which item caused the nausea. Similarly, the final outcome of a chess game depends on every move within the game, so the wisdom of each move can only be evaluated after the game is over. For the apparently simple problem of balancing a pole (Figure 10.6), the consequences of each action (a nudge to the right or left) continue to evolve for many seconds, and are mixed with the effects of previous and subsequent actions. Evaluating the cost or benefit of actions lies at the heart of optimal behaviour, and is called the *temporal credit assignment problem*.

The ability to retrospectively assign credit to each action would be useless if an animal could not use the benefits of hindsight to foresee the likely outcome of its current actions. It follows that an animal's ability to solve the temporal credit assignment problem involves predicting future states of the world around itself. Fortunately, it turns out to be much easier to predict the future if that future is determined by, or at least affected by, the animal's own actions. By implication, the ability of an animal to take actions that maximise rewards depends heavily on its ability to predict the outcome of its actions.

The foregoing exemplifies how reinforcement learning differs from the supervised learning of neural networks in two important respects. First, supervised learning depends on input/output pairs of vectors; so the neural network is informed of the correct output vector for each input it receives. Reinforcement learning is similar inasmuch as each input vector is used to generate an action (in the form of an output vector), but feedback regarding the consequences of that action is simply a scalar reward signal, as shown in Figure 10.1. Consequently, there is no explicit information regarding how to alter each element of the output vector to improve matters.

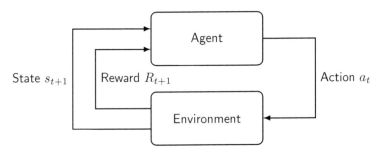

Figure 10.1. Reinforcement learning. An agent uses the current state of the environment to generate an action a_t, which changes the state of the environment to s_{t+1} and usually elicits an immediate reward R_{t+1}.

The second difference is that supervised learning involves immediate feedback. Sometimes this is also the case for reinforcement learning (*immediate reinforcement learning*), but usually the feedback received in reinforcement learning does not appear until some time after the current action (*delayed reinforcement learning*); and when it does appear, the feedback signal depends not only on the current action, but also on actions taken before and after the current action. So the problem addressed by reinforcement learning is substantially harder than the supervised learning problem solved by a neural network. It is noteworthy that reinforcement learning problems are similar to problems encountered in the natural world, where the feedback for actions consists of scalar variables in the form of rewards and punishments, and these are usually delayed until some time after the actions have been executed.

In summary, with supervised learning, the response to each input vector is an output vector that receives immediate vector-valued feedback specifying the correct output, and this feedback refers uniquely to the input vector just received; in contrast, each reinforcement learning output vector (action) receives scalar-valued feedback often some time after the action, and this feedback signal depends on actions taken before and after the current action.

Historically, the origins of reinforcement learning algorithms can be traced back to Shannon (1950), who described a program for playing chess (Shannon also invented *information theory*[107;123]). Even though his program did not learn, he proposed an idea that, to all intents and purposes, is reinforcement learning: 'a higher level program which changes the terms and coefficients involved in the evaluation function depending on the results of games the machine has played' (Shannon's evaluation function corresponds to the action-value function used in reinforcement learning). Indeed, this idea seems to be the inspiration for Samuel (1959), who designed a program for learning to play draughts (checkers). A later version of Samuel's program beat the checkers champion for the U.S. state of Connecticut in 1961. Since that time, reinforcement learning has been developed by many scientists, but its modern incarnation is due principally to Sutton and Barto (2018).

10.2. What's the Problem?

Reinforcement learning uses trial and error to learn a sequence of actions that maximises total reward. The reinforcement learning problem is often analysed as two sub-problems.

Given the current *state* of the agent and its local environment, the first sub-problem involves learning to predict the future total reward or the *return*. This is called *prediction, policy evaluation,* or *value estimation,* and yields a *state-value function.* In reinforcement learning, the state-value function is learned using *temporal difference learning.* This can be used either as a passive predictor of returns, or in parallel with learning a sequence of actions to maximise returns.

The second sub-problem involves finding the action for each successive state that maximises the return. The action taken at each time step is determined by a *policy,* which uses the current estimate of the state-value function to choose an action. Finding action sequences that maximise returns is called *policy improvement.*

In practice, an overall solution can be obtained using a procedure called *policy iteration.* This involves alternately improving the policy (while keeping the estimated state-value function fixed) and improving the estimated state-value function (while keeping the policy fixed), as depicted in Figure 10.4.

The conventional method for solving these sub-problems involves *dynamic programming.* Both reinforcement learning and dynamic programming rely on repeated exposure to a sequence of states or *episodes* to estimate the extent to which each state predicts the average return associated with that state.

However, dynamic programming must wait until the end of each episode before using the return to update the values and actions associated with states encountered along the way. For this reason, dynamic programming is restricted to *offline* updates. In contrast, reinforcement learning can perform *online* updates, which means that its estimates of each state's value and the wisdom of past actions are updated during the course of each episode.

10.3. Key Quantities

The brief glossary below should prove useful while reading this chapter.

- An *episode* is a complete sequence of states (like a game of chess).
- The *policy* π specifies the probability of choosing each of a set of possible actions $\{a_t\}$, given the current state s_t at time t.
- The *reward signal* R_{t+1} is an immediate reward for the current state s_t, which usually results from the action just taken.
- The *return* G_t is the cumulative total reward acquired from time $t+1$ to the end of an episode.
- The *state-value function* $v(s_t)$ is the expected return based on the current state s_t, that is, the return G_t averaged over all instances of the state s_t. The estimate of $v(s_t)$ is $V(s_t)$.
- The *action-value function* $q^\pi(s_t, a_t)$ defines the expected return based on the current state s_t and the action a_t specified by the policy π. The estimate of $q^\pi(s_t, a_t)$ is $Q(s_t, a_t)$.
- The *eligibility trace* is a scalar parameter that indicates how often each state has been visited. Each state has its own eligibility trace, which is given a boost every time that state is visited, before decaying exponentially thereafter at a rate determined by the *trace-decay parameter* λ.
- *Temporal discounting* means that immediate rewards are valued more than future rewards; it is determined by the parameter γ, which affects the state-value and action-value functions.
- The temporal difference error or *TD error* is the difference between the value $v(s_t)$ and the estimated value $V(s_t)$.

It is important to understand the distinction between a reward R (which is immediately available) and a return G (the total cumulative future reward). In particular, a large reward for an action does not necessarily indicate a large return; nor does a small reward for an action necessarily indicate a small return. For example, if a squirrel takes time and effort to bury acorns in the autumn when food is plentiful, then the immediate reward from its efforts is zero, but if those acorns sustain the squirrel through the winter then the return is large. Conversely, if the

147

squirrel eats all the acorns in the autumn, then the immediate reward is large but the return could be construed as negative (e.g. being dead).

When discussing rewards that are anticipated to occur in the future, it is tempting to refer to these as *expected* rewards. However, the term expected has a technical meaning (i.e. average). To avoid confusion, the term expected will be used to refer only to average rewards.

10.4. Markov Decision Processes

Markov decision processes (Watkins, 1989/1992) are important because they embody a set of assumptions relevant to reinforcement learning and *dynamic programming*. The conventional method for solving optimal control problems is *dynamic programming*, devised by Bellman in the 1950s. However, given a particular state, dynamic programming involves enumerating all possible future states, where the number of future states grows exponentially with the number of variables used to define the state. Fortunately, Bellman also came up with *Markov decision processes*, which simplify optimal control problems.

In order to define Markov decision processes, we first need to know about *Markov processes* or *Markov chains*. A Markov process generates a *memoryless* sequence of states in which the next state s_{t+1} depends probabilistically on the current state s_t, but not on previous states. Consequently, the probability of the next state s_{t+1} given the entire history of states prior to s_{t+1} is the same as the probability of s_{t+1} given only the current state s_t:

$$p(s_{t+1}|s_t, s_{t-1}, s_{t-2}, \dots) \quad = \quad p(s_{t+1}|s_t). \qquad (10.1)$$

A Markov decision process is defined in terms of the state s, the action a, the reward r, and the transition probabilities between states. In particular, a Markov decision process relies on the assumption that the next state s_{t+1} and its reward r_{t+1} depend on the current state s_t and action a_t, but not on previous states or actions, so that

$$p(s_{t+1}, r_{t+1}|s_t, a_t, s_{t-1}, a_{t-1}, \dots) = p(s_{t+1}, r_{t+1}|s_t, a_t). \qquad (10.2)$$

Markovian assumptions may seem restrictive, but it is usually possible to transform non-Markovian sequences into sequences that are Markovian or approximately Markovian (see Section 10.10).

10.5. Formalising the Problem

Before delving into the details of reinforcement learning, we should note that the principal objective is simple: to iteratively update the estimated state-value function V to make it increasingly similar to the state-value function v, and to use V to choose actions that maximise returns. We shall see how this is achieved in Section 10.6, but first we need to explore some key quantities,

The state-value function is defined as the expected return,

$$v^\pi(s) \quad := \quad \mathbb{E}_\pi[G_t | s_t = s], \qquad (10.3)$$

where the conditional notation $(|s_t{=}s)$ expresses that $v^\pi(s)$ is the mean taken only over returns G_t for which the state s_t is s; the subscript π in $\mathbb{E}_\pi[G_t]$ indicates the expected value of G_t given that the agent follows policy π.

The fact that an immediate reward is usually valued more highly than the same reward at some future date is reflected in the calculation of the return. Specifically, if the reward at time t is R_t, and if the *discount factor* is $0 \le \gamma < 1$, then the return is

$$
\begin{aligned}
G_t &= R_{t+1} + \gamma R_{t+2} + \gamma^2 R_{t+3} + \gamma^3 R_{t+4} + \cdots && (10.4) \\
&= \sum_{\tau=0}^{T} \gamma^\tau R_{t+\tau+1}. && (10.5)
\end{aligned}
$$

Notice that successive terms get multiplied by an exponentially diminishing quantity; this exponential weighting provided by temporal discounting is shown in Figure 10.2. So if, for example, the reward at each time step is $R = 1$ and if $T = \infty$, then the return is $G_t = 1/(1-\gamma)$, which is also the sum of weightings in Equation 10.5.

The exponential weighting assigned to successive rewards means that an episode can contain an infinite number of rewards without accumulating an infinitely large return. This matters when considering *infinite horizon* tasks (i.e. tasks which could last forever), such as pole balancing (Section 10.10). Crucially, the return can be expressed recursively as

$$G_t = R_{t+1} + \gamma(R_{t+2} + \gamma R_{t+3} + \gamma^2 R_{t+4} + \cdots) \qquad (10.6)$$
$$= R_{t+1} + \gamma G_{t+1}. \qquad (10.7)$$

This, in turn, allows reinforcement problems to be expressed recursively, by making use of the *Bellman equation*.

10.6. The Bellman Equation

The Bellman equation is the linchpin of all reinforcement learning methods. Under Markovian assumptions (Section 10.4), the Bellman equation allows the expectation of all future rewards to be decomposed recursively into the expectation of the sum of two terms: an immediate reward plus a discounted version of all rewards received after the immediate reward. Substituting Equation 10.7 into the state-value function (Equation 10.3) yields

$$v^{\pi}(s) = \mathbb{E}_{\pi}[R_{t+1} + \gamma G_{t+1} | s_t = s] \qquad (10.8)$$

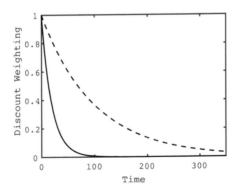

Figure 10.2. The exponential nature of the temporal discount weighting γ^t ensures that immediate rewards are valued more highly than future rewards; shown are the γ^t curves for $\gamma = 0.95$ (solid) and $\gamma = 0.99$ (dashed).

Just to give some idea of where we are heading, the Bellman equation for the policy π is

$$v^\pi(s) \;=\; \mathbb{E}_\pi[R_{t+1} + \gamma v^\pi(s_{t+1})|s_t = s]. \tag{10.9}$$

In words, the Bellman equation says that the value $v(s_t)$ of the state s_t equals the expected sum of two terms: the immediate reward R_{t+1} and the discounted return $\gamma v^\pi(s_{t+1})$ of the next state s_{t+1}. As we shall see, separating the immediate reward from the residual return is crucial for allowing the state-value function to be estimated recursively. To derive this Bellman equation, we rewrite the value function in full:

$$v^\pi(s) = \sum_a \sum_{s'} \pi(a|s)\, p(s'|a, s)$$
$$\times \mathbb{E}_\pi[R_{t+1} + \gamma G_{t+1}|s_t = s, a_t = a, s_{t+1} = s'],$$

where $\pi(a|s)$ is the probability of choosing action a given state s, $p(s'|a, s)$ is the probability of arriving in state s' after action a was executed in state s, and $G_{t+1} = R_{t+2} + \gamma R_{t+3} + \cdots$. The Markovian assumption means that R_{t+2} depends only on s_{t+1} (i.e. not on $s_t = s$ nor on $a_t = a$), so we can decompose the expectation into two terms,

$$\mathbb{E}_\pi[R_{t+1} + \gamma G_{t+1}|s_t = s, a_t = a, s_{t+1} = s']$$
$$= \mathbb{E}_\pi[R_{t+1}|s_t = s, a_t = a, s_{t+1} = s'] + \gamma\,\mathbb{E}_\pi[G_{t+1}|s_{t+1} = s'].$$

The first term on the right is

$$\mathbb{E}_\pi[R_{t+1}|s_t = s, a_t = a, s_{t+1} = s'] \;=\; \sum_R R\, p(R|s, a, s'),$$

and the expectation in the second term on the right is

$$\mathbb{E}_\pi[G_{t+1}|s_{t+1} = s'] \;=\; v^\pi(s'),$$

so the value function is

$$v^\pi(s) \;=\; \sum_a \pi(a|s) \sum_{s'} p(s'|a, s) \left(\left(\sum_R R\, p(R|s, a, s') \right) + \gamma v^\pi(s') \right).$$

Expanding the brackets yields

$$v^\pi(s) = \sum_a \pi(a|s) \sum_{s'} p(s'|a, s) \sum_R R\, p(R|s, a, s')$$
$$+ \gamma \sum_a \pi(a|s) \sum_{s'} p(s'|a, s) v^\pi(s'). \qquad (10.10)$$

The first term on the right is the expected reward after state s, having taken action a as determined by policy $\pi(a|s)$. Similarly, the second term is the expected value $v^\pi(s')$ of the next state s' under policy $\pi(a|s)$. We can now write Equation 10.10 as

$$v^\pi(s) \;=\; \mathbb{E}_\pi[R_{t+1}|s_t = s] + \gamma\mathbb{E}_\pi[v^\pi(s_{t+1})|s_t = s] \qquad (10.11)$$

$$\;=\; \mathbb{E}_\pi[R_{t+1} + \gamma v^\pi(s_{t+1})|s_t = s], \qquad (10.12)$$

which is Equation 10.9 as promised. Note that the recursive nature of the Bellman equation depends critically on the Markov assumption.

If actions are chosen according to an *optimal policy* π^* that maximises the expected return then this defines the *optimal state-value function*

$$v^*(s) \;=\; \underset{a}{\mathrm{argmax}}\; \mathbb{E}_{\pi^*}[R_{t+1} + \gamma v^*(s_{t+1})|s_t = s, a_t = a], \qquad (10.13)$$

where argmax_a means maximising expected return over all actions a.

10.7. Learning State-Value Functions

In order to find the optimal policy (see Section 10.9), we need to estimate the state-value function. Initially, the state-value function is not known, but it can be estimated by observing the sequences of states visited over many episodes (or over many sub-sequences within a single long episode). This is called *policy evaluation* because the states visited are usually the results of actions taken under a given policy.

In an ideal world, over many episodes, the update rule would make the estimated state-value function $V(s_t)$ increasingly similar to the actual state-value function $v^\pi(s_t)$. We can write the update rule as

$$V_{k+1}(s_t) \quad = \quad V_k(s_t) + \epsilon\left(v^\pi(s_t) - V_k(s_t)\right), \qquad (10.14)$$

where $v^\pi(s_t)$ acts as a *target* for the current (kth) estimate $V_k(s_t)$, and ϵ is a learning rate. However, in this imperfect world, we have to use an estimate $V(s_t)$ of $v^\pi(s_t)$ in the formula, which leads to the online temporal difference learning rule. To see where we are heading, here is that rule:

$$V_{k+1}(s_t) \quad = \quad V_k(s_t) + \epsilon\left(R_{t+1} + \gamma V_k(s_{t+1}) - V_k(s_t)\right). \quad (10.15)$$

We begin by defining the error function

$$E \quad = \quad \frac{1}{2}\sum_{t=1}^{\infty}\left(V(s_t) - [R_{t+1} + \gamma v^\pi(s_{t+1})]\right)^2. \qquad (10.16)$$

As above, we are interested in the value of each state, irrespective of the time at which it occurs; so we write the state as simply s without a t subscript. To obtain Equation 10.15, we first need to prove that gradient descent on E yields $V(s) = v^\pi(s)$.

If we knew the gradient of $V(s)$ with respect to E, then we could use the current estimate $V_k(s)$ of $v(s)$ as a basis for iterative updates:

$$V_{k+1}(s) \quad = \quad V_k(s) - \epsilon\,\frac{\partial E}{\partial V_k(s)}, \qquad (10.17)$$

where (omitting the k subscript)

$$\frac{\partial E}{\partial V(s)} = \sum_t (V(s_t) - [R_{t+1} + \gamma v^\pi(s_{t+1})])\frac{\partial V(s_t)}{\partial V(s)}. \qquad (10.18)$$

We define an *indicator function* $\Psi_i(s_t) = \partial V(s_t)/\partial V(s)$, which equals 1 if $s_t = s$ and 0 otherwise (this is analogous to the notation defined in Equation 10.3). Substituting Equation 10.18 into Equation 10.17 yields the offline update rule

$$V_{k+1}(s) = V_k(s) + \epsilon\sum_t \left([R_{t+1} + \gamma v^\pi(s_{t+1})] - V_k(s_t)\right)\Psi_i(s_t). \quad (10.19)$$

It is important to note that $\partial E/\partial V(s) = 0$ at a solution, at which point the total value associated with all N_s instances of the state s is

$$\sum_t V(s_t)\,\Psi_i(s_t) = \sum_t \left[R_{t+1} + \gamma v^\pi(s_{t+1})\right]\Psi_i(s_t), \quad (10.20)$$

where the total number of times that the state s is visited is

$$N_s = \sum_t \Psi_i(s_t). \quad (10.21)$$

By the definition of the indicator function $\Psi_i(s_t)$, $V(s_t)\Psi_i(s_t) = V(s)$, and $V(s)$ has the same value across all N_s instances of s, so

$$\sum_t V(s_t)\,\Psi_i(s_t) = N_s\,V(s). \quad (10.22)$$

Substituting Equation 10.22 into Equation 10.20 and dividing by N_s,

$$V(s) = \frac{1}{N_s}\sum_t [R_{t+1} + \gamma v^\pi(s_{t+1})]\,\Psi_i(s_t), \quad (10.23)$$

which is the average of N_s returns; therefore (for sufficiently large N_s)

$$V(s) = \mathbb{E}_\pi[R_{t+1} + \gamma v^\pi(s_{t+1})|s_t = s] \quad (10.24)$$
$$= v^\pi(s). \quad (10.25)$$

Thus, as promised, gradient descent on E yields a solution at which the estimated value function equals the value function. Close to a solution, the current estimate V_k is a good approximation to v, so we can replace v with V_k in Equation 10.19 to obtain the offline update rule

$$V_{k+1}(s) = V_k(s) + \epsilon \sum_t \left([R_{t+1} + \gamma V_k(s_{t+1})] - V_k(s_t)\right)\Psi_i(s_t), \quad (10.26)$$

where the difference

$$\delta_t = [R_{t+1} + \gamma V(s_{t+1})] - V_k(s_t) \quad (10.27)$$

is known as the *temporal difference error* or TD error. If we update $V(s_t)$ at every time step, we can set $s = s_t$ so that Equation 10.26

reduces to the online update rule

$$V_{k+1}(s_t) = V_k(s_t) + \epsilon \left(R_{t+1} + \gamma V_k(s_{t+1}) - V_k(s_t) \right), \qquad (10.28)$$

which implements *stochastic gradient descent* on E and is the rule promised in Equation 10.15. Provided the changes to $V(s_t)$ are sufficiently small (i.e. provided ϵ is small), convergence as the number of iterations $k \to \infty$ is guaranteed by the *Robbins–Monro theorem*[5].

However, the derivation that leads to the update rule in Equation 10.28 seems hopeful at best. Indeed, Sutton and Barto described this as 'learning a guess from a guess'. Despite such misgivings, it can be proved[128] that the estimate V converges to v^π.

Taking a different perspective, the value function $v^\pi(s_t)$ can be estimated by successive approximation because it is a *fixed point* of the Bellman equation[128]. Starting from an arbitrary estimate $V_k(s)$, this can be modified using the (offline) *expected update* rule

$$V_{k+1}(s) \quad = \quad \mathbb{E}_\pi[R_{t+1} + \gamma V_k(s_{t+1})|s_t = s], \qquad (10.29)$$

where the expected value $\mathbb{E}_\pi$ is estimated over one or more episodes. The *Banach fixed-point theorem* guarantees that, provided $0 \le \gamma < 1$, the estimated value function $V_k(s)$ converges to $v^\pi(s)$ as $k \to \infty$.

The methods described above are *one-step* TD(0) methods because they use the reward R_{t+1} from one time step after the current state to learn. The '0' in TD(0) indicates that this is a special case of the TD(λ) method, described in the next section.

10.8. Eligibility Traces

To solve the temporal credit assignment problem, we need a record of which states have been visited. Ideally, we would like to keep a complete record of every state that has ever been visited, the time it was visited, and the reward received at that time. However, the cost of doing so can be prohibitive. Instead, we can assign an *eligibility trace* to each state. This trace increases when a state is visited, but decreases exponentially thereafter. Consequently, a state that was visited in the distant past has less effect on updates to the state-value function than the same state visited recently. Eligibility traces can also be used in estimating the action-value function, by keeping track of which pairs of states and actions yielded rewards. Because the eligibility trace decays exponentially, it is easy to update online. At every time step the eligibility traces of all states are updated: the eligibility trace of the current state s_t is given a boost, and its update rule is

$$e(s_t) \quad = \quad \gamma\lambda\,e(s_{t-1}) + 1, \tag{10.30}$$

where the trace-decay parameter λ lies between 0 and 1; in contrast, the eligibility trace of every other state s'_t continues to fade exponentially

$$e(s'_t) \quad = \quad \gamma\lambda\,e(s'_{t-1}). \tag{10.31}$$

Thus, the eligibility trace of each state fades but gets boosted when that state is visited (Figure 10.3). Comparing the state-value function v in Equation 10.9 with the eligibility trace e in Equations 10.30 and 10.31, it is apparent that v depends on the discount factor γ but not on the trace-decay parameter λ, whereas e depends on both γ and λ.

Using an eligibility trace, the TD error term (Equation 10.27) in the usual TD(0) update rule (e.g. Equation 10.28) gets multiplied by $e(s_t)$,

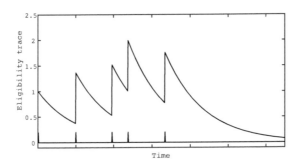

Figure 10.3. The eligibility trace of a state fades exponentially after it is visited, but frequent visits to that state have a cumulative boosting effect. Each vertical bar at the bottom of the graph indicates a time at which this state was visited.

which yields the TD(λ) update rule

$$V_{k+1}(s_t) = V_k(s_t) + \left[\epsilon \times e(s_t) \times \left(R_{t+1} + \gamma V_k(s_{t+1}) - V_k(s_t) \right) \right]. \quad (10.32)$$

The eligibility trace ensures that highly rewarded states, or rewarded states that are visited frequently, tend to dominate the estimated value function. Notice that if $\lambda = 0$ then this TD(λ) update rule is equivalent to the TD(0) update rule in Equation 10.28.

10.9. Learning Action-Value Functions

Once we have an estimate of the optimal state-value function, this can be used to estimate the optimal policy. It might be supposed that improving a policy involves looking ahead over many time steps in order to measure the total reward under each of many candidate policies. However, we can improve a policy by making use of a *greedy algorithm* that looks ahead by a single time step.

The Bellman equation for an action-value function is defined as the expected return for taking action a in state s using policy π:

$$q^\pi(s, a) \quad := \quad \mathbb{E}_\pi[G_t | s_t = s, a_t = a]. \quad (10.33)$$

The policy π defines the probability of choosing action a when in state s. Consequently, the state-value function can be recovered from the action-value function for a given state s by averaging over all actions:

$$v^\pi(s) \quad = \quad \sum_a \pi(a|s) \, q^\pi(s, a). \quad (10.34)$$

Like the state-value function, the action-value function can be expressed recursively by the formula

$$q^\pi(s, a) = \mathbb{E}_\pi[R_{t+1} + \gamma q^\pi(s_{t+1}, a_{t+1}) | s_t = s, a_t = a]. \quad (10.35)$$

The *optimal action-value function* $q^*(s, a)$ is given by the policy that maximises the expected return:

$$q^*(s, a) \quad := \quad \max_\pi q^\pi(s, a). \quad (10.36)$$

In essence, the optimal action-value function specifies the best possible performance for the Markov decision process under consideration. It can be shown that optimal policies employ the optimal state-value function and optimal action-value function.

If the agent takes a sub-optimal action a but thereafter takes actions according to the optimal policy, then this defines a new policy π'. The *policy improvement theorem* guarantees that the policy π is improved by using a new greedy policy π':

$$\pi'(s) \;=\; \underset{a}{\mathrm{argmax}}\; q^{\pi}(s,a) \tag{10.37}$$

$$\;=\; \underset{a}{\mathrm{argmax}}\; \mathbb{E}[R_{t+1} + \gamma v^{\pi}(s_{t+1})|s_t = s, a_t = a], \tag{10.38}$$

where argmax_a means that we seek the action a that maximises $q^{\pi}(s,a)$. In essence, the policy improvement theorem states that an optimal policy is found by choosing the action that leads to the state with the highest value.

It might appear that it is necessary to complete policy evaluation before starting policy improvement. However, notice that there is a reciprocal relationship between the policy π and the state-value function $v(s)$. Specifically, the optimal action (specified by the policy yielding the optimal action-value function $q^*(s,a)$) depends on the

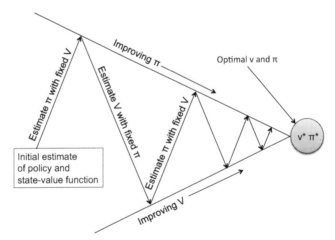

Figure 10.4. Generalised policy iteration: alternating estimates of the optimal policy and value function. Modified from Sutton and Barto (2018).

expected return $v(s)$ anticipated when that action is executed from a given state, and (conversely) the expected return $v(s)$ anticipated depends on the action executed. Consequently, the process of estimating v^* and the process of estimating π^* can be interleaved, in a combined process called *generalised policy iteration*. This involves alternately updating the estimated optimal state-value function whilst holding the policy fixed, and updating the estimated optimal policy whilst holding the state-value function fixed, as shown in Figure 10.4. At first sight, policy iteration looks wildly optimistic — but it works, and can be proved to work under fairly general conditions [128].

SARSA. This is an online TD method that finds an estimate Q of an optimal action-value function q^* and a corresponding optimal policy π^*. As a reminder, the q value is the expected discounted reward for executing action a_t at state s_t and following policy π thereafter. If s_{t+1} is a terminal state then $Q(s_{t+1}, a_{t+1})$ is defined as zero.

The update rule for SARSA is easier to follow if we first define the estimated optimal action as the action a_{t+1}^* that maximises the estimated expected return from the next state s_{t+1}:

$$a_{t+1}^* = \operatorname*{argmax}_{a} Q(s_{t+1}, a). \tag{10.39}$$

Exploration of novel states is encouraged by occasionally choosing an action at random. Rather than using the *greedy policy* defined in Equation 10.39, a ε-greedy policy chooses a random action a_{rand} with probability ε (e.g. $\varepsilon = 0.001$). Specifically, after generating a random value $0 \leq P \leq 1$, the next action taken is $a_{t+1} = a_{t+1}^*$ if $P \geq \varepsilon$ and $a_{t+1} = a_{\mathrm{rand}}$ otherwise.

The ideal rule for updating the estimate Q of the action-value function q would be (if we already knew q^*)

$$Q(s_t, a_t) \leftarrow Q(s_t, a_t) + \epsilon\big(q^*(s_t, a_t) - Q(s_t, a_t)\big). \tag{10.40}$$

(Note the use of an assignment arrow here, which is simply because we need to save space below). If we substitute $q^\pi = q^*$ in Equation 10.35 and follow the reasoning used in estimation of the state-value function in Section 10.6, then the rule for updating the estimate Q of the action-value function q^* is

$$Q(s_t, a_t) \leftarrow Q(s_t, a_t) + \epsilon\big(R_{t+1} + \gamma Q(s_{t+1}, a_{t+1}) - Q(s_t, a_t)\big), \quad (10.41)$$

which is applied after every action taken in a nonterminal state. The name SARSA is an acronym of the five variables used in the rule above, $(s_t, a_t, R_{t+1}, s_{t+1}, a_{t+1})$. SARSA is known as an *on-policy method* because each action a_t is taken according to Q, and Q is updated based on the actions taken. SARSA converges to the optimal policy and action-value function provided all state–action pairs are visited infinitely often [128]. Using eligibility traces yields SARSA(λ), which has one eligibility trace for each state–action pair.

Q-**Learning.** Like SARSA, Q-learning finds an estimate Q of an optimal action-value function q^* and a corresponding optimal policy π^*, but using a subtly different method. In essence, in Q-learning, the target value for Q is based on the next state and the action a_{t+1}^* that would maximise expected returns if this optimal action a_{t+1}^* were to be taken in the next state; in SARSA, the target value for Q is based on the next state and the action that will be taken from that state. Whereas SARSA essentially bootstraps its way to finding an action-

---

SARSA
set $Q(s_T, a) = 0$, where s_T is the terminal state in an episode
foreach *episode* **do**
    initialise state s_t
    choose action a_t from Q using greedy policy
    foreach *step from $t = 1$ to T of episode* **do**
        take action a_t
        get new state s_{t+1} and observe reward R_{t+1}
        choose action a_{t+1} from Q using ε-greedy policy
        use $Q(s_{t+1}, a_{t+1})$ to update the action-value function:
        $Q(s_t, a_t) \leftarrow Q(s_t, a_t) + \epsilon[R_{t+1} + \gamma Q(s_{t+1}, a_{t+1}) - Q(s_t, a_t)]$
        $s_t \leftarrow s_{t+1}$
        $a_t \leftarrow a_{t+1}$
    end
end

value function, Q-learning uses the optimal actions a^*_{t+1} to learn an action-value function; the action-value functions learned by SARSA and by Q-learning can have substantial differences.

Once an action a_t has been taken and the reward R_{t+1} for arriving in that state has been received, the rule for updating Q is

$$Q(s_t, a_t) \leftarrow Q(s_t, a_t) + \epsilon\big(R_{t+1} + \gamma Q(s_{t+1}, a^*_{t+1}) - Q(s_t, a_t)\big), \quad (10.42)$$

where a^*_{t+1} is defined in Equation 10.39. Thus, Q is updated as if the next action were optimal, even though the next action taken is based on the ε-greedy policy. Q-learning is known as an *off-policy method* because actions are taken according to the ε-greedy policy but Q is updated according to the policy implicit in Q (i.e. updates to Q are based on optimal actions a^*_{t+1}).

It may seem obvious that Q-learning is superior to SARSA because Q-learning learns actions guaranteed to maximise estimated returns. However, what is obvious is not always true. If Q is a poor approximation to q^* then the estimate of the best action may be sub-optimal, but it is nevertheless learned as if it were the best action, which can lead to getting stuck in a local minimum. Sutton and Barto

---

Q-Learning
set $Q(s_T, a) = 0$, where s_T is the terminal state in an episode
foreach *episode* **do**
    initialise state s_t
    while *state s_t is not a terminal state* **do**
        choose action a_t from Q using ε-greedy policy
        take action a_t
        get new state s_{t+1} and observe reward R_{t+1}
        get optimal action for state s_{t+1}: $a^*_{t+1} = \text{argmax}_a Q(s_{t+1}, a)$
        use $Q(s_{t+1}, a^*_{t+1})$ to update the action-value function:
        $Q(s_t, a_t) \leftarrow Q(s_t, a_t) + \epsilon[R_{t+1} + \gamma Q(s_{t+1}, a^*_{t+1}) - Q(s_t, a_t)]$
        $s_t \leftarrow s_{t+1}$
    end
end

give an example in which SARSA is shown to be more robust against the effects of noise than Q-learning.

Model-Free and Model-Based Methods. Both SARSA and Q-learning are *model-free methods* because they iteratively accumulate raw transition probabilities in a table or matrix by counting how often each transition is observed. This brute force approach to estimating transition probabilities is robust, but extremely expensive if the number of state transitions is large. An alternative approach involves using a model of the environment that is defined in terms of a small number of parameters. Dynamic programming is model-based, and methods such as Dyna-Q learn a model of the environment in parallel with learning the values of states and actions. Recently, deep learning neural networks have been used as parametric models of the state-value and action-value functions, instantiated as *deep Q-networks*[80;81].

Policy Gradient Methods. Rather than representing the policy as a matrix or table, it can be approximated as a parametric function,

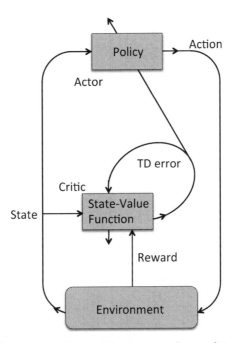

Figure 10.5. The actor–critic architecture can be used to simultaneously update the policy π and the state-value function V.

as implemented by a deep neural network. One advantage of using a parametric function is that the policy can be improved by gradient ascent with respect to the policy parameters. It is noteworthy that the recent successful applications of reinforcement learning described in Section 10.11 adopted this *policy gradient* approach. One of the most successful reinforcement learning methods, REINFORCE[138], relies on a form of stochastic policy gradient. Even though in most applications of reinforcement learning variables are assumed to be discrete, extensions to continuous variables have existed for some time (e.g. Doya, 2000).

Actor–Critic Architectures. Whether an action increases or decreases the return is reflected in the change in the state-value function from one state to the next. Consequently, the state-value function can be considered as a critic, and its outputs can be used to update the policy, implemented as a parametric function (usually in model-based methods such as policy gradient). This *actor–critic architecture* (Figure 10.5) can be used to simultaneously update the policy and the state-value function, and has been used to solve the cart–pole problem (Barto, Sutton, and Anderson, 1983).

Information-Theoretic Methods. Exploration implicitly involves acquiring as much information as possible about the environment. It therefore seems obvious that an exploration strategy based on maximising the information gained from actions should prove useful. Houthooft et al. (2016) proposed a curiosity-driven variational exploration strategy, which explicitly specifies that the next action should be chosen so as to maximise the information gained. Equivalently, this means choosing the action for which the reward is most uncertain. A similar approach due to Eysenbach et al. (2018) provides exploration using maximum-entropy policies. These studies suggest that information-theoretic exploration provides a substantial acceleration for subsequent skill acquisition using reinforcement learning. More generally, the ideas that underpin reinforcement learning have been applied within Friston's free-energy framework to explore computational models of niche construction[7].

10.10. Balancing a Pole

The task of balancing a pole on a cart makes an ideal demonstration problem because it is both easy to understand and hard to solve. The problem consists of applying a series of pulses (nudges) to a cart, which is on a short section of railway track, to ensure that the pole remains as vertical as possible. In this particular implementation, each episode starts with the cart in the centre of the track, and ends when one of three conditions is met: 1) the cart reaches one end of the track; 2) the angle of the pole exceeds 45 degrees; 3) 1,000 actions are taken without violating condition 1 or 2. Feedback R_{t+1} is received immediately after each action. Further details are specified in the box opposite (where feedback parameters were chosen through trial and error).

The cart–pole model has four state variables and three actions, as described in Figure 10.6. The action-value function can therefore be represented as a 7-dimensional matrix $Q(x, \dot{x}, \theta, \dot{\theta}, a_{-1}, a_0, a_{+1})$. The SARSA algorithm learned to balance the pole for (the maximum allowed) 1,000 actions within 500 episodes (see page 165).

We cannot plot a 7-dimensional matrix Q, so we visualise results using the state-value function $V(\theta, \dot{\theta})$, expressed in terms of θ and $\dot{\theta}$ only. This is achieved by marginalising Q over all three actions, the

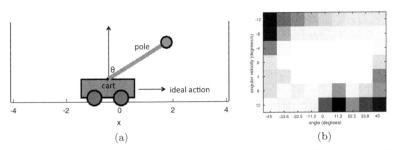

(a)   (b)

Figure 10.6. (a) The cart–pole problem has four state variables: x, the left–right position of the cart; $\dot{x}$, the cart velocity in m/s; θ, the angle of the pole; and $\dot{\theta}$, the angular velocity of the pole in degrees/s. It also involves three actions: a_{-1} = nudge leftwards, a_0 = do nothing, and a_{+1} = nudge rightwards. (b) The state-value function. Non-zero pole angles and high angular speeds have low (dark) state values, especially if the pole motion directs the pole away from vertical ($\theta = 0°$). Diagram (a) from software downloaded from https://github.com/david78k/pendulum, with permission.

SARSA: Balancing a Pole
state vector $\mathbf{s} = (x, \dot{x}, \theta, \dot{\theta})$ where
x=cart position, $\dot{x}$=velocity, θ=pole angle, $\dot{\theta}$=angular velocity
set learning rate $\epsilon = 0.3$, prob of random action $\varepsilon = 0.001$
foreach *episode* **do**
  initialise time $t = 0$
  $\varepsilon \leftarrow \varepsilon \times 0.99$
  set StillBalancingPole $= 1$
  initialise state vector $\mathbf{s}_t = (x, \dot{x}, \theta, \dot{\theta})$
  initialise action a_t to small value
  Main loop
  while *StillBalancingPole and $t \leq 1000$* **do**
    $t = t + 1$
    take an action a_t
    get new state $\mathbf{s}_{t+1} = \text{GetStateVector}(a_t, \mathbf{s}_t)$
    get cart parameters, $[x, \dot{x}, \theta, \dot{\theta}] = \text{GetCartParams}(\mathbf{s}_{t+1})$
    if abs$(x) > 4$ *or* abs$(\theta) > 45°$ **then**
      StillBalancingPole $= 0$
    end
    Get feedback for new state $\mathbf{s}_{t+1}$
    if *StillBalancingPole* **then** reward
      $R_{t+1} = 10 - 1000 * \theta^2 - 5 * \text{abs}(x) - 10 * \text{abs}(\dot{x})$
    else punish
      $R_{t+1} = -10000 - 50 * \text{abs}(x) - 100 * \text{abs}(\theta)$
    end
    Get new action
    if $\varepsilon <$ *a random number* **then**
      $a_{t+1} = \text{ChooseRandomAction}()$
    else
      find a such that $a = \text{argmax}_a Q(\mathbf{s}_{t+1}, a)$ (greedy policy)
      set $a_{t+1} = a$
    end
    Update action-value function Q
    $Q(s_t, a_t) \leftarrow Q(s_t, a_t) + \epsilon[R_{t+1} + \gamma Q(s_{t+1}, a_{t+1}) - Q(s_t, a_t)]$
    Re-assign state and action for next time step
    $\mathbf{s}_t \leftarrow \mathbf{s}_{t+1}, a_t \leftarrow a_{t+1}$
  end
end

position x, and the velocity $\dot{x}$ after learning. The resultant state-value function $V(\theta, \dot{\theta})$ is shown in Figure 10.6b. Experiments by Schulman (2016) suggest that optimal parameter values are $\lambda = 0.96$ and $\gamma = 0.98$. This figure is essentially a graphical representation of Michie and Chambers's (1968) BOXES algorithm, where each state is represented by a box.

Markovian Pole Angles. As stated in Section 10.6, reinforcement learning depends on the assumption that the problem under consideration is a Markov decision process, and therefore that the sequence of states is Markovian. However, many problems involve sequences of states that are clearly not Markovian. For example, the angle of the pole at the next time step depends on its angular velocity, but the velocity depends on the pole angle at *two* consecutive time steps. In this case, defining the state in terms of the *difference* between angles at consecutive time steps (i.e. as velocity) ensures that at least part of the state (the pole angle) is Markovian. More generally, defining the state as a sequence over the recent past is a common strategy for transforming a non-Markovian process into a sequence of states that are approximately Markovian.

10.11. Applications

The list of successful game-playing applications of reinforcement learning is impressive. These game-playing applications follow in the footsteps of an early success in backgammon, known as *TD-Gammon* (Tesauro, 1995), where TD(λ) was used to produce the best backgammon player in the world (Sutton, 2018). An intriguing aspect of TD-Gammon is that it developed a style of playing that was novel, and which was subsequently widely adopted by grandmasters of the game. This foreshadowed the winning strategy of AlphaGo, which also generated novel moves that surprised and (initially) mystified human observers, but which led to successful outcomes.

The game of Go involves several simultaneous short-range and long-range battles for territory, and has about 10^{170} legal board positions — more than the number of atoms in the known universe. In 2016 the widely publicised AlphaGo beat Lee Sedol, an 18-time world champion (Silver et al., 2016). A year later, AlphaGo beat a team of the world's top five players. Whereas AlphaGo initially learned from observing 160,000 human games, AlphaGo Zero learned through sheer trial and error before beating AlphaGo 100 games to none (Silver et al., 2017). Both AlphaGo and AlphaGo Zero relied on a combination of reinforcement learning and deep learning.

Remarkably, without altering the pre-learning parameter values, the algorithm of AlphaGo Zero was then used to learn chess [103]; let's call the result AlphaChess Zero. The best traditional computer chess program (Stockfish) already played at super-human levels of performance. In a tournament of 100 games between Stockfish and AlphaChess Zero, 72 were a draw, and AlphaChess Zero won the remaining 28. As with AlphaGo Zero, some of the moves made by AlphaChess Zero seemed strange, until it was realised that those strange moves were instrumental in winning the game.

Just as TD-Gammon altered the strategies used by humans to play backgammon, so AlphaGo Zero is changing the strategies that humans use to play Go; and it is entirely possible that AlphaChess Zero will do the same for chess. So, in a sense, humans are starting to learn from machines that learn.

The importance of AlphaGo Zero in beating the machine (AlphaGo) that beat the human world champion cannot be overstated. We can try to rationalise the achievements of AlphaGo Zero by pointing out that it played many more games than a human could possibly play in a lifetime. But the fact remains that a computer program has learned to

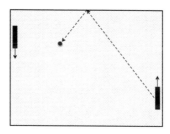

Figure 10.7. The game of pong is a computer version of table tennis. Each player can move the bat vertically to return the ball to the opponent. The arrow on each bat shows the direction of the current movement.

play a game so well that it can beat every one of the 7.7 billion people on the planet. Statistically speaking, that places AlphaGo Zero above the 99.9999999th percentile in terms of performance.

Prior to AlphaGo, success at classic arcade-style Atari games was achieved by a combination of deep learning and reinforcement learning. This resulted in super-human levels of performance in games like pong, which is a computer version of table tennis (Mnih et al., 2013, 2015). The input used by the algorithm is the pixel array seen by human players (Figure 10.7), rather than the x and y positions of objects in the game. Interestingly, the same *deep Q-network* learned to play all 49 different arcade games (Minh et al., 2015).

In some respects, the early successes of reinforcement learning are even more impressive than the later successes, which involved playing games. As most humans know, learning to ride a bicycle is not easy. By simulating the dynamics of a bicycle in software, a reinforcement learning algorithm was able to keep a virtual bicycle upright for long periods of time (Randløv and Alstrøm, 1998). Interestingly, learning was most rapid when a series of incremental sub-goals were used, similar to the scaffolding that adults use when teaching a child to ride a bicycle. More recently, reinforcement learning has been applied to the problems of learning to walk[29;52] and learning to fly. Using a simulation, a glider learned to gain height by circling around thermals. Encouraged by this development, reinforcement learning was then used in a physical glider with considerable success (Figure 1.2a).

10.12. Summary

The Danish philosopher Kierkegaard noted that

Life can only be understood backwards; but it must be lived forwards.
Søren Kierkegaard (1813–1855).

The more information an agent has about which actions led to rewards in the past, the more effectively the agent can modify its actions to increase rewards in the future. Such insights have been harnessed effectively by reinforcement learning to ensure that a life that must be lived forwards can maximise rewards, even if that life can only be understood backwards.

Chapter 11

The Emperor's New AI?

We set sail on this new sea because there is new knowledge to be gained ... for the progress of all people. For space science, like nuclear science and all technology, has no conscience of its own. Whether it will become a force for good or ill depends on man ...
President JF Kennedy, 1963.

11.1. Artificial Intelligence

Artificial intelligence is not only possible, but inevitable. The only question is: when will artificial intelligence arrive?

Before Orville and Wilbur Wright flew the first aeroplane in 1903, sceptics declared that a machine could never fly like a bird[1]. Today, many of us are like those sceptics, doubting that a machine could ever achieve human levels of intelligence. But a compelling counterargument to such scepticism is to note that birds and brains are physical devices, and that they both must obey the same laws of physics. In other words, a bird is a flying machine that happens to be made of organic matter, and a brain is a computational machine that happens to be made of neurons. Based on such observations, it seems obvious, and even inevitable, that a machine can fly even if it is not made of organic matter, and that a computational machine can be intelligent even if it is not made of neurons.

Regarding the question of when artificial intelligence will arrive, consider this. Whereas it took millions of years for the first gliding vertebrate to evolve into a bird that could fly, it took a mere 66 years from the Wright brothers' first flight to Neil Armstrong's 'small step'

---

[1] In 1901, Wilbur had predicted that powered flight would take another 50 years.

onto the moon in 1969. Similarly, even though life probably appeared on Earth as soon as it cooled, it took a further four billion years for the first animals with primitive neurons to evolve, but a mere half a billion years more for natural selection to sculpt those first neurons into the human brain.

As a final example, the first electronic computers were made of vacuum tubes (like old-style tungsten bulbs). To give some idea of the rate of progress, and of our failure to appreciate how quickly progress accelerates, a 1949 article in *Popular Mechanics* magazine declared:

> ... a calculator today is equipped with 18,000 vacuum tubes and weighs 30 tons, computers in the future may have only 1,000 vacuum tubes and perhaps weigh only half a ton.

The first gliding vertebrates could not imagine eagles; the Wright brothers could not imagine humans walking on the moon within 70 years of their historic flight; the 1949 writer for *Popular Mechanics* could not imagine an entire computer inside a phone. Similarly, we almost certainly cannot imagine how progress will have changed this world 50 or 100 years into the future. To do so would be remarkable because, as we have seen from the examples above, the rate of progress seems to accelerate, making long-term prediction almost impossible. Indeed, to paraphrase a famous quotation by JBS Haldane:

> the future is not only stranger than we imagine, it is stranger than we can imagine.

In conclusion, the examples above suggest that, within both natural and man-made domains, progress starts slowly, but then accelerates at a rate that may be exponential. And if progress really is accelerating exponentially, then the answer to the question of when artificial intelligence will arrive is — *soon*.

11.2. Yet Another Revolution?

In its early stages, every technological revolution gets compared to the emperor's new clothes. For example, neural networks are often described as just a type of dressed-up regression analysis. In an otherwise cogent critique of deep learning, Marcus (2018) describes deep learning as 'just mathematics' and 'just a statistical technique'. Other common criticisms are that the achievements of modern neural networks are due to just faster computers, or just more data, or just both — as if no other ingredient is required (such as sustained research effort). Such criticisms come from the nay-sayers of the revolution.

Then there are the cheerleaders, who react as if time-travel has just been invented. Books with exaggerated titles are written, debates with simplified binary choices are held in front of eager audiences, battle lines are drawn, new findings are revealed (whether or not they are new, or findings at all), heroes are identified, and long-forgotten sooth-saying geniuses are rediscovered. However, this frenzy of hyperbole effectively hides whether or not there is a revolution going on and, if there is, what the revolutionaries have discovered that is so revolutionary.

For example, a common theme amongst the binary debaters is whether or not artificial intelligence will destroy the human species. One reason for the popularity of such debates is that having an opinion about artificial intelligence is easy; it does not involve having to know anything much, and (best of all) it does not require having to learn anything new or hard. For the record, I think it is improbable that artificial intelligence will destroy the human species, but the honest answer is that no-one knows for sure. Despite this, almost anyone with or without a PhD in nothing-to-do-with artificial intelligence seems to have a firm opinion on such matters.

Around 2002, I attended a lecture by Geoff Hinton. At the end, a member of the audience asked Hinton whether or not neural networks would ever become 'truly intelligent'. Hinton replied with this parable[2] (paraphrased from memory):

> *In England, when two people get married, tin cans are tied to the newly weds' car with long pieces of string, so that the cans make plenty of noise as they get dragged along the road. It is the car that provides the motive force but it is the cans that make all the noise.*

---

[2]This is a story originally told by the physicist John Wheeler. During a lecture on General Relativity, he drew a car with cans trailing behind, and said, "The car is like physics and the cans are like the philosophers: When the car moves forward the cans make all the noise." (T Sejnowski, personal communication).

Further Reading

The readings given below are a mixture of basic tutorial material and cutting-edge papers that represent new directions of research.

Bishop, CM (1996). *Neural Networks for Pattern Recognition.* Oxford University Press. Technical and comprehensive account of neural networks up to 1996. Gives a particularly detailed account of linear associative models, and has a strong Bayesian perspective.

Goodfellow, B, Bengio, Y, and Courville, A (2016). *Deep Learning.* MIT Press. A comprehensive reference text on modern neural networks.

Marcus, G (2018). Deep Learning: A Critical Appraisal. *arXiv preprint* arXiv:1801.00631. A thoughtful, comprehensive, and cogent critique of modern AI by an author with substantial hands-on experience.

Press, WH, Flannery, BP, Teukolsky, SA, and Vetterling, WT (1989). *Numerical Recipes in C/Fortran etc.* Cambridge University Press. Comprehensive and practical; this is the only book to read on optimisation methods.

Scholarpedia. This online encyclopedia includes excellent tutorials on computational neuroscience. www.scholarpedia.org.

Scholarpedia has an excellent summary of reinforcement learning: http://www.scholarpedia.org/article/Reinforcement_learning. Also see https://en.wikipedia.org/wiki/Reinforcement_learning.

Sejnowski, TJ (2018). *The Deep Learning Revolution.* MIT Press. A fine mixture of historical overview and memoir from one of the pioneers of neural networks.

Silver, D (2018). *Reinforcement Learning* lecture slides. Succinct but, more importantly, reliable and comprehensive account of reinforcement learning algorithms; highly recommended. http://www0.cs.ucl.ac.uk/staff/d.silver/web/Teaching.html

Smith, S (1997). *The Scientist and Engineer's Guide to Digital Signal Processing.* Freely available at https://www.dspguide.com.

Stone JV (2013). *Bayes' Rule: A Tutorial Introduction to Bayesian Analysis*. Sebtel Press. With online Python and MATLAB code. Also published as *Bayes' Rule with MatLab/Python/R*.

Stone, JV (2015). *Information Theory: A Tutorial Introduction*. Sebtel Press. With online Python and MATLAB code.

Sutton, RS and Barto, AG (2018). *Reinforcement Learning: An Introduction*. MIT Press (available free online). Comprehensive account by two of the masters of modern reinforcement learning.

Sutton, RS (1988). Learning to predict by the methods of temporal differences. *Machine Learning*, 3:9–44. A relatively succinct tutorial-style summary of temporal difference learning.

Variational Autoencoders. The topic of variational autoencoders is developing rapidly, so a few key references are supplied here.

A fine video lecture by Ghodsi, A (2017, UC Berkeley) is available at `https://www.youtube.com/watch?v=uaaqyVS9-rM`.

Kingma, DP (2017). *Variational Inference & Deep Learning*. This is Kingma's PhD thesis and explains the variational autoencoder framework in considerable detail. `https://pure.uva.nl/ws/files/17891313/Thesis.pdf`.

Tutorial accounts are given in Doersch (2016)[15], Kim et al. (2015), and Rezende and Viola (2018).

An insightful set of figures regarding conditional variational autoencoders by Isaac Dykeman can be found at `http://ijdykeman.github.io/ml/2016/12/21/cvae.html`, and a more detailed account by Agustinus Kristiadi is at `https://wiseodd.github.io/techblog/2016/12/17/conditional-vae/`.

Finally, for a comprehensive technical summary, see Simeone (2017).

Appendix A

Glossary

action-value function Specifies the value or expected reward $q_\pi(s, a)$ of state s and action a under policy π.

activation function Determines output y for a given input u: $y = f(u)$.

actor–critic methods After an action is executed, the value of its consequence is estimated by a critic, which is instantiated as a state-value function.

algorithm A definite method or sequence of steps.

association A pair of input/output vectors to be learned.

autoencoder A network that maps input vectors to themselves as output vectors via one or more hidden layers.

autograd Software tool (Python) that automatically calculates the derivative of the function implemented by a neural network[141].

average See expected value.

backprop Abbreviation for back propagation, the principal method for training multi-layer networks.

batch Large training sets are presented to a neural network in separate batches. Each batch (typically containing 50–200 vectors) is used to make a single update to the weights.

batch normalization For each batch of training data, the inputs to each layer are normalised to reduce saturation.

Bayes' theorem Provides a rigorous method for interpreting evidence (data) in the context of previous experience. See Appendix E.

Bellman equation For a Markov process, the Bellman equation expresses a recursive relationship between the value of a state and the values of its successor states.

bias unit A unit with a fixed state (usually -1) that supplies input to other units in a network via learned bias weights.

Boltzmann distribution Probability distribution that specifies the probability of each state as a function of its energy. Specifically, the probability that a system is in state s_i which has energy E_i is $p(s_i) = e^{-E_i/T}/Z$, where $Z = \sum_j e^{-E_j/T}$ is the partition function and T is temperature.

Boltzmann machine Generative model based on statistical physics.

CIFAR The CIFAR-10 (Canadian Institute For Advanced Research) training set consists of 50,000 training images and 10,000 test images, divided into 10 classes with 6,000 images per class.

clamp Term used for learning in Boltzmann machines, which means setting the values of visible units to be the same as the elements of a training vector during the wake phase of learning.

content addressable memory If an association between an input and an output vector is learned, and if the input vector evokes that output, then the memory is said to be content addressable.

convolutional network A neural network in which each hidden unit in a layer L_i has a receptive field defined over a small region of units in the previous layer L_{i-1}.

convolution A set of weights defined over a small image region defines a filter. If these weights are applied to every region in an image, this convolves the image with the filter.

cross-entropy A measure of the difference between two distributions $p(x)$ and $q(x)$,

$$H_q(x) = \int_x p(x)\log(1/q(x))\,dx = H(p(x)) + D(p(x)\|q(x)),$$

where $H(p(x))$ is the entropy of $p(x)$ and $D(p(x)\|q(x))$ is the Kullback–Leibler divergence between $p(x)$ and $q(x)$.

deep belief network Generative model with several hidden layers, no intra-layer connections, and directed connections between adjacent layers except for the penultimate hidden layer, which has bidirectional connections to the visible layer.

deep neural network A network with more than one hidden layer of units between the input and output layers.

denoising autoencoder An autoencoder trained to produce outputs that are denoised versions of its inputs.

discount factor Usually denoted by γ. Determines how much future rewards are valued in relation to immediate rewards.

dropout A technique used to decrease over-fitting. During training, a proportion of randomly chosen hidden units are disabled, with different units being disabled on each learning iteration.

early stopping A method used to reduce over-fitting by monitoring progress on a validation set while training on a training set.

eligibility trace See trace decay parameter.

ELBO Evidence lower bound. Rather than maximising the evidence (likelihood) during training, a variational function (which provides a lower bound on the evidence) is maximised instead.

energy function A function defined in terms of the states of units in a network. A set of network states such that connected units have mutually compatible states has a low energy value.

176

episode Usually a single run through a maze, or single play of a game.

error Difference between unit output and target (desired) output.

expected value Given a variable x which can adopt n values, the expected value or expectation is defined as $\mathbb{E}[x] = \sum_{i=1}^{n} p(x_i)x_i$, where $p(x_i)$ is the probability of the variable taking value x_i. Given T samples of x, the expected value is estimated as the mean or average: $\mathbb{E}[x] \approx (1/T) \sum_{t=1}^{T} x_t$.

expressibility The range of functions that a network can represent.

generalisation The ability to extrapolate beyond training data items.

generative model A neural network that models the distribution $p(\mathbf{x})$ of input vectors $\mathbf{x}$ using a small number of hidden units with state $\mathbf{z}$, such that $p(\mathbf{x}|\mathbf{z}) \approx p(\mathbf{x})$.

generative adversarial network A system of two competing networks in which a generator network produces outputs, and a discriminator network decides whether each output is from the generator network or from the training set.

gradient descent If performance is expressed as an error function $E(\mathbf{w})$, then the optimal weights can be found by iteratively changing the network weight vector $\mathbf{w}$ in a direction that is effectively downhill with respect to E. Gradient *ascent* just means performing gradient descent with respect to $-E$.

greedy policy A policy which chooses an action that maximises immediate reward.

Hopfield net Fully interconnected set of units in which stable states correspond to learned associations.

identity matrix A $J \times J$ square matrix $\mathbf{I}$, with ones along the diagonal, and zeroes elsewhere.

inference Using data to estimate the posterior distribution of unknown parameters (e.g. weights or latent variables).

Jensen's inequality For our purposes, Jensen's inequality implies that $\log \mathbb{E}[x] \geq \mathbb{E}[\log x]$. For example, if $x_1 = 512$ and $x_2 = 2$ then $\log \mathbb{E}[x] = \log(514/2) \approx 8 > \mathbb{E}[\log x] = (\log 512 + \log 2)/2 = 4.5$.

Kullback–Leibler divergence A measure of the difference between two probability distributions $p(x)$ and $q(x)$:

$$D(q(x)\|p(x)) = \int_x q(x) \log \frac{q(x)}{p(x)}\, dx. \qquad (A.1)$$

Also called the relative entropy, D is a measure of how surprising the distribution $p(x)$ is, if values of x are chosen with probability $q(x)$. Note that $D(q(x)\|p(x)) \neq D(p(x)\|q(x))$, and $D(q(x)\|p(x)) = 0$ if $q(x) = p(x)$.

labelled data Data in which the class of each input is known; such data can be used to train a network during supervised learning.

likelihood Given data **x** generated by a process with parameters θ, the probability of the data is $p(\mathbf{x}|\theta)$, which is also known as the likelihood of θ. See Appendix D.

linear associative network The simplest neural network, which is essentially a matrix. The output of each unit is the inner product of its weight vector and the input vector.

linear If the transfer (input $\rightarrow$ output) function of a unit is linear, then the output is proportional to the input.

local minimum During gradient descent, the nearest (i.e. local) minimum is usually not the deepest (i.e. global) minimum.

Markov process A sequence of discrete states such that the next state depends only on the current state.

Markov chain Monte Carlo Abbreviated MCMC, this is a general class of methods for providing samples from a multivariate distribution. The Boltzmann machine uses a type of MCMC called Gibbs sampling.

matrix See Appendix C.

maximum likelihood estimation Method of using data to estimate the value of parameters (see Appendix D).

mean See expected value.

MNIST data set The MNIST dataset consists of handwritten images of digits from 0 to 9. It consists of 60,000 images in a training set and 10,000 images in a test set. Each image is 28×28 pixels, with grey-levels between 0 and 255.

Monte Carlo Given a probability distribution $p(x)$ of a variable x, a function of x (e.g. the average) can be estimated based on sampled values of x. If these sampled values are chosen at random, the estimation method is a Monte Carlo method.

multi-layer perceptron A neural network with multiple layers. Usually refers to a backprop network.

mutual information A fundamental measure of association between variables, measured in bits; a generalised form of correlation.

n-step return The discounted total reward for rewards received up to n time steps into the future.

offline update Updating weights after more than one training item has been presented to a network.

off-policy Using actions determined by a fixed policy to estimate the optimal policy (e.g. Q-learning).

one hot vector A binary vector used to indicate one out of n classes. For example, given 10 digit classes (0–9) the class for the digit 3 would be represented as the one hot vector [0 0 0 1 0 0 0 0 0 0]. Used for conditional variational autoencoders.

online update Updating weights immediately after each training item is presented to a network.

on-policy Using actions determined by a policy to estimate the optimal policy (e.g. SARSA).

over-fitting Given noisy data with an underlying trend, an ideal model would fit a function to the trend. Over-fitting occurs when the model fits a function to the noise, or when the fitted function does not interpolate smoothly between widely separated data points.

perceptron In essence, a linear associative network, except that it has one binary output unit with an adjustable threshold.

policy The policy π specifies the probability that action a will be executed next.

policy evaluation Given a state s, the value $v(s)$ of that state depends on the policy π used to decide on the subsequent sequence of actions and states.

policy gradient method If a policy π is determined by a set of parameters $\mathbf{w}$ (e.g. weights in a neural network), then that policy can be optimised by adjusting $\mathbf{w}$ according to the gradient of the return with respect to $\mathbf{w}$.

policy improvement Refining a policy to maximise returns.

policy improvement theorem States that if $q_\pi(s, \pi'(s)) \geq v_\pi(s)$ then $v_{\pi'}(s) \geq v_\pi(s)$.

policy iteration Alternately updating the estimated value function V and the policy π used to choose each action.

pooling A mechanism to implement invariance with respect to a chosen image transformation. For example, if each of three units responds to the digit 5 at a different orientation, then another unit that takes the maximum value of the three units will behave as if it is an orientation-invariant detector of the digit 5.

Q-learning Uses actions specified by a policy to improve the estimated action-value function Q. Called off-policy because the actions used to improve Q are not the actions taken.

rectified linear unit (ReLU) A unit with an output of 0 unless the input is positive ($u > 0$), in which case the output equals the input ($y = u$).

regularisation A method to reduce over-fitting, usually by adding constraint terms to a cost function.

reinforcement learning Class of methods for finding actions and their scalar rewards to maximise returns.

restricted Boltzmann machine A Boltzmann machine with connections between layers but no connections within each layer.

return The cumulative total reward G_t acquired from the state at time $t + 1$ to the end of an episode. If the task has no fixed end point then the return remains finite provided the discount factor $\gamma < 1$.

SARSA Uses actions specified by the current policy implicit in the estimated action-value function Q to improve Q.

simulated annealing An iterative stochastic method for finding the global minimum of a cost function.

state Output of a unit.

state-value function $v(s_t)$ specifies the expected return based on the current state s_t (i.e. $v(s_t) = \mathbb{E}[G_t]$).

stochastic Probabilistic.

stochastic gradient descent Gradient descent based on a random sample of data points.

supervised learning Learning the mapping from a set of input vectors to a corresponding set of output vectors.

temporal difference error Abbreviated *TD error*, this is the error in the expected return predicted by $V(s_t)$.

temporal difference learning Used as part of reinforcement learning to learn value functions and control policy based on differences in predictions. The current estimate of the state-value function or action-value function is used for online updating of that estimate.

tensor In the deep learning literature, a tensor is simply a matrix, which is a corruption of its meaning in mathematics. The term tensor is not used in this book.

top-n Classification performance is often reported as a percentage given a top-n threshold. If inputs are classified as belonging to the top five classes 80% of the time, this is reported as a top-5 performance of 80%. A top-1 performance specifies how often the network classification is the correct class label.

trace-decay parameter Usually denoted by λ, this parameter determines how the value of the reward associated with a state s_t depends on the cumulative rewards that follow s_t, not just on the reward that follows immediately after s_t.

training data Data used to train a neural network, usually split into three sets (training, validation, and test sets).

transfer learning A network trained on a particular type of data (e.g. images of cats) learns a task involving similar data (e.g. dogs).

unit Artificial neuron.

unsupervised learning Learning with unlabelled data. If the data contain well-defined clusters, an unsupervised learning algorithm should represent the data in terms of these clusters.

validation set Part of the training data used to monitor progress on the training set. The validation set is not used for updating weights.

variational autoencoder Autoencoder based on variational principles.

value In reinforcement learning, the value of a state is the expectation of the total future reward resulting from starting in that state.

vector See Appendix C.

weight Value representing the strength of the connection between two units.

Appendix B

Mathematical Symbols

For consistency with different bodies of literature, more than one symbol may represent the same quantity in the list below. However, each symbol represents exactly one physical quantity within each chapter. Scalar variables are in italics (x), and vectors are in bold $(\mathbf{x})$.

$:=$ used to define variables, e.g. $v(s_t) := \mathbb{E}[G_t]$.

$|\mathbf{x}|$ the length of vector $\mathbf{x} = (x_1, \ldots, x_n)$, $|\mathbf{x}| = \sqrt{x_1^2 + \cdots + x_n^2}$.

$\mathbf{x} \cdot \mathbf{y}$ dot or inner product between vectors $\mathbf{x}$ and $\mathbf{y}$ (see Appendix C).

$*$ convolution operator.

a an action.

β inverse of temperature T used in simulated annealing, $\beta = 1/T$.

ε ratio of number of associations in training set to number of weights in neural network; probability of random action.

ϵ learning rate.

E cost function, e.g. difference between outputs and desired outputs.

$\mathbb{E}$ expected value of a variable, $\mathbb{E}[x]$ is the mean of x.

δ_{jt} (delta) error term associated with jth hidden unit for the tth association: for any (hidden or output) unit, $\delta_{jt} = \partial \mathbb{E}_t / \partial u_{jt}$, where u_{jt} is the unit's total input.

f unit activation function, determines unit output for a given input.

F the input/output function computed by a neural network.

G_t return, total future cumulative reward.

γ (gamma) temporal discount factor.

h_{jt} state (output) of jth hidden unit for tth association.

$\mathbf{h}_t$ vector of unit states (outputs) in hidden layer of a neural network, $\mathbf{h}_t = (h_{1t}, \ldots, h_{Jt})$.

i index used to specify a unit in the input layer of a neural network.

j index used to specify a unit in a hidden layer of a neural network.

Mathematical Symbols

J number of latent variables in a variational autoencoder.

k index used to specify a unit in the output layer of a neural network.

λ (lambda) eligibility trace parameter.

L log likelihood, marginal likelihood, or evidence lower bound.

M the total number of learning iterations.

m index used to specify learning iteration.

n the total number of weights in a neural network.

$\mathcal{N}(\mu, \sigma^2)$ Gaussian distribution with mean μ and standard deviation σ; a sample x_t from $\mathcal{N}(\mu, \sigma^2)$ is written as $x_t \sim \mathcal{N}(\mu, \sigma^2)$.

∇ (nabla) vector of derivatives, which points in the direction of steepest ascent (see Section 2.5).

p given a variable x, this denotes the probability density of a particular value x_t of x (e.g. $p(x_t)$) or the probability distribution (e.g. $p(x)$).

$q^\pi(s, a)$ action-value function, specifies the value of state s and action a under policy π.

Q estimate of action-value function q.

R_t immediate reward for being in state s_t at time t.

$\mathbb{R}^n$ an n-dimensional space.

s_t state at time t in reinforcement learning.

t index used to specify an association of a neural network.

T transpose operator (see Appendix C).

T number of vectors/patterns/associations learned; temperature used in simulated annealing, $T = 1/\beta$.

U unit (artificial neuron).

u_t total input to a unit for tth association.

$V(s)$ estimate of state-value function $v(s)$.

$v(s)$ state-value (expected return) of state s used in reinforcement learning.

w_{ij} connection weight between ith input unit and jth hidden unit.

w_{jk} connection weight between jth hidden unit and kth output unit.

$\mathbf{w}$ vector of N weights, $\mathbf{w} = (w_1, \dots, w_N)$.

W matrix of weights.

x_{it} state of ith input unit at tth time step.

$\mathbf{x}_t$ training data or backprop network vector of input layer unit states, $\mathbf{x} = (x_{1t}, \dots, x_{It})$.

y_{kt} state of kth output unit at tth time step.

$\mathbf{y}_t$ vector of states (outputs) in output layer of units, $\mathbf{y} = (y_{1t}, \dots, y_{Kt})$.

$\mathbf{z}_t$ vector of states in hidden layer of backprop network, or in input layer of decoder in a variational autoencoder.

Appendix C

A Vector and Matrix Tutorial

The single key fact to know about vectors and matrices is that each vector represents a point located in space, and a matrix moves that point to a different location. Everything else is just details.

Vectors. A number, such as 1.234, is known as a *scalar*, and a *vector* is an ordered list of scalars. A vector with two components w_1 and w_2 is written as $\mathbf{w} = (w_1, w_2)$. Note that vectors are written in bold type. The vector $\mathbf{w}$ can be represented as a single point in a 2D graph; the location of this point is by convention a distance of w_1 from the origin along the horizontal axis and a distance of w_2 from the origin along the vertical axis.

Adding Vectors. The *vector sum* of two vectors is obtained by adding their corresponding elements. Consider the addition of two pairs of scalars (x_1, x_2) and (w_1, w_2); adding the corresponding elements gives

$$(w_1 + x_1), \quad (w_2 + x_2). \tag{C.1}$$

Clearly, (x_1, x_2) and (w_1, w_2) can be written as vectors:

$$\begin{aligned} \mathbf{z} &= \big((w_1 + x_1), (w_2 + x_2)\big) & \text{(C.2)} \\ &= (x_1, x_2) + (w_1, w_2) \\ &= \mathbf{x} + \mathbf{w}. & \text{(C.3)} \end{aligned}$$

Thus the sum of two vectors is another vector, which is known as the *resultant* of those two vectors.

Subtracting Vectors. Subtracting vectors is implemented similarly by subtracting corresponding elements, so that

$$\begin{aligned} \mathbf{z} &= \mathbf{x} - \mathbf{w} & \text{(C.4)} \\ &= \big((x_1 - w_1), (x_2 - w_2)\big). & \text{(C.5)} \end{aligned}$$

Multiplying Vectors. Consider the result of multiplying the corresponding elements of two pairs of scalars (x_1, x_2) and (w_1, w_2) and adding the two products together:

$$y = w_1 x_1 + w_2 x_2. \tag{C.6}$$

We can write (x_1, x_2) and (w_1, w_2) as vectors and express y as

$$\begin{aligned} y &= (x_1, x_2) \cdot (w_1, w_2) \\ &= \mathbf{x} \cdot \mathbf{w}, \end{aligned} \tag{C.7}$$

where Equation C.7 is to be interpreted as Equation C.6. This multiplication of corresponding vector elements is known as the *inner*, *scalar* or *dot* product, and is often denoted with a dot, as here.

Vector Length. As each vector represents a point in space, it must have a distance from the origin, and this distance is known as the vector's length or *modulus*, denoted by $|\mathbf{x}|$ for a vector $\mathbf{x}$. For a vector $\mathbf{x} = (x_1, x_2)$ with two components, this distance is given by the length of the hypotenuse of a right-angled triangle with sides x_1 and x_2, so

$$|\mathbf{x}| = \sqrt{x_1^2 + x_2^2}. \tag{C.8}$$

Angle between Vectors. The angle θ between two vectors $\mathbf{x}$ and $\mathbf{w}$ is given by

$$\cos \theta = \frac{\mathbf{x} \cdot \mathbf{w}}{|\mathbf{x}| \, |\mathbf{w}|}. \tag{C.9}$$

Crucially, if $\theta = 90°$ then the inner product in the numerator is zero, because $\cos 90° = 0$ irrespective of the lengths of the vectors. Vectors at 90 degrees to each other are known as *orthogonal vectors*.

Row and Column Vectors. Vectors come in two basic flavours, *row vectors* and *column vectors*. A simple notational device to transform a row vector (x_1, x_2) into a column vector (or vice versa) is the *transpose operator*, T:

$$(x_1, x_2)^{\mathsf{T}} = \begin{pmatrix} x_1 \\ x_2 \end{pmatrix}. \tag{C.10}$$

The reason for having row and column vectors is that it is often necessary to combine several vectors into a single *matrix*, which is then used to multiply a single column vector $\mathbf{x}$, defined here as

$$\mathbf{x} = (x_1, x_2)^{\mathsf{T}}. \tag{C.11}$$

In such cases, we need to keep track of which vectors are row vectors and which are column vectors. If we redefine $\mathbf{w}$ as a column vector,

$\mathbf{w} = (w_1, w_2)^\mathsf{T}$, then the inner product $\mathbf{w} \cdot \mathbf{x}$ can be written as

$$y = \mathbf{w}^\mathsf{T}\mathbf{x} \tag{C.12}$$

$$= (w_1, w_2)\begin{pmatrix} x_1 \\ x_2 \end{pmatrix} \tag{C.13}$$

$$= w_1 x_1 + w_2 x_2. \tag{C.14}$$

Here, each element of the row vector $\mathbf{w}^\mathsf{T}$ is multiplied by the corresponding element of the column vector $\mathbf{x}$, and the results are summed. Writing the inner product in this way allows us to simultaneously specify many pairs of such products as a vector–matrix product. For example, if x_1 and x_2 of the vector variable $\mathbf{x}$ have been measured n times (e.g. at n consecutive time steps), then taking the inner product of these pairs of measurements with $\mathbf{w}$ yields n values of the variable y:

$$(y_1, y_2, \ldots, y_n) = (w_1, w_2)\begin{pmatrix} x_{11} & x_{12} & \ldots & x_{1n} \\ x_{21} & x_{22} & \ldots & x_{2n} \end{pmatrix}. \tag{C.15}$$

Here, each (single-element) column y_t is given by the inner product of the corresponding column in $\mathbf{x}$ with the row vector $\mathbf{w}$, so that

$$y = \mathbf{w}^\mathsf{T}\mathbf{x}.$$

Vector–Matrix Multiplication. If we reset the number of times $\mathbf{x}$ has been measured to $n = 1$ for now, we can consider the simple case of how two scalar values y_1 and y_2 are given by the inner products

$$y_1 = \mathbf{w}_1^\mathsf{T}\mathbf{x} \tag{C.16}$$

$$y_2 = \mathbf{w}_2^\mathsf{T}\mathbf{x}, \tag{C.17}$$

where $\mathbf{w}_1 = (w_1, w_2)^\mathsf{T}$ and $\mathbf{w}_2 = (w_3, w_4)^\mathsf{T}$. If we consider the pair of values y_1 and y_2 as a vector $\mathbf{y} = (y_1, y_2)^\mathsf{T}$ then we can rewrite Equations C.16 and C.17 as

$$(y_1, y_2)^\mathsf{T} = (\mathbf{w}_1^\mathsf{T}\mathbf{x}, \mathbf{w}_2^\mathsf{T}\mathbf{x})^\mathsf{T}. \tag{C.18}$$

Combining the column vectors $\mathbf{w}_1$ and $\mathbf{w}_2$ defines a *matrix* W:

$$W = (\mathbf{w}_1, \mathbf{w}_2)^\mathsf{T} = \begin{pmatrix} w_1 & w_2 \\ w_3 & w_4 \end{pmatrix}. \tag{C.19}$$

We can now rewrite equation C.18 as

$$(y_1, y_2)^\mathsf{T} = \begin{pmatrix} w_1 & w_2 \\ w_3 & w_4 \end{pmatrix}(x_1, x_2)^\mathsf{T}, \tag{C.20}$$

or more succinctly as $\mathbf{y} = W\mathbf{x}$. This defines the standard syntax for vector–matrix multiplication. Note that the column vector $(x_1, x_2)^\mathsf{T}$ is multiplied by the first row in W to obtain the row y_1 and is multiplied by the second row in W to obtain the row y_2. Just as the vector $\mathbf{x}$ represents a point on a plane, so the point $\mathbf{y}$ represents a (usually different) point on the plane. Thus *the matrix W implements a linear geometric transformation of points from $\mathbf{x}$ to $\mathbf{y}$.*

If $n > 1$ then the tth column $(y_{1t}, y_{2t})^\mathsf{T}$ in $\mathbf{y}$ is obtained as the product of tth column $(x_{1t}, x_{2t})^\mathsf{T}$ in $\mathbf{x}$ with the row vectors in W:

$$
\mathbf{y} = \begin{pmatrix} y_{11} & \cdots & y_{1n} \\ y_{21} & \cdots & y_{2n} \end{pmatrix} \tag{C.21}
$$

$$
= \begin{pmatrix} w_1 & w_2 \\ w_3 & w_4 \end{pmatrix} \begin{pmatrix} x_{11} & \cdots & x_{1n} \\ x_{21} & \cdots & x_{2n} \end{pmatrix} \tag{C.22}
$$

$$
= W\mathbf{x}. \tag{C.23}
$$

Note that $\mathbf{y}$ has the same number of rows as W and the same number of columns as $\mathbf{x}$.

The Outer Product. If an m-element column vector $\mathbf{x}$ is multiplied by an n-element row vector $\mathbf{y}^\mathsf{T}$ then the result is a matrix W with m rows and n columns. For example, if $m = 2$ and $n = 3$ then

$$
W = \mathbf{x}\,\mathbf{y}^\mathsf{T} \tag{C.24}
$$

$$
= \begin{pmatrix} x_1 \\ x_2 \end{pmatrix} (y_1, y_2, y_3) \tag{C.25}
$$

$$
= \begin{pmatrix} x_1 y_1 & x_1 y_2 & x_1 y_3 \\ x_2 y_1 & x_2 y_2 & x_2 y_3 \end{pmatrix}. \tag{C.26}
$$

Transpose of Vector–Matrix Product. If $\mathbf{y} = W\mathbf{x}$ then the transpose $\mathbf{y}^\mathsf{T}$ of this vector–matrix product is

$$
\mathbf{y}^\mathsf{T} = (W\mathbf{x})^\mathsf{T} = \mathbf{x}^\mathsf{T} W^\mathsf{T}, \tag{C.27}
$$

where W^T is obtained by swapping off-diagonal elements:

$$
W^\mathsf{T} = \begin{pmatrix} w_1 & w_2 \\ w_3 & w_4 \end{pmatrix}^\mathsf{T} = \begin{pmatrix} w_1 & w_3 \\ w_2 & w_4 \end{pmatrix}. \tag{C.28}
$$

Matrix Inverse. By analogy with scalar algebra, if $\mathbf{y} = W\mathbf{x}$ then $\mathbf{x} = W^{-1}\mathbf{y}$, where W^{-1} is the inverse of W. If the columns of a matrix are orthogonal then $W^{-1} = W^\mathsf{T}$.

Appendix D

Maximum Likelihood Estimation

A popular method for estimating the values of parameters is maximum likelihood estimation (MLE). Because it is often assumed that data have a Gaussian distribution, we use MLE to estimate the mean of Gaussian data here. Given Gaussian data, the probability (density) of observing a value x_i is

$$p(x_i|\mu,\sigma) \;\; = \;\; c\,e^{-(\mu-x_i)^2/(2\sigma^2)}, \tag{D.1}$$

where μ is the mean (centre) of the Gaussian distribution, σ is the standard deviation, which is a measure of the spread of the distribution, and $c = 1/\sqrt{2\pi\sigma^2}$ is a constant which ensures that the distribution has a total value (integral) of 1. A graph of a typical Gaussian distribution is shown in Figure 8.10, which has a mean labelled as x' and a standard deviation of $\sigma = 1$. We wish to estimate the mean μ.

A sample $\mathbf{x}$ of N values of x can be represented as the vector $\mathbf{x} = (x_1, \ldots, x_N)$. If these samples are mutually independent, then

$$p(\mathbf{x}|\mu) \;\; = \;\; \prod_{i=1}^{N} p(x_i|\mu), \tag{D.2}$$

where we have omitted σ for simplicity. Maximum likelihood estimation consists in finding an estimate $\hat{\mu}$ of μ that is maximally consistent with the data $\mathbf{x}$. More precisely, $p(\mathbf{x}|\mu)$ is the probability of the observed data given μ. However, because we are interested in finding the optimal value of μ, we consider $p(\mathbf{x}|\mu)$ to be a function of μ, called the *likelihood function*. Consequently, even though $p(\mathbf{x}|\mu)$ is the probability of observing the data $\mathbf{x}$, it is called the likelihood of μ.

In the process of estimating μ, we could simply 'try out' different values of μ in Equation D.2 to see which value $\hat{\mu}$ is most consistent with the data $\mathbf{x}$, that is, which value $\hat{\mu}$ of μ makes the data most probable. The result represents our best estimate of μ. Note that a

different set of data would yield a different likelihood function, with a
different value for the maximum likelihood estimate $\hat{\mu}$.

At first, this way of thinking about the data seems odd. It just sounds
wrong to speak of the probability of the data, which are the things we
have already observed — so why would we care how probable they are?
In fact, we do not care about the probability of the data *per se*, but we
do care how probable those data are in the context of the parameters
we wish to estimate.

In practice, we usually choose to deal with log likelihoods rather than
likelihoods. Because the log function is monotonic, the estimate $\hat{\mu}$ of μ
that maximises $p(\mathbf{x}|\mu)$ also maximises $\log p(\mathbf{x}|\mu)$, where

$$\log p(\mathbf{x}|\mu) \quad = \quad \log \prod_{i=1}^{N} p(x_i|\mu) \tag{D.3}$$

$$= \quad \sum_{i=1}^{N} \log p(x_i|\mu). \tag{D.4}$$

Substituting Equation D.1 into Equation D.4 gives

$$\log p(\mathbf{x}|\mu) \quad = \quad k - \sum_{i=1}^{N} \frac{(\mu - x_i)^2}{2\sigma^2}, \tag{D.5}$$

where $k = -N \log c$. A common notation for the log likelihood is $L(\mu)$.
If the standard deviation $\sigma = 1$ then this becomes

$$L(\mu) \quad = \quad k - \frac{1}{2} \sum_{i=1}^{N} (\mu - x_i)^2. \tag{D.6}$$

Maximising $L(\mu)$ is equivalent to minimising $-L(\mu)$, which resembles
the equation used for *least-squares estimation* (LSE), so LSE is a form
of MLE. At a maximum, $dL(\mu)/d\mu = 0$ and so (because $dk/d\mu = 0$)

$$\frac{dL(\mu)}{d\mu} \quad = \quad -\frac{1}{2} \sum_{i=1}^{N} \frac{d(\mu - x_i)^2}{d\mu} \tag{D.7}$$

$$= \quad -\sum_{i=1}^{N} (\mu - x_i). \tag{D.8}$$

Thus, if we set $dL(\mu)/d\mu$ to zero and solve for μ, then we obtain the
maximum likelihood estimate $\hat{\mu}$ of μ, where $\hat{\mu}$ turns out to be the
mean, that is, $\hat{\mu} = (1/N) \sum x_i$. Finally, note that MLE corresponds to
Bayesian estimation with a uniform prior distribution[122].

Appendix E

Bayes' Theorem

Bayes' theorem is essentially a rigorous method for interpreting evidence (data) in the context of previous experience or knowledge. Bayes' theorem is also known as *Bayes' rule*[112;122].

If we construe each possible value of a parameter as one of many possible answers then Bayesian inference is not guaranteed to provide the correct answer. Instead, it provides the probability that each of a number of alternative answers is true, and these probabilities can then be used to find the answer that is most probably true. In other words, Bayesian inference provides an informed guess. While this may not sound like much, it is far from random guessing. Indeed, it can be shown that no other procedure can provide a better guess, so that Bayesian inference can be justifiably interpreted as the output of a perfect guessing machine, a perfect inference engine. This perfect inference engine is fallible, but it is provably less fallible than any other.

For notational convenience, we denote a variable by x, and a particular value of x is indicated with a subscript (e.g. x_t).

Conditional Probability. The conditional probability that $y = y_t$ given that $x = x_t$ is defined as

$$p(y_t|x_t) \quad = \quad p(x_t, y_t)/p(x_t), \qquad \text{(E.1)}$$

where $p(x_t, y_t)$ is the *joint probability* that $x = x_t$ and $y = y_t$. Equation E.1 holds true for all values of y, so the *conditional distribution* is

$$p(y|x_t) \quad = \quad p(x_t, y)/p(x_t), \qquad \text{(E.2)}$$

where $p(x_t, y)$ is a cross-section of the *joint probability distribution* $p(x, y)$ at $x = x_t$. When considered over all values of x, this yields a family of conditional distributions (one member for each value of x)

$$p(y|x) \quad = \quad p(x, y)/p(x). \qquad \text{(E.3)}$$

E Bayes' Theorem

The Product Rule: Multiplying both sides of Equation E.3 by $p(x)$ yields the *product rule* (also known as the *chain rule*)

$$p(x, y) \;=\; p(y|x)p(x). \tag{E.4}$$

The Sum Rule and Marginalisation: The *sum rule* is also known as the *law of total probability*. In the case of a discrete variable, given a joint distribution $p(x, y)$, the *marginal distribution* $p(y)$ is obtained by *marginalisation* (summing) over values of x:

$$p(y) \;=\; \sum_t p(x_t, y). \tag{E.5}$$

If we apply the product rule, we get

$$p(y) \;=\; \sum_t p(y|x_t)p(x_t). \tag{E.6}$$

In the case of a continuous variable, the sum and product rules become

$$p(y) = \int_x p(x, y)\, dx \;=\; \int_x p(y|x)p(x)\, dx. \tag{E.7}$$

Bayes' Theorem: If we swap x and y in Equation E.4 then

$$p(y, x) = p(x|y)p(y). \tag{E.8}$$

Because $p(x, y) = p(y, x)$, we have

$$p(y|x)p(x) \;=\; p(x|y)p(y). \tag{E.9}$$

Dividing both sides of Equation E.9 by $p(y)$ yields Bayes' theorem:

$$p(y|x) \;=\; \frac{p(x|y)p(y)}{p(x)}. \tag{E.10}$$

If we have an observed value x_t of x, then Bayes' theorem can be used to infer the *posterior probability distribution* of y:

$$p(y|x_t) \;=\; \frac{p(x_t|y)p(y)}{p(x_t)}. \tag{E.11}$$

where $p(y)$ is the *prior probability distribution* of y, $p(x_t|y)$ is the conditional probability that $x = x_t$, which defines the *likelihood function* of y, and $p(x_t)$ is the *marginal likelihood* or *evidence* (see Appendix D).

References

[1] Ackley, DH, Hinton, GE, and Sejnowski, TJ. A learning algorithm for Boltzmann machines. *Cog. Sci.*, 9:147–169, 1985.

[2] Alemi, AA, Fischer, I, Dillon, JV, and Murphy, K. Deep variational information bottleneck. *arXiv e-prints*, 2016. arXiv:1612.00410.

[3] Bai, S, Kolter, Z, and Koltun, V. An empirical evaluation of generic convolutional and recurrent networks for sequence modeling. *arXiv e-prints*, 2018. arXiv:1803.01271.

[4] Barto, AG, Sutton, RS, and Anderson, CW. Neuronlike adaptive elements that can solve difficult learning control problems. *IEEE Trans. Sys. Man Cyb.*, 13(5):834–846, 1983.

[5] Bishop, CM. *Neural Networks for Pattern Recognition*. Oxford University Press, 1996.

[6] Blum, A and Rivest, RL. Training a 3-node neural network is NP-complete. In *NIPS*, pages 494–501, 1989.

[7] Bruineberg, J, Rietveld, E, Parr, T, van Maanen, L, and Friston, KJ. Free-energy minimization in joint agent-environment systems: A niche construction perspective. *J. Theor. Biol.*, 455:161–178, 2018.

[8] Burda, Y, Grosse, R, and Salakhutdinov, R. Importance weighted autoencoders. *arXiv e-prints*, 2015. arXiv:1509.00519.

[9] Burgess, CP, Higgins, I, Pal, A, Matthey, L, Watters, N, Desjardins, G, and Lerchner, A. Understanding disentangling in β-VAE. *arXiv e-prints*, 2018. arXiv:1804.03599.

[10] Cho, K, van Merrienboer, B, Gulcehre, C, Bahdanau, D, Bougares, F, Schwenk, H, and Bengio, Y. Learning phrase representations using RNN encoder-decoder for statistical machine translation. *arXiv e-prints*, 2014. arXiv:1406.1078.

[11] Choromanska, A, Henaff, M, Mathieu, M, Ben Arous, G, and LeCun, Y. The loss surfaces of multilayer networks. *arXiv e-prints*, 2014. arXiv:1412.0233.

[12] Cybenko, G. Continuous valued neural networks with two hidden layers are sufficient. Technical report, Department of Computer Science, Tufts University, Medford, Massachusetts, 1988.

[13] Cybenko, G. Approximation by superposition of a sigmoidal function. *Maths Contr. Sig. Sys.*, 2:303–314, 1989.

[14] Dayan, P and Watkins, CJCH. Q-Learning. *Machine Learning*, 8(3):279–292, 1992.

References

[15] Doersch, C. Tutorial on variational autoencoders. *arXiv e-prints*, 2016. arXiv:1606.05908.

[16] Doya, K. Reinforcement learning in continuous time and space. *Neural Comptutation*, 12(1):219–245, 2000.

[17] Du, SS, Lee, JD, Li, H, Wang, L, and Zhai, X. Gradient descent finds global minima of deep neural networks. *arXiv e-prints*, 2018. arXiv:1811.03804.

[18] Elbayad, M, Besacier, L, and Verbeek, J. Pervasive attention: 2D convolutional neural networks for sequence-to-sequence prediction. *arXiv e-prints*, 2018. arXiv:1808.03867.

[19] Elman, JL. Finding structure in time. *Cog. Sci.*, 14(2):179–211, 1990.

[20] Eysenbach, B, Gupta, A, Ibarz, J, and Levine, S. Diversity is all you need: Learning diverse skills without a reward function. *arXiv e-prints*, 2018. arXiv:1802.06070.

[21] Gallagher, M, Downs, T, and Wood, I. Ultrametric structure in autoencoder error surfaces. In *ICANN 98*, pages 177–182. Springer, 1998.

[22] Geman, S and Geman, D. Stochastic relaxation, Gibbs distributions and the Bayesian restoration of images. *J. Appl. Statist.*, 20:25–62, 1993.

[23] Gers, FA, Schmidhuber, J, and Cummins, F. Learning to forget: Continual prediction with LSTM. *Neural Computation*, 12(10):2451–2471, 2000.

[24] Glorot, X and Bengio, Y. Understanding the difficulty of training deep feedforward neural networks. In *Proc. 13th Int. Conf. AI and Statistics*, pages 249–256, 2010.

[25] Goodfellow, IJ, Pouget-Abadie, J, Mirza, M, Xu, B, Warde-Farley, D, Ozair, S, Courville, A, and Bengio, Y. Generative adversarial networks. *arXiv e-prints*, 2014. arXiv:1406.2661.

[26] Gorman, RP and Sejnowski, TJ. Analysis of hidden units in a layered network trained to classify sonar targets. *Neural Networks*, 1(1):75–89, 1988.

[27] Greener, JG, Moffat, L, and Jones, DT. Design of metalloproteins and novel protein folds using variational autoencoders. *Scientific Reports*, 8(1):16189, 2018.

[28] Guilliard, I, Rogahn, R, Piavis, J, and Kolobov, A. Autonomous thermalling as a partially observable Markov decision process. *arXiv e-prints*, 2018. arXiv:1805.09875.

[29] Haarnoja, T, Zhou, A, Ha, S, Tan, J, Tucker, G, and Levine, S. Learning to walk via deep reinforcement learning. *arXiv e-prints*, 2018. arXiv:1812.11103.

[30] Harvey, I and Stone, JV. Unicycling helps your French: Spontaneous recovery of associations by learning unrelated tasks. *Neural Computation*, 8:697–704, 1996.

[31] Hayakawa, H, Inui, T, and Kawato, M. Computational theory and neural network model of perceiving shape from shading in monocular

depth perception. In *IJCNN-91-Seattle*, pages 649–654, 1991.

[32] He, K, Zhang, X, Ren, S, and Sun, J. Deep residual learning for image recognition. *arXiv e-prints*, 2015. arXiv:1512.03385.

[33] He, K, Zhang, X, Ren, S, and Sun, J. Identity mappings in deep residual networks. In *ECCV 2016*, pages 630–645. Springer, 2016.

[34] Hebb, DO. *The Organization of Behavior: A Neuropsychological Theory*. Wiley, New York, 1949.

[35] Helmbold, D and Long, P. Surprising properties of dropout in deep networks. *Journal of Machine Learning Research*, 18(1):7284–7311, 2017.

[36] Hertz, J, Krogh, A, and Palmer, RG. *Introduction to the Theory of Neural Computation*. Addison-Wesley, 1991.

[37] Higgins, I, Matthey, L, Glorot, X, Pal, A, Uria, B, Blundell, C, Mohamed, S, and Lerchner, A. Early visual concept learning with unsupervised deep learning. *arXiv e-prints*, 2016. arXiv:1606.05579.

[38] Hinton, G. Deep learning: A technology with the potential to transform health care. *JAMA*, 320(11):1101–1102, 2018.

[39] Hinton, GE. A parallel computation that assigns canonical object-based frames of reference. *Proc. 7th Int. Joint Conf. AI*, pages 683–685, 1981.

[40] Hinton, GE. Shape representation in parallel systems. In *Proc. 7th Int. Joint Conf. AI*, pages 1088–1096, 1981.

[41] Hinton, GE. A practical guide to training restricted Boltzmann machines. In *Neural Networks: Tricks of the Trade*, pages 599–619. Springer, 2012.

[42] Hinton, GE, Osindero, S, and Teh, Y. A fast learning algorithm for deep belief nets. *Neural Computation*, 18(7):1527–1554, 2006.

[43] Hinton, GE and Salakhutdinov, RR. Reducing the dimensionality of data with neural networks. *Science*, 313(5786):504–507, 2006.

[44] Hinton, GE, Sejnowski, TJ, and Ackley, DH. Boltzmann machines: Constraint satisfaction networks that learn. Technical report, Department of Computer Science, Carnegie-Mellon University, 1984.

[45] Hinton, GH, Osindero, S, and Teh, YW. Is the early visual system optimised to be energy efficient? *Neural Computation*, 18(7):1527–1554, 2006.

[46] Hochreiter, S and Schmidhuber, J. Long short-term memory. *Neural Computation*, 9(8):1735–1780, 1997.

[47] Hopfield, JJ. Neural networks and physical systems with emergent collective computational abilities. *Proc. Nat. Acad. Sci. USA*, 79(8):2554–2558, 1982.

[48] Hopfield, JJ. Neurons with graded response have collective computational properties like those of two-state neurons. *Proc. Nat. Acad. Sci. USA*, 81:3088–3092, 1984.

[49] Houthooft, R, Chen, X, Duan, Y, Schulman, J, De Turck, F, and Abbeel, P. VIME: Variational information maximizing exploration. *arXiv e-prints*, 2016. arXiv:1605.09674.

[50] Hsu, W, Zhang, Y, and Glass, J. Unsupervised domain adaptation for robust speech recognition via variational autoencoder-based data augmentation. *arXiv e-prints*, 2017. arXiv:1707.06265.

[51] Huang, G, Liu, Z, Maaten, L, and Weinberger, KQ. Densely connected convolutional networks. In *Proc. IEEE Conf. Computer Vision and Pattern Recognition*, pages 4700–4708, 2017.

[52] Hwangbo, J and et al. Learning agile and dynamic motor skills for legged robots. *Science Robotics*, 4(26):eaau5872, 2019.

[53] Ioffe, S and Szegedy, C. Batch normalization: Accelerating deep network training by reducing internal covariate shift. *arXiv preprint arXiv:1502.03167*, 2015.

[54] Jordan, MI. Serial order: A parallel distributed approach. Technical report, Institute for Cognitive science, University of California, San Diego, 1986. ICS Report 8604.

[55] Karras, T, Aila, T, Laine, S, and Lehtinen, J. Progressive growing of GANs for improved quality, stability, and variation. *arXiv e-prints*, 2017. arXiv:1710.10196.

[56] Kavasidis, I, Palazzo, S, Spampinato, C, Giordano, D, and Shah, M. Brain2Image: Converting brain signals into images. In *Proc. 25th ACM Int. Conf. Multimedia*, pages 1809–1817. ACM, 2017.

[57] Kim, Y, Wiseman, S, and Rush, AM. A tutorial on deep latent variable models of natural language. *arXiv e-prints*, 2015. arXiv:1812.06834.

[58] Kingma, DP. *Variational Inference & Deep Learning*. PhD thesis, University of Amsterdam, 2017.

[59] Kingma, DP, Mohamed, S, Rezende, DJ, and Welling, M. Semi-supervised learning with deep generative models. In *Advances in Neural Information Processing Systems*, pages 3581–3589, 2014.

[60] Kingma, DP and Welling, M. Auto-encoding variational Bayes. *arXiv e-prints*, 2013. arXiv:1312.6114.

[61] Kohonen, T. Correlation matrix memories. *IEEE Trans. Computers*, 100(4):353–359, 1972.

[62] Krizhevsky, A, Sutskever, I, and Hinton, GE. Imagenet classification with deep convolutional neural networks. In *Advances in Neural Information Processing Systems*, pages 1097–1105, 2012.

[63] Larochelle, H, Bengio, Y, Louradour, J, and Lamblin, P. Exploring strategies for training deep neural networks. *Journal of Machine Learning Research*, 10(Jan):1–40, 2009.

[64] Larsen, A, Sønderby, S, Larochelle, H, and Winther, O. Autoencoding beyond pixels using a learned similarity metric. *arXiv e-prints*, 2015. arXiv:1512.09300.

[65] Le Roux, N and Bengio, Y. Representational power of restricted Boltzmann machines and deep belief networks. *Neural Computation*, 20(6):1631–1649, 2008.

[66] LeCun, Y, Boser, B, Denker, JS, Henderson, RE, Hubbard, W, and Jackel, LD. Backpropagation applied to handwritten ZIP code recognition. *Neural Computation*, 1:541–551, 1989.

[67] LeCun, Y, Bottou, L, Bengio, Y, and Haffner, P. Gradient-based learning applied to document recognition. *Proc. IEEE*, 86(11):2278–2324, 1998.

[68] Lettvin, JV, Maturana, HR, McCulloch, WS, and Pitts, WH. What the frog's eye tells the frog's brain. *Proceedings of the Institute of Radio Engineers*, pages 1940–1951, 1959.

[69] Lim, J, Ryu, S, Kim, JW, and Kim, WY. Molecular generative model based on conditional variational autoencoder for de novo molecular design. *arXiv e-prints*, 2018. arXiv:1806.05805.

[70] Lister, R. Annealing networks and fractal landscapes. In *IEEE Int. Conf. Neural Networks (San Francisco)*, pages 257–262, 1993.

[71] Lister, R and Stone, JV. An empirical study of the time complexity of various error functions with conjugate gradient back propagation. *IEEE Int. Conf. Artificial Neural Networks (ICNN'95, Perth, Australia)*, 1995.

[72] Longuet-Higgins, HC. The non-local storage of temporal information. *Proc. R. Soc. Lond. B*, 171(1024):327–334, 1968.

[73] Longuet-Higgins, HC, Willshaw, DJ, and Buneman, OP. Theories of associative recall. *Quarterly Reviews of Biophysics*, 3(2):223–244, 1970.

[74] Maaløe, L, Fraccaro, M, Liévin, V, and Winther, O. BIVA: A very deep hierarchy of latent variables for generative modeling. *arXiv e-prints*, 2019. arXiv:1902.02102.

[75] MacKay, DJC. *Information Theory, Inference, and Learning Algorithms*. Cambridge University Press, 2003.

[76] Marcus, G. Deep learning: A critical appraisal. *arXiv e-prints*, 2018. arXiv:1801.00631.

[77] McCulloch, WS and Pitts, W. A logical calculus of the ideas immanent in nervous activity. *Bull. Math. Biophysics*, 5:115–133, 1943.

[78] Michie, D and Chambers, RA. BOXES: An experiment in adaptive control. *Machine Intelligence*, 2(2):137–152, 1968.

[79] Minsky, M and Papert, S. *Perceptrons: An Introduction to Computational Geometry*. MIT Press, 1969.

[80] Mnih, V et al. Playing Atari with deep reinforcement learning. *arXiv e-prints*, 2013. arXiv:1312.5602.

[81] Mnih, V et al. Human-level control through deep reinforcement learning. *Nature*, 518(7540):529, 2015.

[82] Mozer, MC. Neural net architectures for temporal sequence processing. In *Santa Fe Institute Studies in the Sciences of Complexity*, volume 15, pages 243–243. Addison-Wesley, 1993.

[83] Oord, A, Kalchbrenner, N, and Kavukcuoglu, K. Pixel recurrent neural networks. *arXiv e-prints*, 2016. arXiv:1601.06759.

[84] Pearlmutter, BA. Learning state space trajectories in recurrent neural networks. *Neural Computation*, 1(2):263–269, 1989.

[85] Pezeshki, M, Fan, L, Brakel, P, Courville, A, and Bengio, Y. Deconstructing the ladder network architecture. *arXiv e-prints*, 2015. arXiv:1511.06430.

[86] Polykovskiy, D et al. Entangled conditional adversarial autoencoder for de novo drug discovery. *Mol. Pharma.*, 15(10):4398–4405, 2018.

[87] Pomerleau, DA. ALVINN: An autonomous land vehicle in a neural network. In *NIPS*, pages 305–313, 1989.

[88] Press, WH, Flannery, BP, Teukolsky, SA, and Vetterling, WT. *Numerical Recipes in C*. Cambridge University Press, 1989.

[89] Radford, A, Metz, L, and Chintala, S. Unsupervised representation learning with deep convolutional generative adversarial networks. *arXiv e-prints*, 2015. arXiv:1511.06434.

[90] Randløv, J and Alstrøm, P. Learning to drive a bicycle using reinforcement learning and shaping. In *Proc. 15th Int. Conf. Machine Learning (ICML'98)*, pages 463–471, 1998.

[91] Rasmus, A, Berglund, M, Honkala, M, Valpola, H, and Raiko, T. Semi-supervised learning with ladder networks. In *NIPS*, pages 3546–3554, 2015.

[92] Rasmus, A., Valpola, H., Honkala, M., Berglund, M., and Raiko, T. Semi-supervised learning with ladder networks. *arXiv e-prints*, 2015. arXiv:1507.02672.

[93] Reddy, G, Celani, A, Sejnowski, TJ, and Vergassola, M. Learning to soar in turbulent environments. *Proc. Nat. Acad. Sci. USA*, 113(33):E4877–E4884, 2016.

[94] Rezende, DJ, Mohamed, S, and Wierstra, D. Stochastic backpropagation and approximate inference in deep generative models. *arXiv e-prints*, 2014. arXiv:1401.4082.

[95] Rezende, DJ and Viola, F. Taming variational autoencoders. *arXiv e-prints*, 2018. arXiv:1810.00597.

[96] Rosenblatt, F. The perceptron: A probabilistic model for information storage and organization in the brain. *Psychological Review*, 65(6):386–408, 1958.

[97] Rumelhart, DE, Hinton, GE, and Williams, RJ. Learning representations by back-propagating errors. *Nature*, 323:533–536, 1986.

[98] Sabour, S, Frosst, N, and Hinton, GE. Dynamic routing between capsules. In *NIPS*, pages 3859–3869, 2017.

[99] Salakhutdinov, R and Larochelle, H. Efficient learning of deep Boltzmann machines. In *Proc. 13th Int. Conf. AI and Statistics*, pages 693–700, 2010.

[100] Samuel, AL. Some studies in machine learning using the game of checkers. *IBM Journal of Research and Development*, 3(3):210–229, 1959.

[101] Schäfer, A M and Zimmermann, HG. Recurrent neural networks are universal approximators. In *Int. Conf. Artificial Neural Networks*, pages 632–640. Springer, 2006.

[102] Schulman, J. *Optimizing Expectations: From Deep Reinforcement Learning to Stochastic Computation Graphs*. PhD thesis, University of California, Berkeley, 2016.

[103] Sejnowski, TJ. *The Deep Learning Revolution*. MIT Press, 2018.

[104] Sejnowski, TJ and Rosenberg, CR. NETtalk. *Complex Systems*, 1(1), 1987.

[105] Selfridge, OG. Pandemonium: A paradigm for learning. In *The Mechanisation of Thought Processes*. National Physical Laboratory, 1958.

[106] Shannon, CE. Programming a computer for playing chess. *The London, Edinburgh, and Dublin Philosophical Magazine and Journal of Science*, 41(314):256–275, 1950.

[107] Shannon, CE and Weaver, W. *The Mathematical Theory of Communication*. University of Illinois Press, 1949.

[108] Silver, D et al. Mastering the game of Go with deep neural networks and tree search. *Nature*, 529:484–503, 2016.

[109] Silver, D et al. Mastering the game of Go without human knowledge. *Nature*, 550(7676):354–359, 2017.

[110] Simard, P, LeCun, Y, and Denker, J. Efficient pattern recognition using a new transformation distance. In *NIPS*, pages 50–58, 1992.

[111] Simeone, O. A brief introduction to machine learning for engineers. *arXiv e-prints*, 2017. arXiv:1709.02840.

[112] Sivia, DS. *Data Analysis: A Bayesian Tutorial*. Oxford University Press, 1996.

[113] Smolensky, P. Information processing in dynamical systems: Foundations of harmony theory. Technical report, Department of Computer Science, University of Colorado at Boulder, 1986.

[114] Solla, SA, Sorkin, GB, and White, SR. Configuration space analysis for optimization problems. In Bienstock, E, editor, *Disordered Systems and Biological Organisation*, pages 283–293. Springer, 1986.

[115] Stone, JV. Connectionist models: Theoretical status, form, and function. *AISB*, 66, 1988.

[116] Stone, JV. Learning sequences with a connectionist model. Invited paper presented to the *Rank Prize Funds Symposium on Neural Networks*, February 1989.

[117] Stone, JV. The optimal elastic net: Finding solutions to the travelling salesman problem. *Proc. Int. Conf. Artificial Neural Networks*, pages 170–174, 1992.

[118] Stone, JV. Learning perceptually salient visual parameters through spatiotemporal smoothness constraints. *Neural Computation*, 8(7):1463–1492, 1996.

[119] Stone, JV. *Independent Component Analysis: A Tutorial Introduction*. MIT Press, 2004.

[120] Stone, JV. Distributed representations accelerate evolution of adaptive behaviours. *PLoS Comp. Biol.*, 3(8):e147, 2007.

[121] Stone, JV. *Vision and Brain*. MIT Press, 2012.

[122] Stone, JV. *Bayes' Rule: A Tutorial Introduction to Bayesian Analysis*. Sebtel Press, 2013.

[123] Stone, JV. *Information Theory: A Tutorial Introduction*. Sebtel Press, 2015.

References

[124] Stone, JV and Harper, N. Temporal constraints on visual learning. *Perception*, 28:1089–1104, 1999.

[125] Stone, JV, Hunkin, NM, and Hornby, A. Predicting spontaneous recovery of memory. *Nature*, 414:167–168, 2001.

[126] Sun, C, Shrivastava, A, Singh, S, and Gupta, A. Revisiting unreasonable effectiveness of data in deep learning era. In *IEEE Int. Conf. Computer Vision (ICCV)*, pages 843–852. IEEE, 2017.

[127] Sutskever, I, Vinyals, O, and Le, QV. Sequence to sequence learning with neural networks. *arXiv e-prints*, 2014. arXiv:1409.3215.

[128] Sutton, RS and Barto, AG. *Reinforcement Learning: An Introduction*, volume 1. MIT Press, 2018.

[129] Szegedy, C et al. Going deeper with convolutions. In *Proc. IEEE Conf. Computer Vision and Pattern Recognition*, pages 1–9. 2015.

[130] Tesauro, G. Temporal difference learning and TD-Gammon. *Communications of the ACM*, 38(3):58–68, 1995.

[131] Tishby, N, Pereira, FC, and Bialek, W. The information bottleneck method. *arXiv e-prints*, 2000. arXiv:physics/0004057.

[132] Tramel, EW, Gabrié, M, Manoel, A, Caltagirone, F, and Krzakala, F. Deterministic and generalized framework for unsupervised learning with restricted Boltzmann machines. *Phys. Rev. X*, 8:041006, 2018.

[133] Vincent, P, Larochelle, H, Lajoie, I, Bengio, Y, and Manzagol, P. Stacked denoising autoencoders: Learning useful representations in a deep network with a local denoising criterion. *Journal of Machine Learning Research*, 11(Dec):3371–3408, 2010.

[134] Wang, H and Raj, B. On the origin of deep learning. *arXiv e-prints*, 2017. arXiv:1702.07800.

[135] Watkins, CJCH. *Learning from Delayed Rewards*. PhD thesis, King's College, Cambridge, 1989.

[136] Widrow, B and Hoff, ME. Adaptive switching circuits. *1960 WESCON Convention Record, Part IV*, pages 96–104, 1960.

[137] Williams, PM. Bayesian regularization and pruning using a Laplace prior. *Neural Computation*, 7(1):117–143, 1995.

[138] Williams, RJ. Simple statistical gradient-following algorithms for connectionist reinforcement learning. *Machine Learning*, 8(3-4):229–256, 1992.

[139] Williams, RJ and Zipser, D. A learning algorithm for continually running fully recurrent neural networks. *Neural Computation*, 1(2):270–280, 1989.

[140] Wu, H and Gu, X. Towards dropout training for convolutional neural networks. *Neural Networks*, 71:1–10, 2015.

[141] Yuret, D. Knet: Beginning deep learning with 100 lines of Julia. In *Machine Learning Systems Workshop at NIPS*, 2016.

[142] Zemel, RS, Mozer, C, and Hinton, GE. TRAFFIC: Recognizing objects using hierarchical reference frame transformations. In Tourzesky, DS, editor, *Advances in Neural Information Processing Systems*, pages 266–273. Morgan Kaufmann, 1990.

Index

action-value function, 147, 157, 175
activation function, 13, 38, 175
actor–critic, 163, 175
adaline, 12
AlexNet, 129
algorithm, 175
AlphaGo, 166
AlphaGo Zero, 166
analysis by synthesis, 98, 141
arcade-style game, 168
association, 12, 175
Atari game, 168
autoassociative network, 26
autoencoder, 175
autograd, 41, 175
average, 175

backprop, 7, 37, 175
Banach fixed-point theorem, 155
Barto, A, 8, 145
basin of attraction, 68
batch, 175
batch normalization, 54, 175
Bayes' rule, 190
Bayes' theorem, 108, 111, 175, 189
Bellman equation, 175
BFGS method, 56
bias unit, 40, 175
bicycle, 1, 168
Boltzmann distribution, 75, 175
Boltzmann machine, 6, 175

chain rule, 21
CIFAR, 131, 176
clamp, 176
conditional probability, 189
conditional variational autoencoder, 119
conjugate gradients, 56

content addressable memory, 6, 66, 176
contrastive divergence, 87
convolution, 122, 125, 176
convolutional network, 122, 176
correlograph, 12
cross-entropy, 54, 79, 96, 176

deep autoencoder networks, 93
deep belief network, 92, 176
deep Boltzmann machine, 92
deep neural network, 176
deep Q-network, 162, 168
deep RBM, 85
delayed reinforcement learning, 145
delta rule, 18
denoising autoencoder, 176
DenseNet, 131
direction of steepest descent, 18
discount factor, 149, 176
discriminator network, 137
dropout, 52, 129, 176
dynamic programming, 146

early stopping, 51, 176
ELBO, 110, 176
eligibility trace, 147, 176
embedding, 103
energy function, 176
energy landscape, 68
energy-based networks, 63
episode, 146, 177
error, 177
error function, 15
evidence lower bound, 110, 176
exclusive OR, 32, 48
expectation, 148
expected value, 177
expressibility, 86, 177
exploding gradients, 52
extreme gradients, 52

fast gradient sign method, 137

feature map, 125
free-energy framework, 163
Friston, K, 163

generalisation, 6, 177
generative adversarial
networks, 177
generative model, 97, 177
generator network, 137
Gibbs sampling, 98
glider, 168
global minimum, 58
Goodfellow, I, 136
GoogLeNet, 130
graceful degradation, 6
gradient descent, 15, 177
greedy algorithm, 157
greedy policy, 159, 177

Hebb's postulate, 5
Hessian matrix, 56
heuristic, 16
hidden unit, 72
Hinton, G, 71, 171
holophone, 12
Hopfield net, 6, 177
Hopfield, J, 63

identity matrix, 177
immediate reinforcement learning, 145
indicator function, 153
inference, 108, 177
infinite horizon, 150
information bottleneck, 97, 98
information theory, 145

Jensen's inequality, 177

Kohonen, T, 12
Kullback–Leibler divergence,
78, 111, 177

labelled data, 177
ladder autoencoder networks,
132
latent variables, 100
least mean square, 18
least-squares estimation, 188
LeCun, Y, 125
likelihood, 178, 189
likelihood function, 188, 190
linear, 178
linear associative network, 11,
12, 178

linearly separable, 30, 31
LMS rule, 18
local minimum, 58, 178
log likelihood, 81
LSTM, 140
Lyapunov function, 70

manifold, 104
marginal likelihood, 105, 108,
190
Markov chain, 148
Markov decision process, 148,
166
Markov process, 148, 178
Matlab, ii
maximum
likelihood estimation,
81, 114, 178, 187
MCMC, 77, 178
mean, 178
minimal description length, 100
MNIST data set, 94, 96, 178
model evidence, 105, 108
model-free methods, 162
momentum term, 56
Monte Carlo, 178
multi-layer perceptron, 37, 178
mutual information, 178

n-step return, 178
NETtalk, 7
NetTalk, 60
neuron, 2
niche construction, 163
NP-complete, 58

off-policy, 161, 178
offline update, 178
on-policy, 160, 179
one hot vector, 119, 178
one-step TD, 155
online update, 178
outer product, 66, 186
over-fitting, 49, 179

partition function, 75, 80
perceptron, 5, 12, 179
perceptron convergence theorem, 30
phonemes, 7
pixelRNN, 141
policy, 147, 179
policy evaluation, 152, 179
policy gradient, 163, 179
policy improvement, 146, 157,
179

policy improvement theorem, 158, 179
policy iteration, 146, 159, 179
pong, 168
pooling, 127, 179
posterior probability, 189
posterior probability distribution, 190
pre-training, 55
prior, 105, 189
prior distribution, 190
product rule, 189, 190
pruning, 52
Python, ii
PyTorch, ii

Q-learning, 160, 179

radial basis function, 128
rectified linear unit, 129, 179
regularisation, 52, 179
reinforcement learning, 8, 143, 179
  delayed, 145
  immediate, 145
ReLU, 129
reparametrisation trick, 117
ResNet, 130
restricted Boltzmann machine, 179
return, 146, 147, 179
reward, 147
Robbins–Monro theorem, 155
Rosenblatt, F, 12, 27

Samuel, A, 8, 145
SARSA, 179
second-order methods, 56
Sejnowski, T, 71
semi-supervised networks, 132
Shannon, C, 8, 145
sigmoid, 37
simulated annealing, 73, 180
sleep, 72, 83
softmax function, 96
stacked RBM, 87, 92
state, 180
state-value function, 146, 147, 180
statistical mechanics, 7
step function, 64
stochastic, 180
stochastic gradient descent, 155, 180
sub-sampling, 126

sum rule, 189, 190
supervised learning, 180
Sutton, R, 145

tangent prop, 135
TD error, 147
TD(λ), 156
TD-Gammon, 166
temporal convolutional networks, 141
temporal credit assignment problem, 144
temporal difference error, 180
temporal difference learning, 146, 180
temporal discounting, 147
tensor, 180
thermal equilibrium, 76
time complexity, 58
top-n, 180
top-5 classification, 129
total reward, 147
trace-decay parameter, 180
training data, 180
transfer learning, 180
transpose operator, 24, 186

unfolding, 61
unit, 180
unsupervised learning, 180

validation set, 180
value, 180
vanishing gradients, 52
variational autoencoder, 84, 174
variational lower bound, 112
visible unit, 72

wake, 72, 83
weight sharing, 126
Wheeler, J, 171
Widrow–Hoff rule, 18
Willshaw, D, 12

XOR, 32, 48

ZIP codes, 62

A Note From the Author

I sincerely hope that you enjoyed (or, at least, that you learned a little) from reading this book. If you did (or even if you didn't) then I would be grateful if you would write a review, either on Goodreads or Amazon.

If you think you are not sufficiently expert to write a review then you are precisely the type of reader that other readers value the most. After all, a book with the words, "A Tutorial Introduction" in its title should be read mainly by non-experts.

James V Stone.

Made in the USA
Columbia, SC
09 November 2022

70768297R00120